Microsoft®

# Word 2002



Marquee Series

NITA RUTKOSKY Pierce College at Puyallup – Puyallup, Washington

DENISE SEGUIN Fanshawe College – London, Ontario

EMCParadigm

# CONTENTS



†These sections are not included in *Office XP, Brief Edition.*

**The Marquee Series Team:** Michael Sander, Developmental Editor; Jennifer Wreisner, Senior Designer; Leslie Anderson, Michelle Lewis, and Desktop Solutions, Desktop Production; Desiree Faulkner, Tester; Sharon O'Donnell, Copyeditor; Lynn Reichel, Proofreader; and Nancy Fulton, Indexer.

**Publishing Team:** George Provol, Publisher; Janice Johnson, Director of Product Development; Tony Galvin, Acquisitions Editor; Lori Landwer, Marketing Manager; Shelley Clubb, Electronic Design and Production Manager.

**Acknowledgment:** The authors and publisher wish to thank the following reviewer for her technical and academic assistance in testing exercises and assessing instruction: Mary A. Walthall, Ph.D., St. Petersburg College, Clearwater Campus, Clearwater, FL

**Library of Congress Cataloging-in-Publication Data**
Rutkosky, Nita Hewitt.
Microsoft Word 2002 / Nita Rutkosky, Denise Seguin.
p.cm. – (Marquee series)
Includes index.
ISBN 0-7638-1479-2 (text) – ISBN 0-7638-1480-6 (text & CD)
1. Microsoft Word. 2. Word processing. I. Seguin, Denise. II. Title. III. Series

Z52.5.M52 R94 2002b
652.5'5369—dc21 2001040582



Text + CD: 0-7638-1480-6
Order Number: 05559



Published by **EMC**Paradigm
875 Montreal Way
St. Paul, MN 55102
(800) 535-6865
E-mail: educate@emcp.com
Web site: www.emcp.com



Printed in the United States of America

10 9 8 7 6 5 4 3 2 1

# WORD SECTION 1

# Creating and Editing a Document

Microsoft Word 2002 is a word processing program you can use to create documents such as letters, reports, research papers, brochures, newsletters, and much more. Word is a full-featured word processing program that provides a wide variety of editing and formatting features as well as sophisticated visual features. In this section you will learn the skills and complete the projects described here.

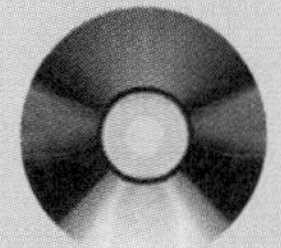

*Note: Before beginning this section, copy to a floppy disk or other folder the* Word S1 *subfolder from the* Word *folder on the CD that accompanies this textbook, and then make* Word S1 *the active folder. Steps on copying a folder, deleting a folder, and making a folder active are on the inside back cover of this textbook.*

## Skills

- Complete the word processing cycle
- Move the insertion point
- Insert, replace, and delete text
- Scroll and navigate in a document
- Select and delete text
- Use Undo and Redo
- Check the spelling and grammar in a document
- Use AutoCorrect
- Use Thesaurus
- Use the Help feature
- Highlight text
- Preview a document
- Print a document
- Insert the date and time in a document
- Close a document
- Create a document using a template
- Create a folder
- Save a document in a different format

## Projects

Prepare a document describing a special vacation package and edit and format three documents describing various vacation specials offered by First Choice Travel.

Prepare a memo regarding a movie site using a memo template; edit an internal memo; prepare a memo regarding catering and costuming for a film; and prepare a letter to the manager of The Waterfront Bistro requesting catering information.

Prepare a memo regarding the distribution schedule.

Edit a letter to Marquee Productions regarding costuming for a film.

## 1.1 Completing the Word Processing Cycle

The process of creating a document in Microsoft Word generally follows a word processing cycle. The steps in the cycle vary but typically include: opening Word; creating and editing the document; saving, printing, and closing the document; and then closing Word.

**PROJECT:** As an employee of First Choice Travel, you have been asked to create a short document containing information on a travel package offered by First Choice Travel.

## STEPS

1. At the Windows desktop, click the Start button **Start** on the Taskbar.

   Clicking the Start button causes a pop-up menu to display.

2. At the Start pop-up menu, point to *Programs*.

   A side menu displays when you point to an option on the Start pop-up menu that displays with a right-pointing triangle after it.

3. Click *Microsoft Word* on the *Programs* side menu.

   Depending on your system configuration, the steps to open Word may vary.

4. At the Word document screen, identify the various features by comparing your screen with the one shown in Figure W1.1.

   See Table W1.1 for a description of the screen features. Figure W1.1 shows the Standard and Formatting toolbars on two rows. Your screen may show them on one row.

5. At the Word document screen, key (type) the text shown in Figure W1.2.

   Key the text as shown. When you key *adn* and then press the spacebar, the AutoCorrect feature will automatically correct it to *and*. When you key *teh* and then press the spacebar, AutoCorrect corrects it to *the*. Do not press the Enter key to end a line of text. Word will automatically wrap text to the next line.

**FIGURE W1.1** Word Document Screen

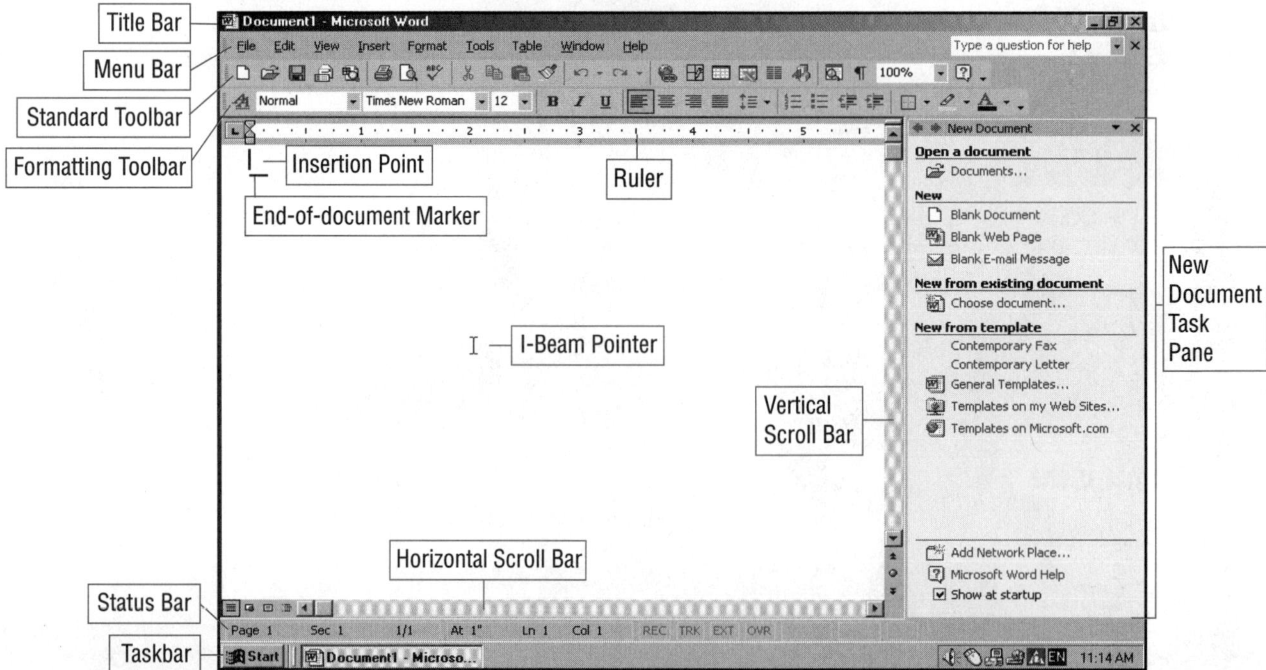

**FIGURE W1.2**

> Are you spontaneous adn enjoy doing something on a moment's notice? If this describes you, then you will be interested in First Choice Travel's Moment's Notice Travel Package. For teh low price of $499 you can fly from New York to London for a four-day stay. The catch to this incredible deal is that you must make your reservations within the next week and complete your London stay within thirty days.

6. Save the document by clicking the Save button on the Standard toolbar.
7. At the Save As dialog box, make sure the *Word S1* folder on your disk is the active folder, key **Word S1-01** in the File name text box, and then click the Save button.

The Save in option at the Save As dialog box displays the active folder. If you need to make the *Word S1* folder on your disk in drive A the active folder, click the down-pointing triangle at the right of the Save in option and then click *3½ Floppy (A:)*. Double-click *Word S1* in the list box. After keying the document name, you can press the Enter key instead of clicking the Save button.

8. Print the document by clicking the Print button on the Standard toolbar.
9. Close the document by clicking File on the Menu bar and then clicking Close at the drop-down menu.

**TABLE W1.1** Document Screen Features

| Feature | Description |
|---|---|
| **Title Bar** | Displays document name followed by program name |
| **Menu Bar** | Contains a list of options to manage and customize documents |
| **Standard Toolbar** | Contains buttons that are shortcuts for the most popular commands |
| **Formatting Toolbar** | Contains buttons that can quickly apply formatting to text |
| **Ruler** | Used to set margins, indents, and tab |
| **I-beam Pointer** | Used to move the insertion point or to select text |
| **Task Pane** | Presents features to help user identify and use more of the program. The name of the task pane and features in the task pane change depending on actions being performed |
| **Insertion Point** | Indicates the location of where the next character entered at the keyboard will appear |
| **End-of-document Marker** | Indicates the end of the document |
| **Scroll Bars** | Used to view various parts of the document |
| **Status Bar** | Displays position of insertion point and working mode buttons |
| **Taskbar** | Used to select one of a number of active programs |

# In Addition

## Correcting Errors

The AutoCorrect feature automatically corrects certain words as they are being keyed. For example, key *teh* and press the spacebar, and AutoCorrect changes it to *the*. Word also contains a feature called Spell It that inserts a wavy red line below words that are not contained in the Spelling dictionary or not corrected by AutoCorrect. If the word containing a wavy red line is correct, you can leave it as written. The wavy red line does not print. If the word is incorrect, edit it.

## 1.2 Moving the Insertion Point; Inserting, Replacing, and Deleting Text

Many documents that are created need to have changes made to them. These changes may include adding text, called *inserting*, or removing text, called *deleting*. To insert or delete text, move the insertion point to certain locations without erasing the text through which it passes. To insert text, position the insertion point in the desired location and then key the text. If you want to key over something, switch to the *Overtype* mode by pressing the Insert key. Delete text in a document by pressing the Backspace key or Delete key.

**PROJECT:** First Choice Travel marketing staff members have reviewed your document on vacation specials and have recommended a few changes. You need to create a revised version.

### STEPS

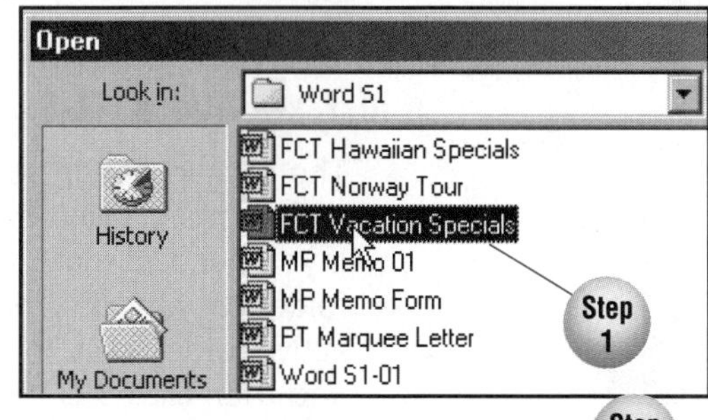


1. At the Word document screen, click the Open button on the Standard toolbar. At the Open dialog box, make sure the *Word S1* folder on your disk is the active folder, and then double-click *FCT Vacation Specials* in the list box.

PROBLEM? If the FCT Vacation Specials document does not display in the Open dialog box, check with your instructor.

2. Click File and then Save As. At the Save As dialog box, key **Word S1-02** in the File name text box, and then press Enter.

   If you open an existing document, make changes to it, and then want to save it with the same name, click the Save button on the Standard toolbar. If you want to keep the original document and save the document with the changes with a new name, click File and then Save As.

3. Position the mouse pointer at the beginning of the second paragraph and then click the left mouse button. (This moves the insertion point to the location of the mouse pointer.)

4. Press the up, down, left, and right arrow keys located to the right of the regular keys on the keyboard.

   Use the information shown in Table W1.2 to practice moving the insertion point in the document.

5. Press Ctrl + Home, click at the beginning of the paragraph that begins *Sign up today for…*, and then key **Ocean Vista Cruise Lines announces the inaugural voyage of the Pacific Sky ocean liner.**

   By default, text you key in a document is inserted in the document and existing text is moved to the right.

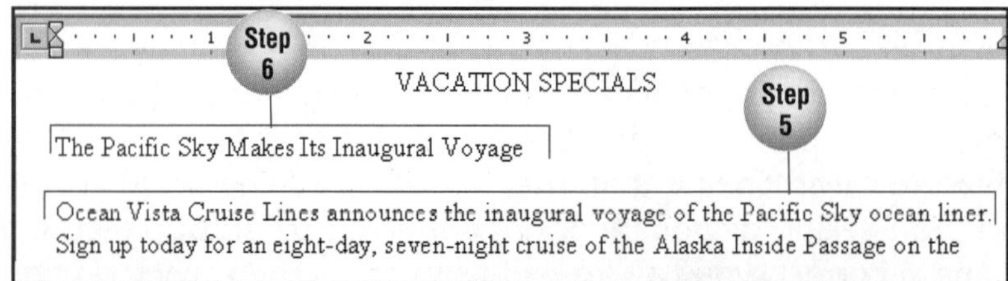

6 Click at the beginning of the heading *Ocean Vista Cruise Lines*, press the Insert key on the keyboard, and then key **The Pacific Sky Makes Its Inaugural Voyage**.

Pressing the Insert button turns on *Overtype* and anything you key will replace existing text. When *Overtype* is on, the letters *OVR* display in black on the Status bar.

7 Press the Insert key to turn off *Overtype*.

8 Press Ctrl + End (this moves the insertion point to the end of the document) and then click on any character in the last sentence in the document (the sentence that begins *Let First Choice Travel take…*).

9 Press the Backspace key until the insertion point is positioned at the left margin and then press the Delete key until you have deleted the remainder of the sentence.

Pressing the Backspace key deletes any characters left of the insertion point. Press the Delete key to delete any characters to the right of the insertion point.

10 Click the Save button on the Standard toolbar.

Clicking the Save button saves the document with the same name (Word S1-02).

**TABLE W1.2** Insertion Point Movements

| Location | Press |
|---|---|
| **End of line** | End key |
| **Beginning of line** | Home key |
| **Up one screen** | Pg Up key |
| **Down one screen** | Pg Down key |
| **Beginning of document** | Ctrl + Home |
| **End of document** | Ctrl + End |

# In Addition

## Expanding Drop-Down Menus

When you click an option on the Menu bar, only the most popular options display (considered first-rank options). To expand the drop-down menu, click the down-pointing triangles that display at the bottom of the menu, click an option on the Menu bar and then pause on the menu for a few seconds, or double-click the option on the Menu bar. Second-rank options display on the expanded drop-down menu with a lighter gray background. If you choose a second-rank option, it becomes a first-rank option the next time the drop-down menu is displayed. If you want all menu options to display, click Tools and then Customize. At the Customize dialog box, click the Options tab. Click in the Always show full menus check box to insert a check mark and then click the Close button.

**Open a Document**
1 Click Open button.
2 Double-click document name.

## 1.3 Scrolling and Navigating in a Document

In addition to moving the insertion point to a specific location, you can use the mouse to move the display of text in the document screen. Use the mouse with the horizontal scroll bar and/or the vertical scroll bar to scroll through text in a document. The horizontal scroll bar displays toward the bottom of the Word screen and the vertical scroll bar displays toward the right side. Scrolling in a document changes the text displayed but does not move the insertion point. The Select Browse Object button located at the bottom of the vertical scroll bar contains options for browsing through a document. Scrolling in a document changes the text displayed while browsing in a document moves the insertion point.

**PROJECT:** To minimize the need for additional editing, you have decided to carefully review the First Choice Travel vacation specials document on screen.

## STEPS

1. With Word S1-02 open, move the insertion point to the beginning of the document by pressing Ctrl + Home.
2. Position the mouse pointer on the down scroll triangle on the vertical scroll bar and then click the left mouse button several times.

   This scrolls down the lines of text in the document. Scrolling changes the display of text but does not move the insertion point.

3. Position the mouse pointer on the vertical scroll bar below the scroll box and then click the left mouse button a couple of times.

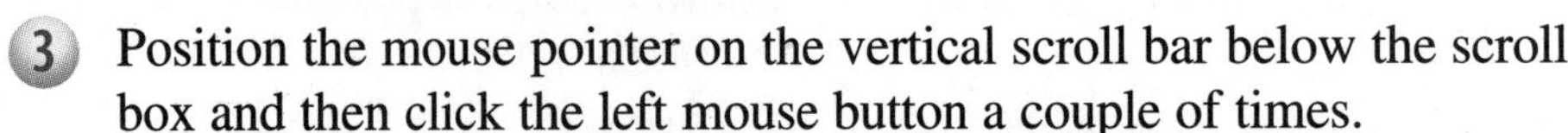

   The scroll box on the vertical scroll bar indicates the location of the text on the document screen in relation to the remainder of the document. Clicking on the vertical scroll bar below the scroll box scrolls down one screen of text at a time.

4. Position the mouse pointer on the scroll box on the vertical scroll bar, hold down the left mouse button, drag the scroll box to the top of the vertical scroll bar, and then release the mouse button.

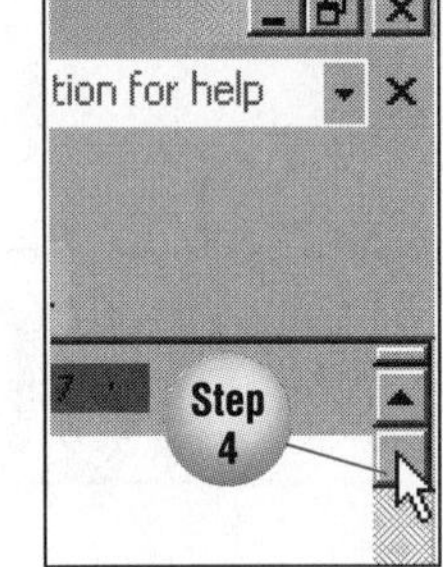


   Dragging the scroll box to the top of the vertical scroll bar displays text at the beginning of the document.

5. Click the Select Browse Object button and then click the Go To option.

   The location of the Go To option may vary. It may be the first option from the left in the bottom row. Position the arrow pointer on the option and the name of the option displays at the bottom of the palette. Use other options at the palette to browse to document features such as a field, endnote, footnote, comment, section, heading, and graphic.

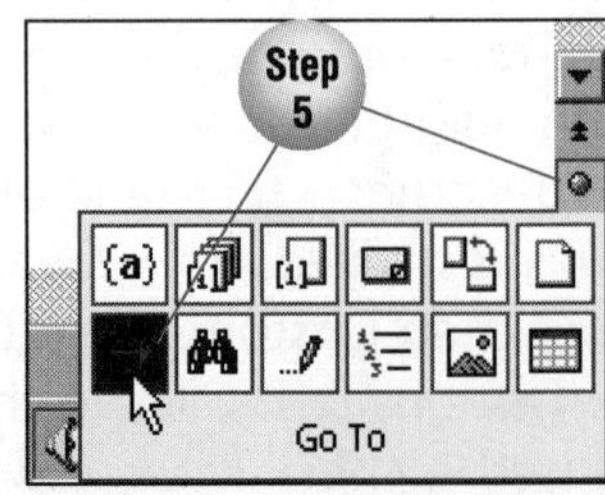

6 At the Find and Replace dialog box with the Go To tab selected, key **2** in the Enter page number text box, press the Enter key, and then click Close.

With options at the Find and Replace dialog box with the Go To tab selected, you can move the insertion point to various locations in a document such as a specific page, section, line, bookmark, and so on.

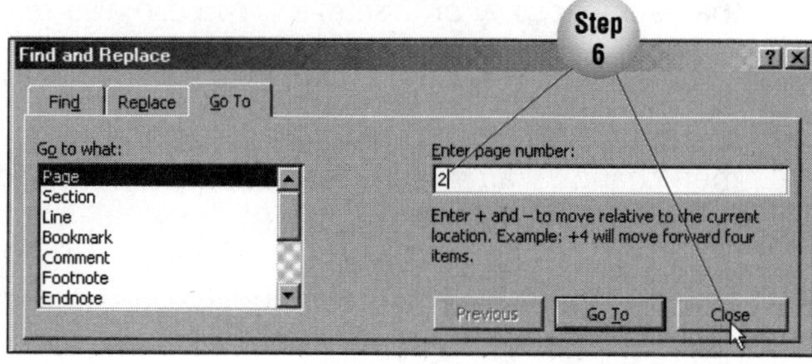


7 Click the Previous Page button located above the Select Browse Object button.

Clicking the Previous Page button moves the insertion point to the beginning of the previous page. The full names of and the task completed by the Previous and Next buttons vary depending on the last navigation completed.

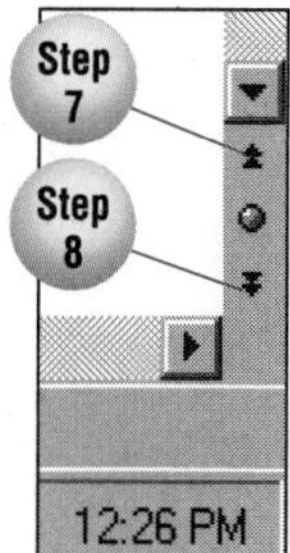


8 Click the Next Page button located below the Select Browse Object button.

9 Press Ctrl + Home to move the insertion point to the beginning of the document.

10 Save the document by clicking the Save button on the Standard toolbar.

# In Addition

## Smart Tags and Option Buttons

**Smart Tags:** Using a smart tag, you can perform actions in Word that you would normally need to open another program to perform. For example, if you key a date, Word inserts a purple dotted line below the date, indicating a smart tag. Position the mouse pointer on the date and a smart tag icon displays. Click the icon and then choose an action from the pop-up menu such as scheduling a meeting in Outlook.

**Option Buttons:** As you insert and edit text in a document, you may notice an option button popping up in your text. The name and appearance of this option button varies depending on the action. If a word you key is corrected by AutoCorrect, if you create an automatic list, or if autoformatting is applied to text, the AutoCorrect Options button appears. Click this button to undo the specific automatic action. If you paste text in a document, the Paste Options button appears near the text. Click this button to display options for controlling how the pasted text is formatted.

**Display Find and Replace Dialog Box**
1 Click Select Browse Object button.
2 Click Go To option.

## 1.4 Selecting and Deleting Text; Using Undo and Redo

Previously, you learned to delete text by pressing the Backspace key or Delete key. You can also select text and then delete it, replace it with other text, or apply formatting to selected text. If you make a change to text, such as deleting selected text, and then change your mind, use the Undo and/or Redo buttons on the Standard toolbar.

**PROJECT:** To minimize the need for additional editing, you have decided to carefully review the First Choice Travel vacation specials document on screen.

### STEPS

1. With Word S1-02 open, position the mouse pointer at the beginning of the word *Behold* (located immediately after the first bullet). Hold down the left mouse button, drag to the right until the word is selected, and then release the mouse button. (The letters in *Behold* display in white on a black background.)

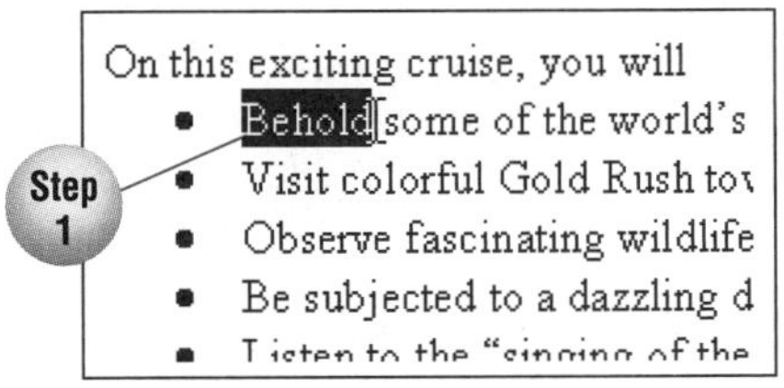

On this exciting cruise, you will
- Behold some of the world's
- Visit colorful Gold Rush to
- Observe fascinating wildlife
- Be subjected to a dazzling d

Step 1

2. Key **View**.

   When you key *View,* it takes the place of *Behold.* If you select text and then decide you want to deselect it, click in the document window outside the selected text.

3. Move the insertion point to the beginning of the word *Glacier* (located in the second paragraph) and then press the F8 function key on the keyboard. Press the right arrow key until the words *Glacier Bay and* are selected.

   Pressing the F8 function key turns on the *Extend* mode and the *EXT* letters display in black on the Status bar. With the *Extend* mode on, use the insertion point movement keys to select text.

PROBLEM? If you select the wrong text and want to deselect it, press the Esc key to turn off the *Extend* mode, and then press any arrow key.

Step 3

The Pacific Sky cruises through Glacier Bay and the Alaskan Ports of Skagway, Haines, and Juneau. The beautiful port city of Vancouver, British Columbia.

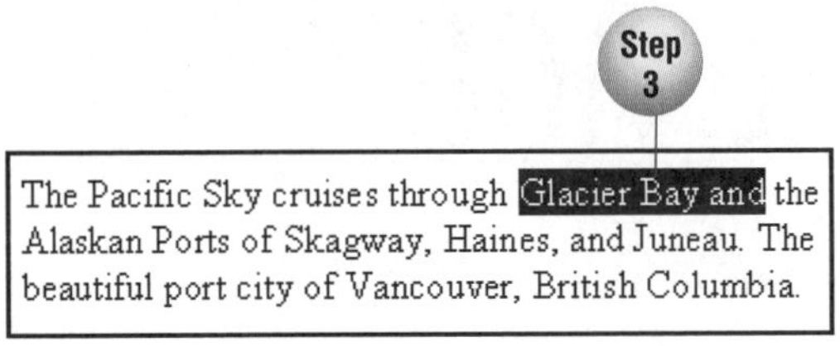

4. Press the Delete key.

   Pressing the Delete key deletes the selected text. If you want to cancel a selection, press the Esc key, and then press any arrow key.

5. Position the mouse pointer on any character in the first sentence that begins *Ocean Vista Cruise Lines announces…*, hold down the Ctrl key, click the mouse button, and then release the Ctrl key.

   Holding down the Ctrl key while clicking the mouse button selects the entire sentence.

6. Press the Delete key to delete the selected sentence.

7 Click the Undo button on the Standard toolbar.

When you click the Undo button, the deleted sentence reappears. Clicking the Undo button reverses the last command or deletes the last entry you keyed. Click the down-pointing triangle at the right of the Undo button and a drop-down list displays containing changes made to the document since it was opened. Click an action and the action, along with any preceding actions, is undone.

8 Click the Redo button on the Standard toolbar.

Clicking the Redo button deletes the selected sentence. If you click the Undo button and then decide you do not want to reverse the original action, click the Redo button.

9 Position the mouse pointer between the left edge of the screen and the first line of text in the second paragraph until the pointer turns into an arrow pointing up and to the right (instead of the left) and then click the left mouse button.

The space between the left edge of the screen and the text is referred to as the selection bar. Use the selection bar to select specific amounts of text. Refer to Table W1.3 for more information on selecting text.

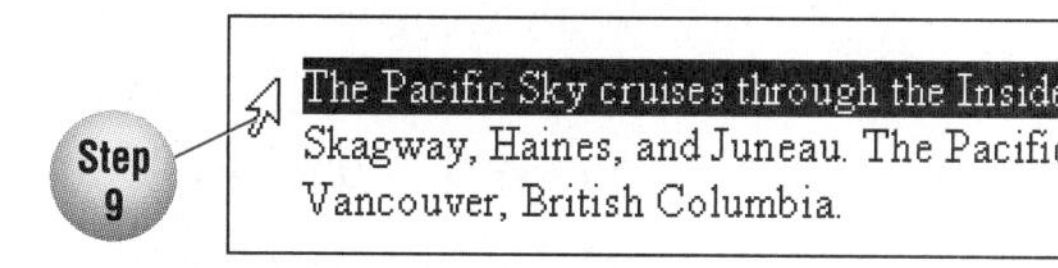


10 Deselect the text by clicking in the document outside the selected area.

11 Save the document by clicking the Save button on the Standard toolbar.

**TABLE W1.3** Selecting with the Mouse

| To Select | Complete These Steps Using the Mouse |
|---|---|
| **A word** | Double-click the word |
| **A line of text** | Click in the selection bar to the left of the line |
| **Multiple lines of text** | Drag in the selection bar to the left of the lines |
| **A sentence** | Hold down the Ctrl key and then click anywhere in the sentence |
| **A paragraph** | Double-click in the selection bar next to the paragraph or triple-click anywhere in the paragraph |
| **Multiple paragraphs** | Drag in the selection bar |
| **An entire document** | Triple-click in the selection bar |

# In Addition

## Undoing Multiple Actions

Word maintains actions in temporary memory. If you want to undo an action performed earlier, click the down-pointing triangle to the right of the Undo button. This causes a drop-down menu to display. To make a selection from this drop-down menu, click the desired action. Any actions preceding a chosen action are also undone. You can do the same with the actions in the Redo drop-down list. To display the Redo drop-down list, click the down-pointing triangle to the right of the Redo button. To redo an action, click the desired action. Any actions preceding the chosen action are also redone. Multiple actions must be undone or redone in sequence.

## 1.5 Checking the Spelling and Grammar in a Document

Use Word's spelling checker to find and correct misspelled words and find duplicated words (such as *and and*). The spelling checker compares words in your document with words in its dictionary. If a match is found, the word is passed over. If no match for the word is found, the spelling checker stops, selects the word, and offers replacements. The grammar checker will search a document for errors in grammar, style, punctuation, and word usage. The spelling checker and the grammar checker can help you create a well-written document but do not replace the need for proofreading.

**PROJECT:** Continuing with the editing process, you are ready to check the spelling and grammar in the First Choice Travel vacation specials document.

### STEPS

1. With Word S1-02 open, press Ctrl + Home to move the insertion point to the beginning of the document, and then click the Spelling and Grammar button on the Standard toolbar.
2. When the word *inagural* is selected, make sure *inaugural* is selected in the Suggestions list box, and then click the Change button in the Spelling and Grammar dialog box.

   Refer to Table W1.4 for an explanation of the buttons in the Spelling and Grammar dialog box.

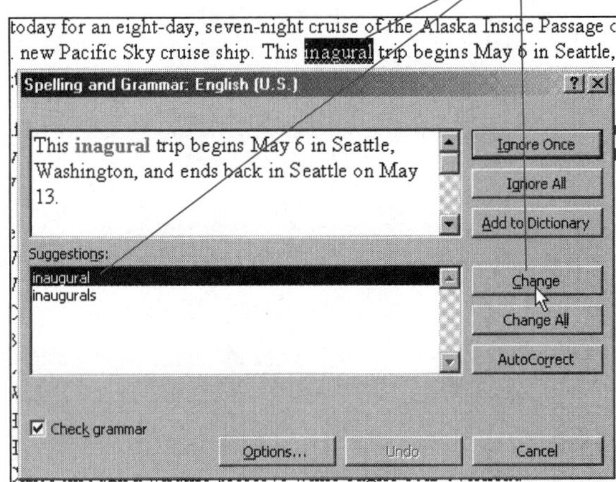


**TABLE W1.4** Spelling and Grammar Dialog Box Buttons

| Button | Function |
|---|---|
| Ignore Once | During spell checking, skips that occurrence of the word; in grammar checking, leaves the currently selected text as written. |
| Ignore All | During spell checking, skips that occurrence of the word and all other occurrences of the word in the document. |
| Ignore Rule | During grammar checking, leaves the currently selected text as written and also ignores the current rule for the remainder of the grammar check in the document. |
| Add to Dictionary | Adds the selected word to the main spelling checker dictionary. |
| Change | Replaces the selected word in the sentence with the selected word in the Suggestions list box. |
| Change All | Replaces the selected word in the sentence with the selected word in the Suggestions list box and all other occurrences of the word in the document. |
| AutoCorrect | Inserts the selected word and the correct spelling of the word in the AutoCorrect dialog box. |
| Undo | Reverses the most recent spelling and grammar action. |
| Next Sentence | Accepts manual changes made to a sentence and then continues grammar checking. |
| Options | Displays a dialog box with options for customizing a spelling and grammar check. |

3. When the sentence that begins *Space are limited...* is selected, click the Explain button, and then read the information on Subject-Verb Agreement that displays in the yellow box above the Office Assistant.

   Clicking the Explain button turns on the display of the Office Assistant. The yellow box above the Office Assistant provides information on the grammar rule.

4. Make sure *Space is* is selected in the Suggestions list box and then click the Change button.

PROBLEM ? If you accidentally click outside the Spelling and Grammar dialog box, resume the checking by clicking the Resume button.

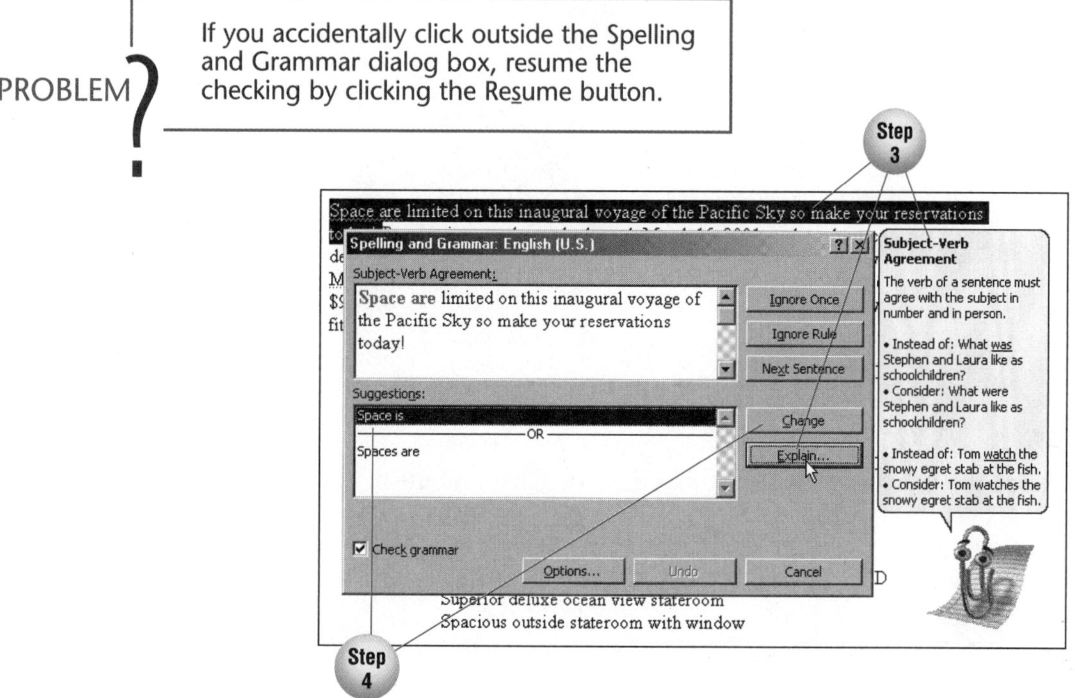


5. When the word *the* is selected (this word is repeated twice), click the Delete button in the Spelling and Grammar dialog box.

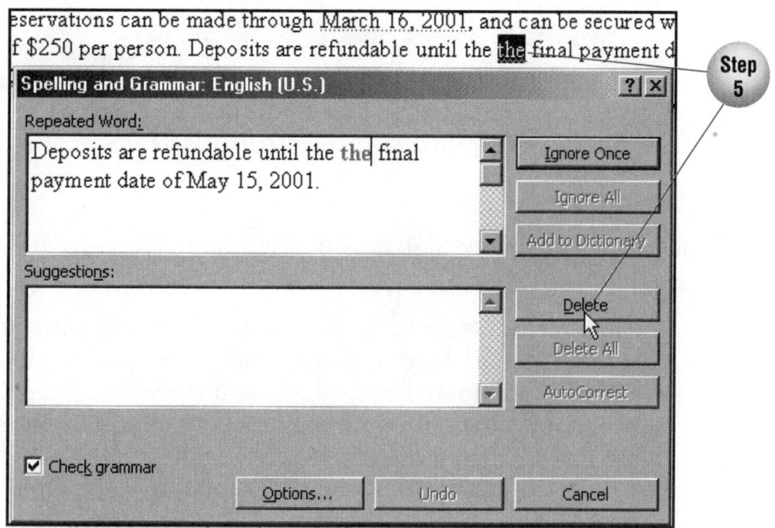


*(continued)*

6 When the sentence that begins *You could spent the weekend…* is selected, read the information on Verb Form that displays in the yellow box above the Office Assistant. Make sure *spend* is selected in the Suggestions list box and then click the Change button.

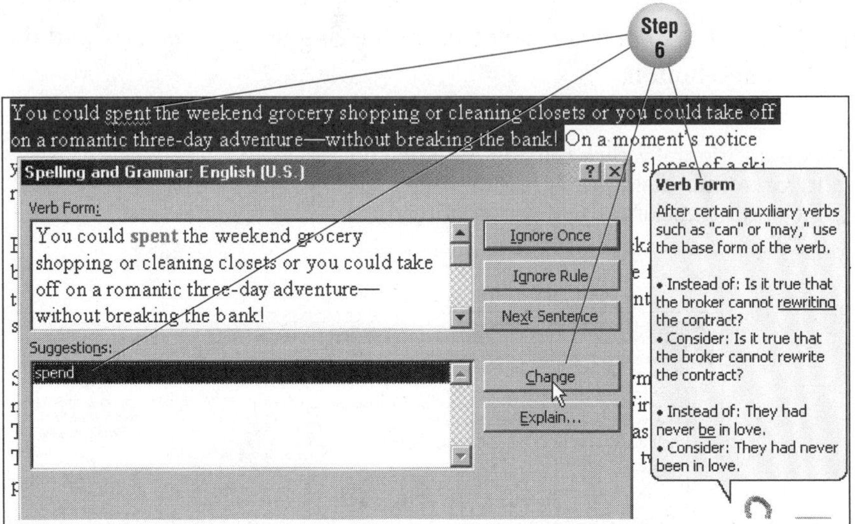


7 When the word *utah* is selected, click the Change button.

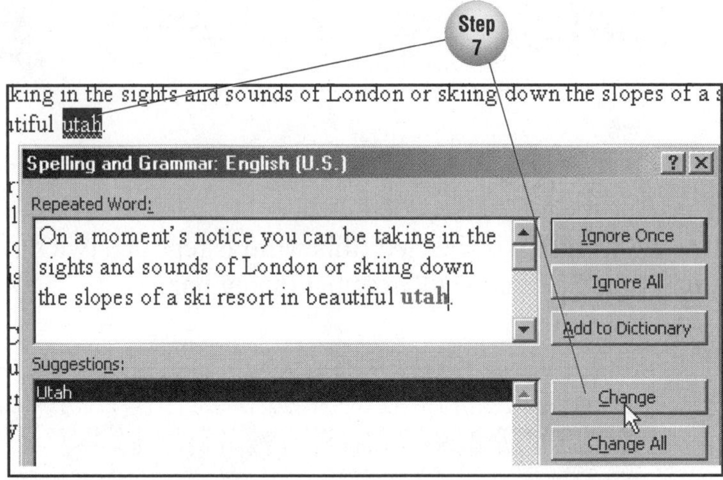


8 When the Readability Statistics dialog box displays, read the information, and then click the OK button.

The Readability Statistics dialog box displays a variety of information about the document such as word, character, paragraph, and sentence counts; and the average length of sentences, words, and characters. Readability percentages also display toward the bottom of the dialog box. Refer to Table W1.5 for a description of the percentages. If the Readability Statistics dialog box does not display, you can turn it on by clicking Tools and then Options. At the Options dialog box, click the Spelling & Grammar tab, insert a check mark in the Show readibility statistics check box, and then click OK.

9. Click the Save button on the Standard toolbar to save the changes made to the document.

**TABLE W1.5** Readability Statistics

| | |
|---|---|
| **Flesch Reading Ease** | The Flesch reading ease is based on the average number of syllables per word and the average number of words per sentence. The higher the score, the greater the number of people who will be able to understand the text in the document. Standard writing generally scores in the 60–70 range. |
| **Flesch-Kincaid Grade Level** | This is based on the average number of syllables per word and the average number of words per sentence. The score indicates a grade level. Standard writing is generally written at the seventh or eighth grade level. |

# In Addition

## Editing While Checking Spelling and Grammar

When checking a document, you can temporarily leave the Spelling and Grammar dialog box, make corrections in the document, and then resume checking. For example, suppose while spell checking you notice a sentence that you want to change. To correct the sentence, move the I-beam pointer to the location in the sentence where the change is to occur, click the left mouse button, and then make the changes to the sentence. To resume checking, click the Resume button, which was formerly the Ignore button.

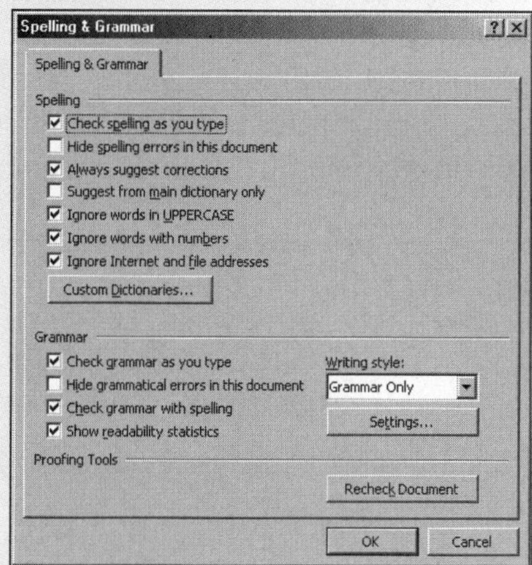


## Changing Spelling Options

Control spelling and grammar checking options at the Spelling & Grammar dialog box shown at the right. Display this dialog box by clicking the Options button at the Spelling and Grammar dialog box. You can also display this dialog box by clicking Tools and then Options. At the Options dialog box, click the Spelling & Grammar tab.

# 1.6 Using AutoCorrect and the Thesaurus

The AutoCorrect feature automatically detects and corrects some typographical errors, misspelled words, and incorrect capitalizations. In addition to correcting errors, you can use the AutoCorrect feature to insert frequently used text. Use the Thesaurus program to find synonyms, antonyms, and related words for a particular word. Synonyms are words that have the same or nearly the same meaning and antonyms are words with opposite meanings.

**PROJECT:** You need to insert additional text in the First Choice Travel vacation specials document. To speed up the process, you will add an entry to AutoCorrect. You will also use Thesaurus to find synonyms for specific words in the document.

## STEPS

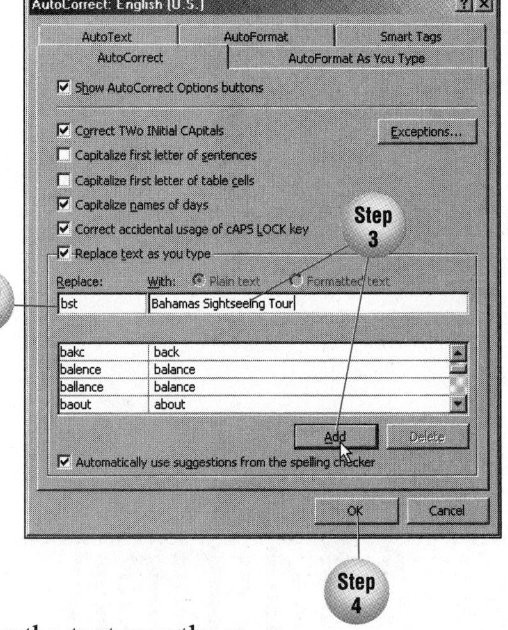


1. With Word S1-02 open, click Tools and then AutoCorrect Options.
2. At the AutoCorrect dialog box with the AutoCorrect tab selected, key **bst** in the Replace text box, and then press the Tab key.
3. Key **Bahamas Sightseeing Tour** in the With text box and then click the Add button.
4. Click OK to close the dialog box.
5. Press Ctrl + End to move the insertion point to the end of the document and then move the insertion point a double space below the last bulleted item.
6. Key the text shown in Figure W1.3. (Key the text exactly as shown. AutoCorrect will correct *bst* to *Bahamas Sightseeing Tour*.)

**FIGURE W1.3**

> bst
>
> The Bahamas consist of over 700 islands and cays, all with friendly people, beautiful beaches, and magnificent dive spots. First Choice Travel offers the bst to explore these exciting and breathtaking islands. Sign up for the bst and experience the bustling city of Nassau, which offers everything from parasailing to casino gaming. Call us to discover how you can join the bst at an incredibly low price.

7. Click anywhere in the word *breathtaking* located in the second sentence in the paragraph you just keyed.
8. Click Tools, point to Language, and then click Thesaurus.

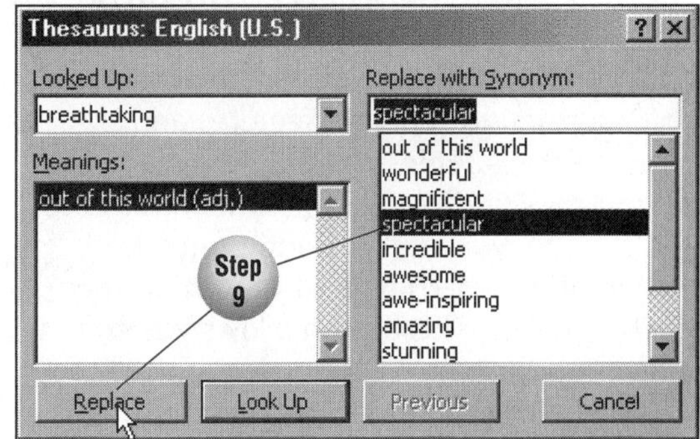


9 At the Thesaurus dialog box, click *spectacular* in the Replace with Synonym list box, and then click the Replace button.

10 Position the mouse pointer on the word *bustling* located in the third sentence in the paragraph you just keyed and then click the *right* mouse button.

PROBLEM ? If the shortcut menu does not display, check to make sure you clicked the *right* mouse button.

11 At the shortcut menu that displays, point to Synonyms, and then click *lively* at the side menu.

12 Click the Save button to save the document with the same name.

13 Click Tools and then AutoCorrect Options.

14 At the AutoCorrect dialog box, click the down-pointing triangle in the list box scroll bar until *bst* displays and then click *bst*.

15 Click the Delete button.

16 Click OK to close the dialog box.

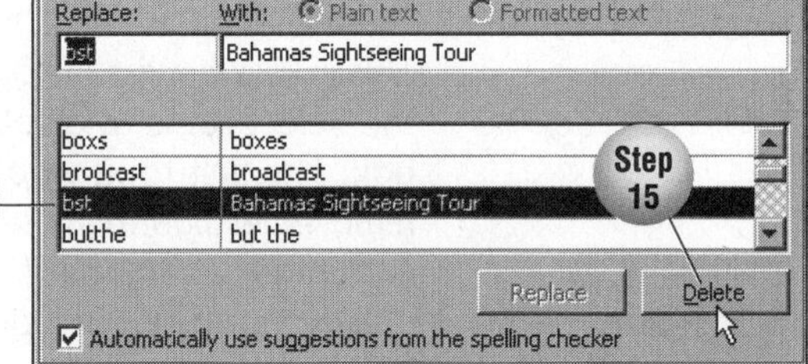


# In Addition

## Using the Thesaurus Dialog Box

At the Thesaurus dialog box, a list of words displays in the Meanings list box. Depending on the word you are looking up, the words in the Meanings list box may display followed by *(n.)* for *noun*, *(adj.)* for *adjective*, or *(adv.)* for *adverb*. You might also see the words *Antonym*, and *Related Words*. The first word in the Meanings list box is selected by default and synonyms for that word are displayed in the Replace with Synonym list box. The Replace with Synonym list box may also display an antonym for a word. You can view synonyms in the Replace with Synonym list box for the words shown in the Meanings list box by clicking the desired word.

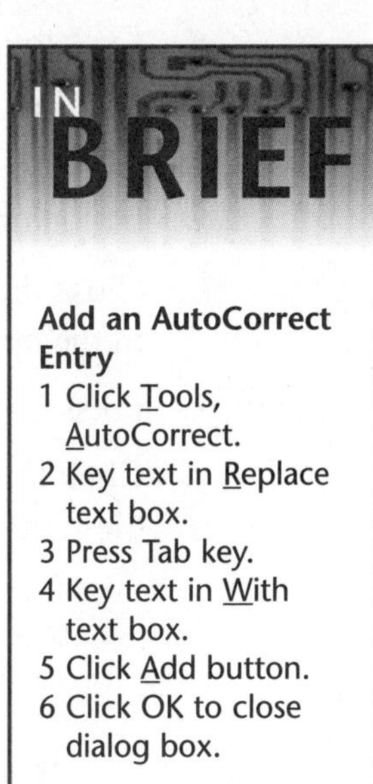

IN BRIEF

**Add an AutoCorrect Entry**

1 Click Tools, AutoCorrect.
2 Key text in Replace text box.
3 Press Tab key.
4 Key text in With text box.
5 Click Add button.
6 Click OK to close dialog box.

# 1.7 Using the Help Feature; Highlighting Text

Microsoft Word includes a Help feature that contains information on Word features and commands. For example, you might want to find information on Word's highlighting feature. With the Help feature, you can find and print the information about the Highlight button on the Formatting toolbar. This button allows you to highlight important information electronically, similar to the way you might highlight with a marker or highlighter pen sentences in books, magazines, and papers.

**PROJECT:** You want to identify specific text in the First Choice Travel document for other marketing team members to evaluate. You will use the Help feature to search for and print information on highlighting text and then highlight specific text in the vacation specials document.

## STEPS

1. With Word S1-02 open, click the Microsoft Word Help button located at the right side of the Standard toolbar.

2. At the Microsoft Word Help window that displays, click the Show button.

   The Show button is located toward the top of the Help window. When you click the Show button it changes to the Hide button.

3. Click the Answer Wizard tab, key **How do I highlight text?** in the What would you like to do? text box, and then press Enter.

   This displays a list of topics in the Select topic to display list box. The first topic *Apply or remove highlighting* is selected and information about the topic displays at the right side of the Help window.

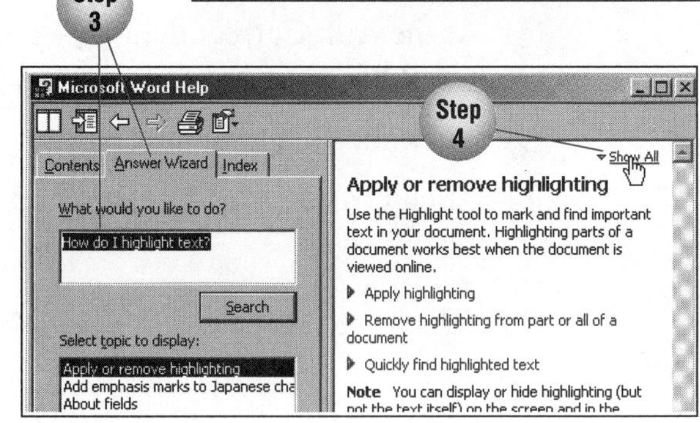


4. Click the *Show All* hyperlink that displays in the upper right corner of the Help window.

   This displays all information about the topic.

5. Read the information that displays in the Help window and then click the Print button on the Help window toolbar. At the Print dialog box, click the OK button.

6. Close the Microsoft Word Help window by clicking the Close button located in the upper right corner of the window.

7. Press Ctrl + Home to move the insertion point to the beginning of the document.

8. Click the Highlight button located toward the right side of the Formatting toolbar.

   If the Standard and Formatting toolbars display on one row, separate the toolbars by clicking Tools and then Customize. At the Customize dialog box with the Options tab selected, click the Show Standard and Formatting toolbars on two rows option to insert a check mark, and then click the Close button.

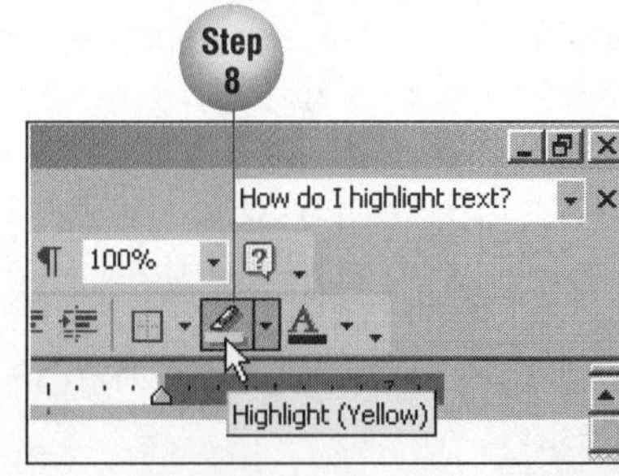

9 Select the sentence *This inaugural trip begins May 6 in Seattle, Washington, and ends back in Seattle on May 13.* that displays in the first paragraph in the *The Pacific Sky Makes Its Inaugural Voyage* section.

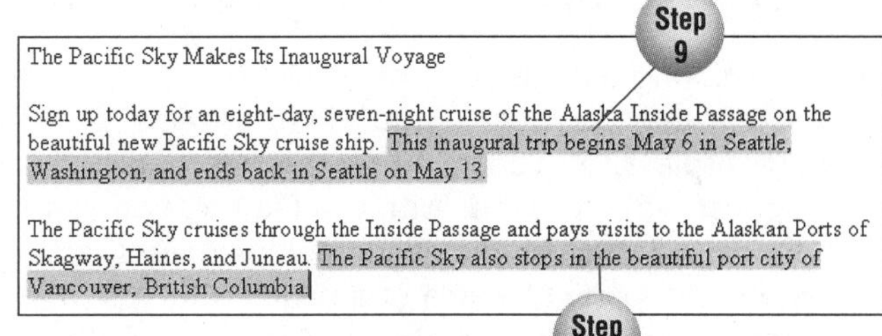


10 Select the sentence *The Pacific Sky also stops in the beautiful port city of Vancouver, British Columbia.* that displays in the second paragraph in the *The Pacific Sky Makes Its Inaugural Voyage* section.

11 Click the Highlight button on the Formatting toolbar to turn off highlighting.

12 Click the down-pointing triangle at the right side of the Highlight button and then click *None* at the palette.

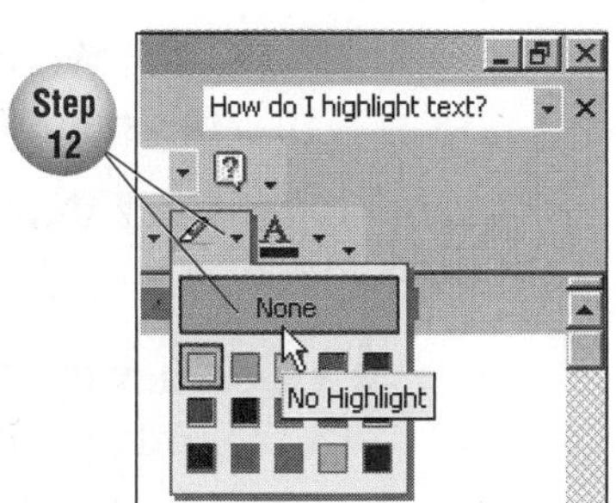


13 Select the sentence *The Pacific Sky also stops in the beautiful port city of Vancouver, British Columbia.*

This removes the highlighting from the sentence.

14 Click the down-pointing triangle at the right side of the Highlight button and then click the yellow color (first color from the left in the top row).

15 Click the Highlight button to turn off highlighting.

16 Click the Save button to save the document.

# In Addition

## Getting Help Using the Ask a Question Box

Click the text inside the Ask a Question box located at the right side of the Menu bar (this removes the text), key a help question, and then press Enter. A list of topics matching keywords in your question displays below the Ask a Question box. Click the desired topic and a Help window displays with information about the topic.

## Turning On/Turning Off the Office Assistant

Microsoft Office offers an Office Assistant that will automatically provide topics and tips on tasks you perform as you work. You can turn on the display of the Office Assistant by clicking Help and then Show the Office Assistant. Turn off the display of the assistant by clicking Help and then Hide the Office Assistant. If you turn on the display of the assistant and then decide to turn it off (rather than just hiding it), click the Office Assistant and then click the Options button that displays in the yellow box. At the Office Assistant dialog box, click the Use the Office Assistant to remove the check mark, and then click OK.

## In Brief

**Use Help**
1 Click Microsoft Word Help button.
2 Click Answer Wizard tab.
3 Key question.
4 Press Enter.

**Highlight Text**
1 Click Highlight button.
2 Select text.
3 Click Highlight button.

## 1.8 Previewing and Printing a Document

Before printing a document, previewing a document may be useful. Word's Print Preview feature displays the document on the screen as it will appear when printed. With this feature, you can view a partial page, single page, multiple pages, or zoom in on a particular area of a page. With options at the Print dialog box, you can specify the number of copies to print and also specific pages for printing.

**PROJECT:** You are ready to print certain sections of the First Choice Travel vacation specials document. But first you will preview the document on screen.

### STEPS

1. With Word S1-02 open, press Ctrl + Home to move the insertion point to the beginning of the document.
2. Click the Print Preview button on the Standard toolbar.

   This displays the Word S1-02 document in Print Preview.
3. Click the Multiple Pages button on the Print Preview toolbar. This causes a grid to appear immediately below the button.

   Refer to Figure W1.4 for the names of the buttons on the Print Preview toolbar.

**FIGURE W1.4** Print Preview Toolbar

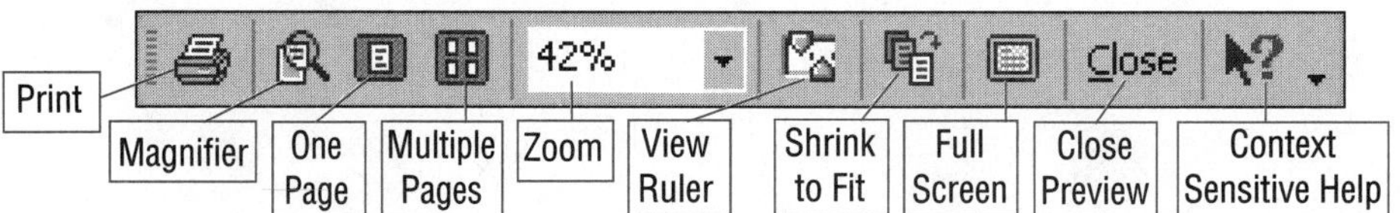


4. At the grid that displays, drag the mouse down and to the right until the message at the bottom of the grid displays as *2 X 2 Pages*, and then click the left mouse button.
5. Click the One Page button on the Print Preview toolbar.
6. Click the down-pointing triangle at the right of the Zoom button 42% and then click *75%* at the drop-down list.

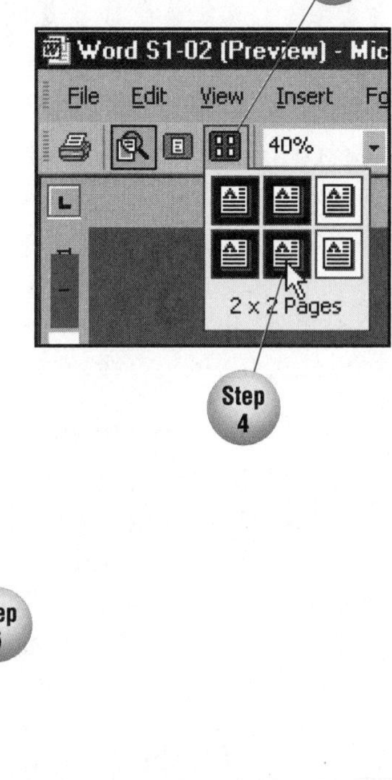

7 Click the One Page button on the Print Preview toolbar.

8 Click the Close button to close Print Preview.

9 Print only page 2 of the document by clicking File and then Print.

10 At the Print dialog box, click in the Pages text box in the Page range section, and then key **2**.

11 Click OK.

12 Move the insertion point to any character in page 3 and then print page 3 by clicking File and then Print.

13 At the Print dialog box, click the Current page option in the Page range section.

14 Click OK.

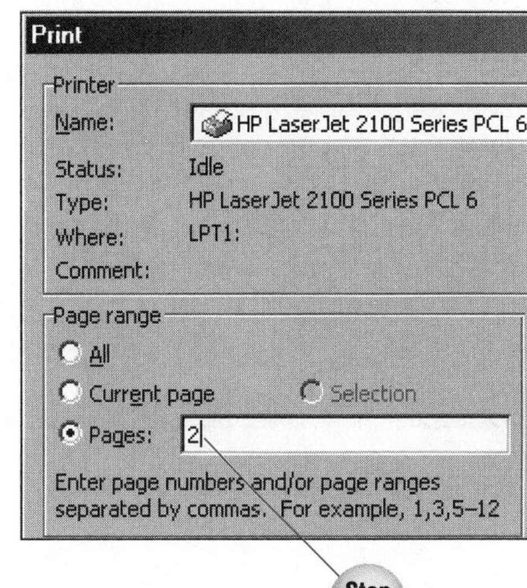


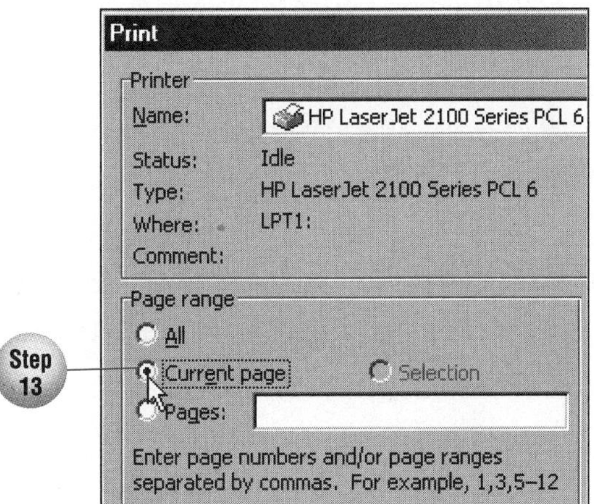


# In Addition

## Printing a Range of Pages

With the Pages option in the Page range section of the Print dialog box, you can identify a specific page, multiple pages, and/or a range of pages for printing. If you want specific multiple pages printed, use a comma to indicate *and* and use a hyphen to indicate *through*. For example, to print pages 2 and 5, you would key **2,5** in the Pages text box. To print pages 6 through 10, you would key **6-10**.

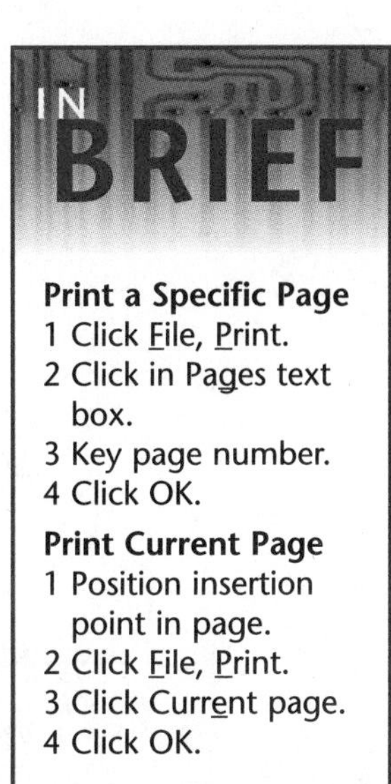

## In Brief

**Print a Specific Page**
1 Click File, Print.
2 Click in Pages text box.
3 Key page number.
4 Click OK.

**Print Current Page**
1 Position insertion point in page.
2 Click File, Print.
3 Click Current page.
4 Click OK.

## 1.9 Inserting the Date and Time; Closing a Document

Insert the current date and/or time with options at the Date and Time dialog box. The Date and Time dialog box contains a list of date and time options in the Available formats list box. If the Update automatically option at the Date and Time dialog box does not contain a check mark, the date and/or time are inserted in the document as normal text that can be edited in the normal manner. The date and/or time can also be inserted in a document as a field. The advantage to inserting the date or time as a field is that the field can be updated with the Update Field key, F9. To insert the date and/or time as a field, insert a check mark in the Update automatically check box at the Date and Time dialog box. To update a date or time inserted as a field, click the date or time and then press the Update Field key, F9.

**PROJECT:** Your team is satisfied with the recent revisions to the First Choice Travel vacation specials document. To track document versions, you need to date the document before closing the file.

### STEPS

1. With Word S1-02 open, press Ctrl + End to move the insertion point to the end of the document.
2. Press the Enter key twice.
3. Key your name and then press Enter.
4. Key **Date:** and then press the spacebar once.
5. Click Insert and then Date and Time.
6. At the Date and Time dialog box, click the third option from the top in the Available formats list box.

   Your date will vary from what you see in the Date and Time dialog box below.
7. Click in the Update automatically check box to insert a check mark.
8. Click OK to close the dialog box.

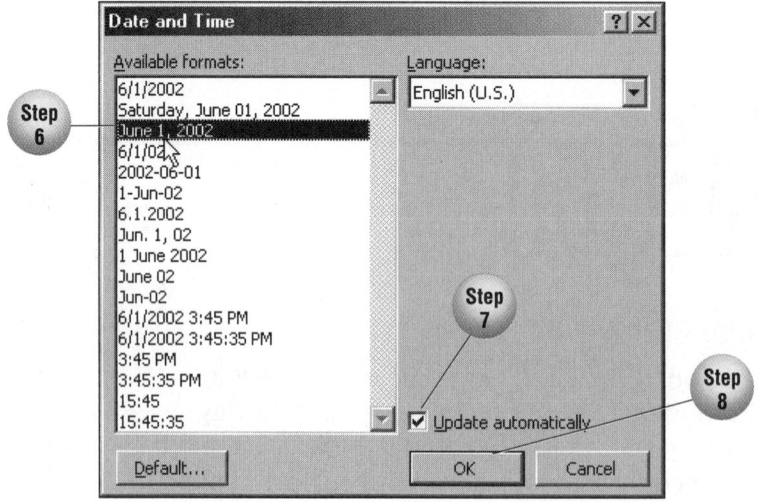


9. Press Enter once.
10. Key **Time:** and then press the spacebar once.

11. Click Insert and then Date and Time.
12. At the Date and Time dialog box, click the fifteenth option from the top in the Available formats list box.
13. Make sure the Update automatically check box contains a check mark and then click OK to close the dialog box.

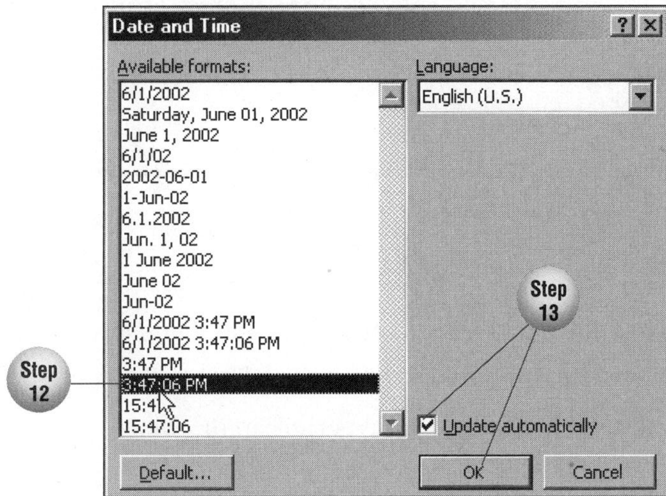


14. Print the entire document by clicking the Print button on the Standard toolbar.
15. Update the time by clicking the time and then pressing the F9 key.

    Clicking F9, the Update Field key, updates the time.
16. Print only page 3 of the document.
17. Click the Save button to save the document.
18. Close the document by clicking File and then Close.

## In Addition

### Closing Multiple Documents

If you have more than one document open, you can close all open documents at the same time. To do this, hold down the Shift key, and then click File on the Menu bar. This causes the File drop-down menu to display with the Close All option instead of the Close option. Click Close All to close all open documents.

**Display Date and Time Dialog Box**
Click Insert, Date and Time

## 1.10 Creating a Document Using a Template

Word includes a number of template documents that are formatted for specific uses. Each Word document is based on a template document with the *Normal* template the default. With Word templates, you can easily create a variety of documents such as letters, memos, and awards, with specialized formatting. Templates are available at the Templates dialog box. This dialog box contains several tabs for displaying a variety of templates. Double-click the desired template and a template document is opened with certain formatting already applied.

**PROJECT:** Marquee Productions, a client of First Choice Travel, is planning to film a movie in Toronto. As Melissa Gehring, manager of the Los Angeles office of First Choice Travel, you are sending a memo to the manager of the Toronto office regarding flight and hotel information.

### STEPS

1. At a blank document screen, click File and then New.

   This displays the New Document Task Pane at the right side of the screen.

2. Click the *General Templates* hyperlink in the New Document Task Pane.

3. At the Templates dialog box, click the Memos tab.

   View the various templates available by clicking each of the tabs at the Templates dialog box.

4. Double-click *Contemporary Memo*.

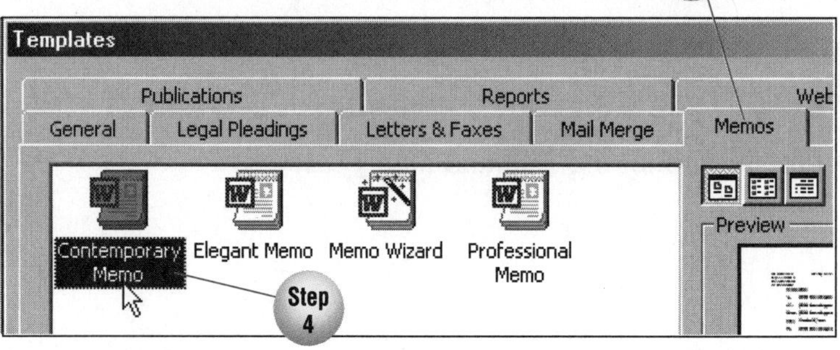


5. At the contemporary memo template document, position the mouse pointer on the word *here* in the bracketed text *[Click **here** and type name]* after *To:* and then click the left mouse button.

6. Key **Alex Torres, Manager, Toronto Office**.

7. Click the word *here* in the bracketed text *[Click **here** and type name]* after *CC:* and then key **Terry Blessing, President**.

8. Click the word *here* in the bracketed text *[Click **here** and type name]* after *From:* and then key **Melissa Gehring, Manager, Los Angeles Office**.

9. Click the word *here* in the bracketed text *[Click **here** and type subject]* after *Re:* and then key **Marquee Productions Movie Site**.

10. Select the text in the memo from *How To Use This Memo Template* to just past the period at the end of the last paragraph of text.

11 Key the text shown in Figure W1.5.

When you begin keying the text, the selected text is automatically deleted.

**FIGURE W1.5**

Marquee Productions will be filming a movie in and around the Toronto area from July 8 through August 30. Robert Velarde, site coordinator for Marquee Productions, has requested scheduling and pricing information on flights from Los Angeles to Toronto and information on lodging.

Approximately 45 people from Marquee Productions will need flight reservations and hotel rooms. Please research this information and locate the best group rates. I would like the information by the end of the week.

Memorandum

**To:** Alex Torres, Manager, Toronto Office

**CC:** Terry Blessing, President

**From:** Melissa Gehring, Manager, Los Angeles Office

**Date:** (current date)

**Re:** Marquee Productions Movie Site

Marquee Productions will be filming a movie in and around the Toronto area from July 8 through August 30. Robert Velarde, site coordinator for Marquee Productions, has requested scheduling and pricing information on flights from Los Angeles to Toronto and information on lodging.

Approximately 45 people from Marquee Productions will need flight reservations and hotel rooms. Please research this information and locate the best group rates. I would like the information by the end of the week.

Step 11

12 Click the Save button on the Standard toolbar.

13 At the Save As dialog box, key **Word S1-03** and then press Enter.

14 Click the Print button on the Standard toolbar.

15 Close the document by clicking File and then Close.

# In Addition

## Displaying a New Blank Document Screen

By default, a Word document is based on the Normal template. You can choose a different template at the Templates dialog box or use the default template. If you close a document and then want to create another document based on the Normal template, click the New Blank Document button on the Standard toolbar or press the shortcut key, Ctrl + N.

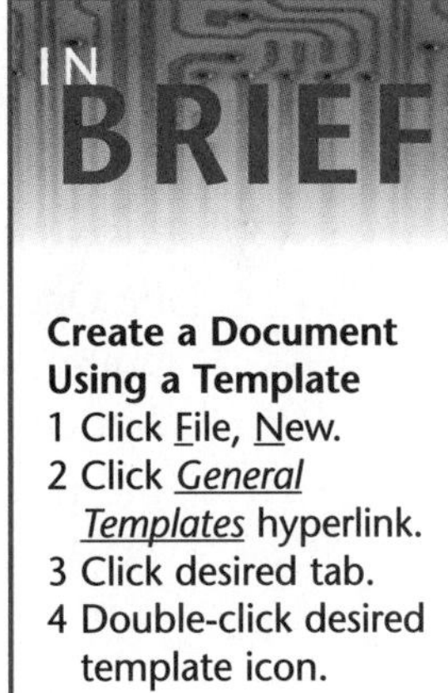

**IN BRIEF**

**Create a Document Using a Template**

1 Click File, New.
2 Click *General Templates* hyperlink.
3 Click desired tab.
4 Double-click desired template icon.

## 1.11 Managing Documents

As you continue working with documents, consider document management tasks such as creating a folder and copying, moving, and deleting documents. Many document management tasks can be completed at the Open dialog box. Document management tasks can be completed on one document or selected documents. By default, Word saves a file as a Word document and adds the extension *.doc* to the name. This extension identifies the file as a Word document. With the Save as type option at the Save As dialog box, you can save a document in a different format such as a Web page, a plain text file, a WordPerfect or Works file, or an earlier version of Word.

**PROJECT:** Since First Choice Travel will be communicating with Marquee Productions, you decide to create a folder into which you will insert Marquee Productions documents and save one document in a different format.

## STEPS

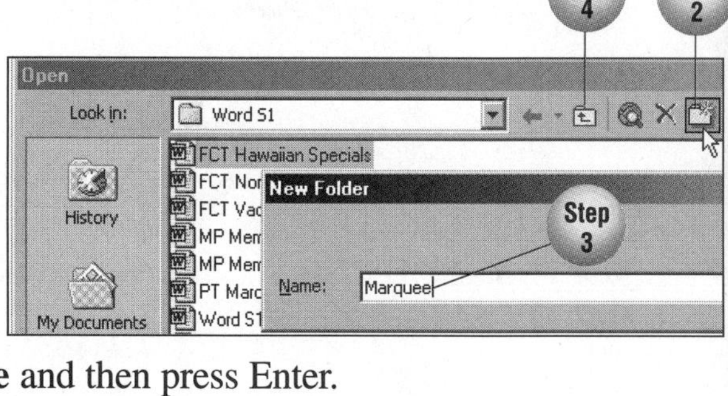


1. Click the Open button on the Standard toolbar
2. At the Open dialog box with *Word S1* the active folder, click the Create New Folder button on the dialog box toolbar.
3. At the New Folder dialog box, key **Marquee** and then press Enter.

   The new folder becomes the active folder.
4. Click the Up One Level button on the Open dialog box toolbar to return to the previous folder.
5. Click the document *MP Memo 01* in the Open dialog box list box. Hold down the Ctrl key, click *MP Memo Form*, click *Word S1-02*, click *Word S1-03,* and then release the Ctrl key.

   Use the Ctrl key to select nonadjacent documents. Use the Shift key to select adjacent documents.

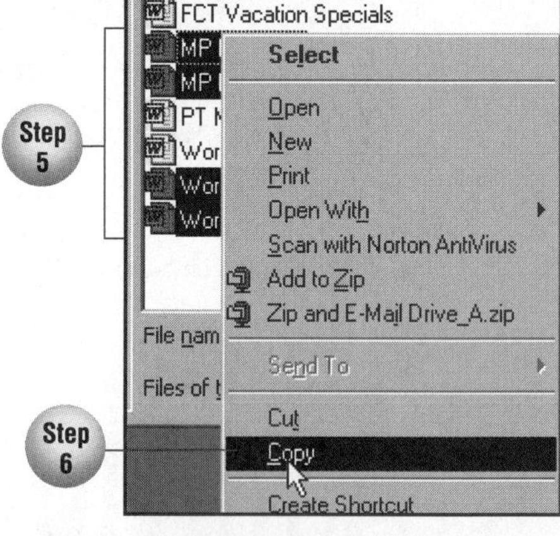


6. Right-click on any selected document and then click Copy at the shortcut menu.
7. Double-click the *Marquee* file folder.

   File folders display in the Open dialog box list box before documents. File folders display preceded by a file folder icon and documents display preceded by a document icon .
8. Position the mouse pointer in a white portion of the Open dialog box list box, click the *right* mouse button, and then click Paste at the shortcut menu.

   The copied documents are inserted in the *Marquee* folder.

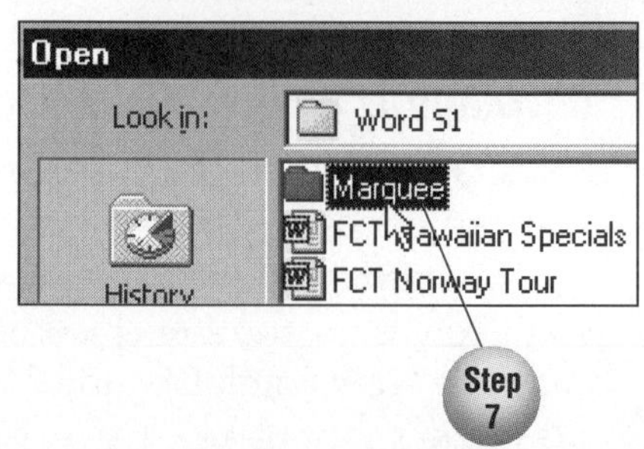

9 You need to send the Word S1-02 document to a colleague who does not use Microsoft Word, so you decide to save it as a plain text document. At the Open dialog box with the *Marquee* folder active, double-click *Word S1-02*.

10 Click File and then Save As. At the Save As dialog box, key **Word S1-02 Plain Text** in the File name text box.

11 Click the down-pointing triangle at the right side of the Save as type list box, click the down-pointing triangle until *Plain Text* displays, click *Plain Text*, and then click the Save button.

Saving a document as plain text removes most of the formatting.

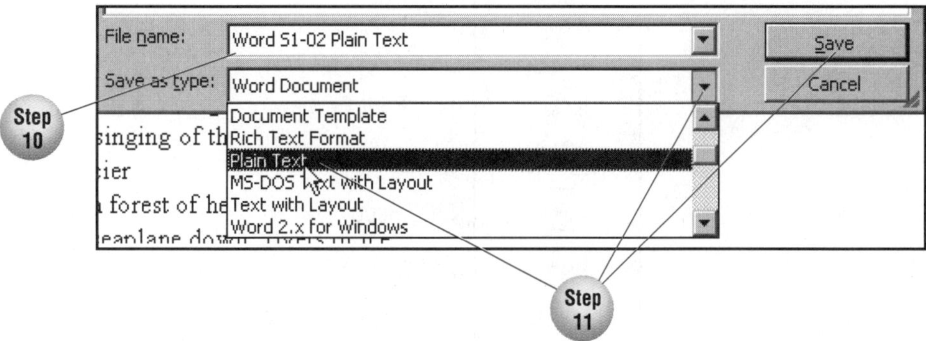


12 At the File Conversion dialog box, click OK.

The first time you save a document as plain text, you may need to install conversion files.

13 Click File and then Close to close the document.

14 Open Word S1-02 Plain Text, click the Print button on the Standard toolbar, and then close the document.

When you open Word S1-02 Plain Text, notice how most of the formatting has been removed from the text.

15 Display the Open dialog box and then click the Up One Level button on the dialog box toolbar.

16 Delete the *Marquee* folder by clicking once on the folder to select it and then clicking the Delete button on the dialog box toolbar.

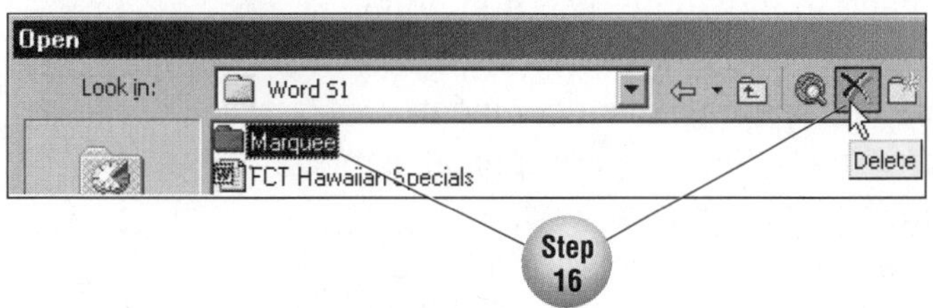


17 At the message asking if you are sure want to delete the folder and all of its contents, click the Yes button.

18 Close the Open dialog box.

19 Exit Word by clicking File and then Exit.

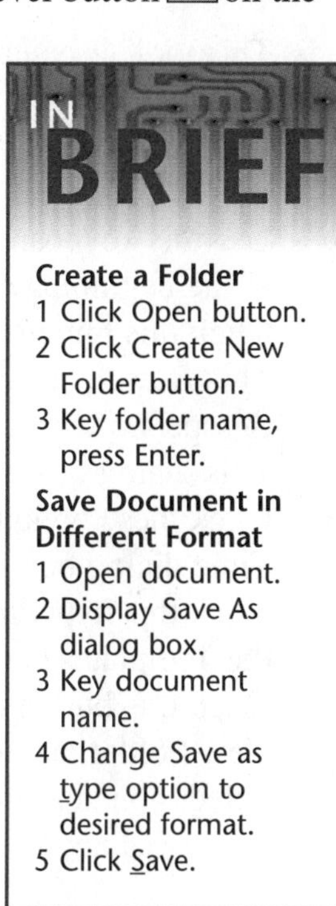

**IN BRIEF**

**Create a Folder**
1 Click Open button.
2 Click Create New Folder button.
3 Key folder name, press Enter.

**Save Document in Different Format**
1 Open document.
2 Display Save As dialog box.
3 Key document name.
4 Change Save as type option to desired format.
5 Click Save.

# FEATURES SUMMARY

| Feature | Button | Menu | Keyboard |
|---|---|---|---|
| AutoCorrect dialog box | | Tools, AutoCorrect Options | |
| Close a document | | File, Close | Ctrl + W |
| Date and Time dialog box | | Insert, Date and Time | |
| Exit Word | | File, Exit | |
| Highlighting | | | |
| Preview a document | | File, Print Preview | Ctrl + F2 |
| Print document | | File, Print | Ctrl + P |
| Redo the last command or entry | | Edit, Redo | Ctrl + Y |
| Save a document | | File, Save | Ctrl + S |
| Save As dialog box | | File, Save As | F12 |
| Spelling and grammar check | | Tools, Spelling and Grammar | F7 |
| Thesaurus dialog box | | Tools, Language, Thesaurus | Shift + F7 |
| Undo the last command or entry | | Edit, Undo | Ctrl + Z |

# PROCEDURES CHECK

**Completion:** In the space provided at the right, indicate the correct term, command, or option.

1. This toolbar contains buttons for working with documents such as the Open and Save buttons. ________________
2. Click this option at the File drop-down menu to save a previously named document with a new name. ________________
3. Use this keyboard command to move the insertion point to the beginning of the document. ________________
4. Click this button to check the spelling in a document. ________________
5. This feature detects and corrects some typographical errors, misspelled words, and incorrect capitalizations. ________________
6. This dialog box displays a list of synonyms for a word. ________________
7. Click these options on the Menu bar to display the Date and Time dialog box. ________________
8. Click this hyperlink at the New Document Task Pane to display the Templates dialog box. ________________
9. Click this button on the Open dialog box toolbar to display the New Folder dialog box. ________________
10. Select nonadjacent documents at the Open dialog box by holding down this key while clicking each document. ________________

# SKILLS REVIEW

## Activity 1: MOVING THE INSERTION POINT; SCROLLING; INSERTING TEXT

1 Open FCT Hawaiian Specials.
2 Save the document with Save As and name it Word S1-R1.
3 Practice moving the insertion point to the following locations:
   a Move the insertion point to the end of the document.
   b Move the insertion point back to the beginning of the document.
   c Scroll to the end of the document.
   d Scroll back to the beginning of the document.
   e Move the insertion point to the beginning of the second page.
   f Move the insertion point to the beginning of the document.
4 Move the insertion point between the words *the* and *Pacific* in the first sentence below the *White Sands Charters* heading and then key **spectacular**.
5 Move the insertion point to the beginning of the paragraph below the *Air Adventures* heading and then key the sentence **Experience beautiful coastlines, magnificent waterfalls, and fly inside an active volcano.**
6 Save Word S1-R1.

## Activity 2: SELECTING AND DELETING TEXT

1 With Word S1-R1 open, select and then delete the words *Depending on weather, marine conditions, and access, your* located in the third sentence in the paragraph below the *White Sands Charters* heading.
2 Capitalize the *g* in *guides*. (This word now begins the sentence.)
3 Select and then delete the last sentence in the Air Adventures section (the sentence that reads *Chart untouched areas from the moonscapes of volcanic craters to thundering waterfalls and rugged coastlines.*).
4 Undo the deletion.
5 Redo the deletion.
6 Select and then delete the fourth bulleted item in the Bicycle Safari section (the text that reads *Vista dining*).
7 Undo the deletion.
8 Deselect the text.
9 Save Word S1-R1.

## Activity 3: CHECKING THE SPELLING AND GRAMMAR IN A DOCUMENT

1 With Word S1-R1 open, move the insertion point to the beginning of the document.
2 Complete a spelling and grammar check on the document (*Molokini* is spelled correctly).
3 Save Word S1-R1.

## Activity 4: CREATING AN AUTOCORRECT ENTRY; USING THESAURUS; INSERTING THE DATE AND TIME

1 With Word S1-R1 open, add the following to the AutoCorrect dialog box: insert *HA* in the Replace text box and *Hawaiian* in the With text box.
2 Move the insertion point to the end of the document and then key the text shown in Figure W1.6.
3 After keying the text, use Thesaurus and make the following changes:
   a Change *lavish* to *sumptuous.*
   b Change *exceptional* to *extraordinary.*
4 Insert the current date and time by completing the following steps:
   a Move the insertion point to the end of the document.
   b Press the Enter key twice.
   c Insert the current date (you choose the format).
   d Press the Enter key.
   e Insert the current time (you choose the format).
5 Save, print, and then close Word S1-R1.

**FIGURE W1.6** Activity 4

> Luau Legends
>
> Enjoy a spectacular HA dinner show featuring lavish prime rib and authentic HA buffet. This uniquely HA experience includes a traditional lei greeting, exceptional food and beverages, magic music of the islands, and Hawaii's finest performers. Join us each evening beginning at 7:00 p.m. for an evening of delicious HA food and spectacular performances.

## Activity 5: CREATING A MEMO USING A TEMPLATE

1 Use the Contemporary Memo template and create a memo with the following information:
   a The memo is to Hanh Postma, Manager, European Distribution.
   b Send a copy of the memo to Roman Deptulski, Manager, Overseas Distribution.
   c The memo is from Sam Vestering, Manager, North American Distribution.
   d The subject (Re:) of the memo is Distribution Schedule.
   e Key the text in Figure W1.7 as the body of the memo.
2 Save the completed memo and name it Word S1-R2.
3 Print and then close Word S1-R2.

**FIGURE W1.7** Activity 5

> I am preparing the quarterly distribution report and would like you to send your schedule to me as soon as possible. Please use the Excel worksheet provided by the Distribution Department and then e-mail the completed worksheet to me. I will send you the master schedule by the end of next month.

# PERFORMANCE PLUS

### Activity 1: INSERTING TEXT IN A MEMO

1 Open MP Memo 01.
2 Save the document with Save As and name it Word S1-P1.
3 Insert the words *or Buffalo* between *Toronto* and *area* in the second sentence in the body of the memo.
4 Move the insertion point to the end of the paragraph in the body of the memo and then add the following sentence: **We are anticipating having lunches and snacks catered on the set.**
5 Press the Enter key twice and then key the two paragraphs of text shown in Figure W1.8.
6 Save the memo again with the same name (Word S1-P1).
7 Print and then close Word S1-P1.

**FIGURE W1.8** Activity 1

Since the film is a period piece, we need to locate a company that can research, locate, and/or design costumes for the movie. When you locate a costume company, please request information on time needed to research, locate, or sew costumes.

Please have the information on catering and costuming available for the production meeting on Thursday, May 9.

### Activity 2: PREPARING A MEMO

1 Open MP Memo Form.
2 Save the document with Save As and name it Word S1-P2.
3 Insert the following information after the specified heading:

| | |
|---|---|
| **To:** | Robert Velarde, Site Coordinator |
| **From:** | Camille Matsui, Production Assistant |
| **Date:** | (Insert current date) |
| **Re:** | Catering and Costuming Businesses |

4 Move the insertion point a triple space below the *Re:* heading and then write the body of the memo using the following information (write the information in paragraph form—do not use bullets):
   - You contacted the Chamber of Commerce in Buffalo and Toronto and determined that King Street Eatery in downtown Toronto and The Waterfront Bistro in Buffalo were the best choices.
   - You have sent a letter to each catering business requesting menus and a pricing guide.
   - The only costuming company you could find was Performance Threads in Niagara Falls, Canada. You sent a letter to that company requesting information on research, costume design, and pricing.
   - You hope to have the information available before the production meeting.

5 Complete a spelling and grammar check on the memo (proper names are spelled correctly).

6 Save the memo again with the same name (Word S1-P2).
7 Print and then close Word S1-P2.

### Activity 3: ADDING A PARAGRAPH TO A LETTER

1 Open PT Marquee Letter.
2 Save the document with Save As and name it Word S1-P3.
3 Move the insertion a double space below the paragraph of text in the letter and then add the following information (write the information in paragraph form—do not use bullets):
   - Costume research takes approximately two to three weeks.
   - If appropriate costumes cannot be found, costumes are sewn.
   - Anticipate five working days for a costume to be sewn.
   - Include the number of costumes and approximate sizes.
   - A price estimate will be provided before costumes are purchased or sewn.
4 Use Thesaurus to replace *regarding* in the first sentence in the letter to an appropriate synonym.
5 Complete a spelling and grammar check on the letter.
6 Save the document with the same name (Word S1-P3).
7 Print and then close Word S1-P3.

### Activity 4: FINDING INFORMATION ON CHANGING GRAMMAR CHECKING OPTIONS

1 Use the Microsoft Word Help feature to learn how to set grammar preferences. After learning about the preferences, click Tools and then Options to display the Options dialog box. Click the Spelling & Grammar tab and then explore the options at the dialog box. Change the Writing style option to Grammar & Style.
2 Open FCT Norway Tour.
3 Save the document with Save As and name it Word S1-P4.
4 Complete a spelling and grammar check on the document (*Myrdal* is spelled correctly).
5 Save the document again with the same name (Word S1-P4).
6 Display the Options dialog box, change the Writing style option back to Grammar Only, and then close the dialog box.
7 Print and then close Word S1-P4.

### Activity 5: LOCATING ONLINE TECHNICAL RESOURCES

1 Use the Microsoft Word Help feature to help you find out what technical resources are available online. (Key the question **How do I connect to Microsoft technical resources?** in the Answer Wizard text box. Click the *Show All* hyperlink to display all of the information.
2 Print and then read the information that displays about online services.
3 Connect to at least two of the resources. Print the first Web page that displays at each of the two resources.
4 Using the information you learned, prepare a memo to your instructor describing the online technical resources available.
5 Save the memo and name it Word S1-P5.
6 Print and then close Word S1-P5.

# WORD

## SECTION 2

# Formatting Characters and Paragraphs

As you work with Word, you will learn a number of commands and procedures that affect how the document appears when printed. The appearance of a document on the document screen and how it looks when printed is called the *format*. Formatting can include such elements as changing the font, aligning and indenting text, changing line and paragraph spacing, setting tabs, and inserting elements such as bullets and numbers. In this section you will learn the skills and complete the projects described here.

*Note: Before beginning this section, delete the* Word S1 *folder on your disk. Next, copy to your disk the* Word S2 *subfolder from the* Word *folder on the CD that accompanies this textbook, and then make* Word S2 *the active folder.*

## Skills

- Apply fonts and font effects
- Use Format Painter
- Repeat a command
- Align text in paragraphs
- Indent text
- Change line and paragraph spacing
- Insert bullets and numbering
- Insert symbols
- Set tabs and tabs with leaders
- Add borders and shading to text
- Apply styles
- Create an outline-style numbered list

## Projects

Edit and format fact sheets on Oslo, Norway, and Petersburg, Alaska; format a document on traveling by train in Europe; format documents on vacation packages in Oregon and Nevada and cross-country skiing vacation packages; and use the Internet to find information on museums and galleries in Toronto and then use that information to prepare a letter to Marquee Productions.

Prepare a letter to the chair of the Theatre Arts Division at Niagara Peninsula College requesting 20 theatre interns.

Prepare a movie distribution schedule.

## 2.1 Applying Fonts and Font Effects Using the Formatting Toolbar

The Formatting toolbar contains several buttons for applying font and font effects to text. Click the Bold button to apply bold formatting, click the Italic button to apply italic formatting, or click the Underline button to underline selected text. The default font used by Word is Times New Roman. Change this default with the Font button and change text size with the Font Size button. The default font color is black. Change this default color with the Font Color button. To view all buttons on the Formatting toolbar at once, display the Formatting toolbar on a line separate from the Standard toolbar.

**PROJECT:** You are working on a series of fact sheets that First Choice Travel is creating about the cities included in its special tours. The first fact sheet is about Oslo, Norway. You have been asked to improve the appearance of the document by applying different kinds of fonts and effects to the text.

### STEPS

1. Open FCT Oslo. Save the document with Save As and name it Word S2-01.
2. Make sure the Standard and Formatting toolbars display on separate rows. If they do not, click Tools and then Customize. At the Customize dialog box with the Options tab selected, click the Show Standard and Formatting toolbars on two rows option to insert a check mark, and then click the Close button.

   The toolbars will display in separate rows each time you open Word.
3. Select *OSLO FACT SHEET* and then click the Bold button **B** on the Formatting toolbar.
4. Select *History* and then click the Underline button **U** on the Formatting toolbar.
5. Select and then underline the remaining headings including *Population*; *Commerce and Industry*; *Climate*; *Holiday, Sport, and Leisure*; and *Sightseeing Tours*.
6. Select the words *Memorial Park* located in the first paragraph below the *History* heading and then click the Italic button *I* on the Formatting toolbar.
7. Click Edit and then Select All to select the entire document.

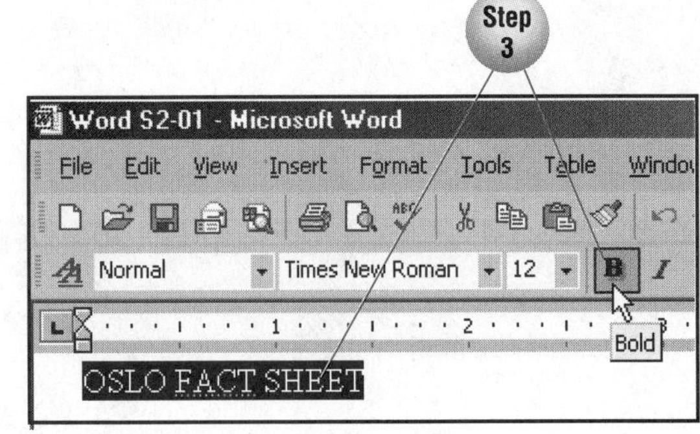


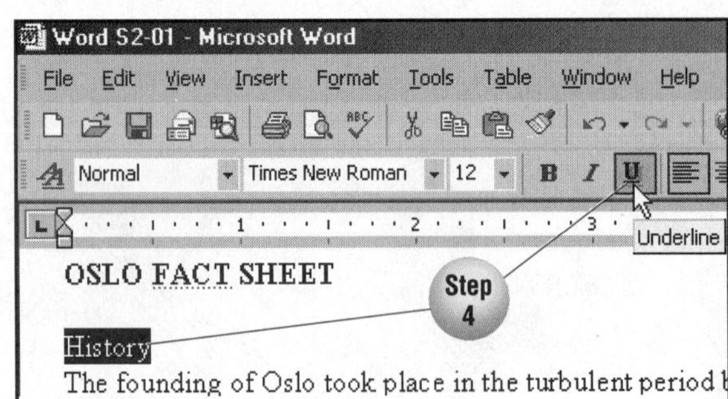

8. Click the down-pointing triangle at the right side of the Font button Times New Roman on the Formatting toolbar. Click the down-pointing triangle to scroll down the list until *Bookman Old Style* is visible and then click it. (If this font is not available, choose another font.)

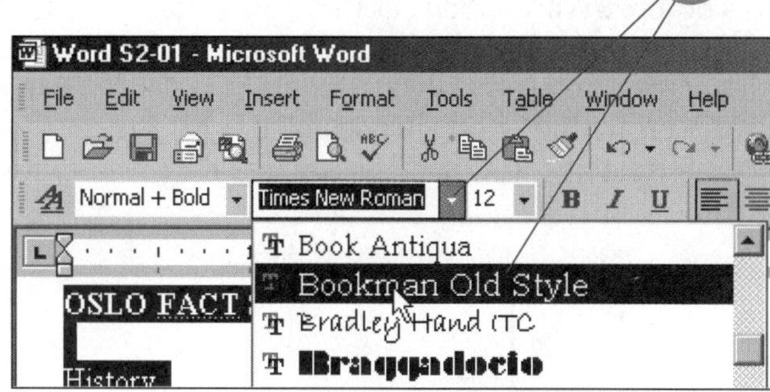


9. Click the down-pointing triangle at the right side of the Font Size button 12 on the Formatting toolbar and then click *11* at the drop-down list.

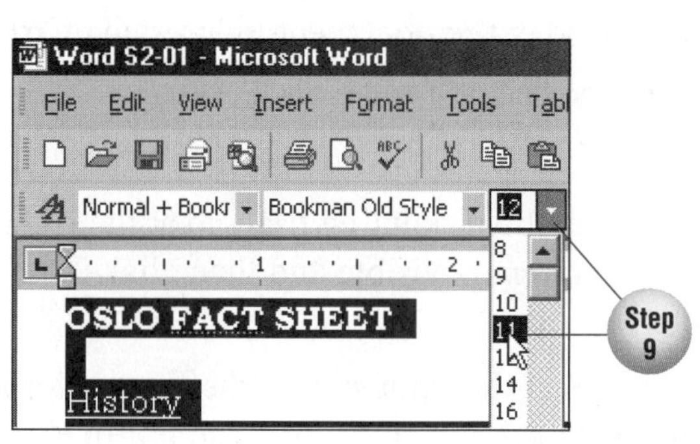


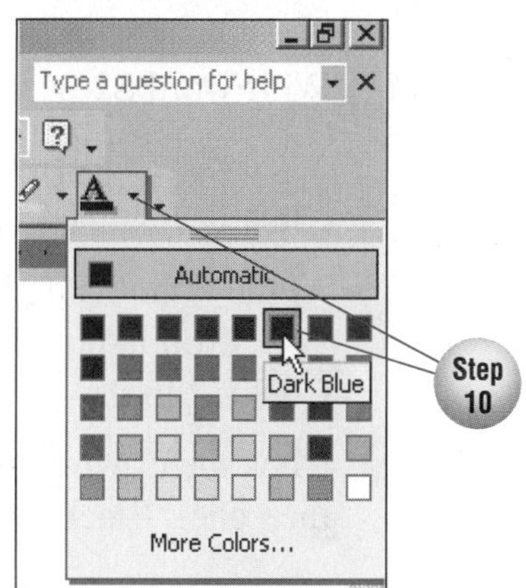


10. Click the down-pointing triangle at the right side of the Font Color button on the Formatting toolbar and then click the Dark Blue color at the color palette (sixth color from the left in the top row).
11. Deselect the text by clicking outside the selected text.
12. Save Word S2-01.
13. Print Word S2-01.

# In Addition

## Using Typefaces

A typeface is a set of characters with a common design and shape. Word refers to typeface as *font*. Typefaces can be decorative or plain and are either monospaced or proportional. A monospaced typeface allots the same amount of horizontal space for each character while a proportional typeface allots a varying amount of space for each character. Proportional typefaces are divided into two main categories: *serif* and *sans serif*. A serif is a small line at the end of a character stroke. Consider using a serif typeface for text-intensive documents because the serifs help move the reader's eyes across the page. Use a sans serif typeface for headings, headlines, and advertisements that are not text intensive.

**In Brief**

**Display Toolbars on Separate Lines**

1. Click Tools, Customize.
2. Insert check mark in Show Standard and Formatting toolbars on two rows option.
3. Click Close button.

## 2.2 Changing the Font at the Font Dialog Box; Using the Format Painter

In addition to buttons on the Formatting toolbar, you can apply font formatting with options at the Font dialog box. With options at this dialog box, you can change the font, font size, and font style; change the font color; choose an underlining style; and apply formatting effects. Once you apply character formatting to text, you can copy that formatting to different locations in the document using the Format Painter.

**PROJECT:** The changes you made to the Oslo fact sheet have enhanced the readability and visual appeal of the text. Now you will turn your attention to the headings.

### STEPS

1. With Word S2-01 open, select the entire document by pressing Ctrl + A.

   Ctrl + A is the shortcut key to select the entire document.

2. Click Format and then Font.
3. At the Font dialog box, click the down-pointing triangle at the right side of the Font list box until *Times New Roman* is visible and then click *Times New Roman*. Click *12* in the Size list box.
4. Click the down-pointing triangle at the right side of the Font color list box and then click Black at the color palette (first color from the left in the top row).

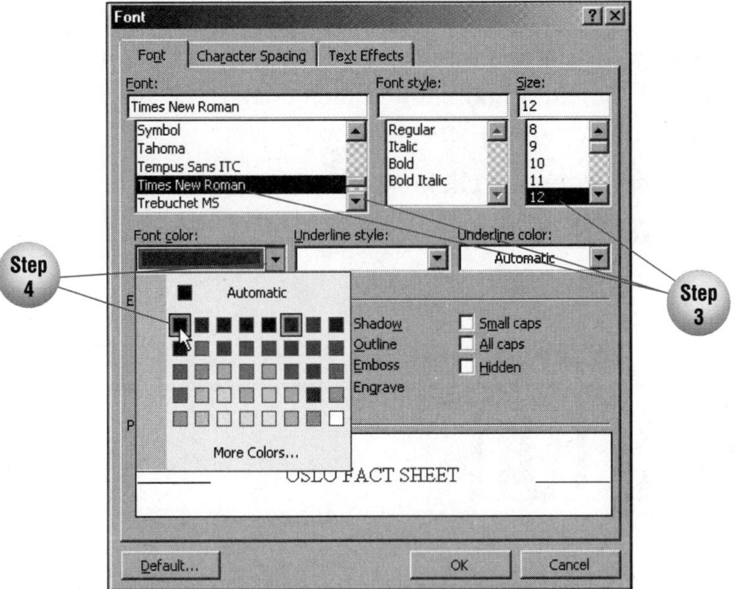


5. Click OK to close the dialog box.
6. Deselect the text by clicking in the document outside the selected text.
7. Select *History*, click the Underline button **U** on the Formatting toolbar, and then click the Bold button **B**.

   Clicking the Underline button removes underlining from the heading and clicking the Bold button applies bold formatting.

8 Click the down-pointing triangle at the right side of the Font button [Times New Roman] on the Formatting toolbar and then click *Arial* at the drop-down list.

9 Deselect the heading.

10 Click once on any character in the heading *History* and then double-click the Format Painter button on the Standard toolbar.

When Format Painter is active, the mouse pointer displays with a paintbrush attached.

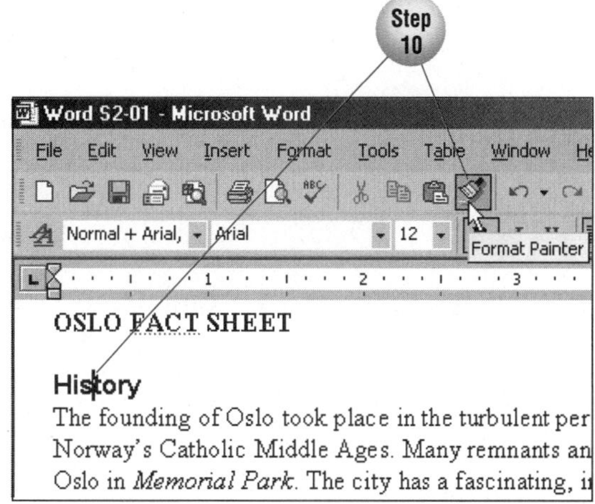


11 Select the heading *Population*. (You will need to scroll down the document to display this heading.)

12 Select individually the remaining headings (*Commerce and Industry*; *Climate*; *Holiday, Sport, and Leisure*; and *Sightseeing Tours*).

PROBLEM?

If the pointer displays without a paintbrush attached, you clicked the Format Painter button only once. To format text in more than one location, you must double-click the Format Painter button.

13 Click once on the Format Painter button.

14 Deselect the heading.

15 Save Word S2-01.

**Change Font at Font Dialog Box**
1 Click Format, Font.
2 Choose desired font.
3 Click OK.

**Apply Formatting with Format Painter**
1 Apply formatting.
2 Double-click Format Painter button.
3 Select text.
4 Click Format Painter button.

# In Addition

## Changing the Default Font

Microsoft Word uses a default font for text (usually 12-point Times New Roman). You can change this default font by choosing the desired font, font style, and font size at the Font dialog box and then clicking the Default button. At the message telling you that the change will affect all new documents based on the Normal template, click the Yes button. Once the default font is changed, the new font is in effect each time you open Word.

## 2.3 Applying Effects Using the Font Dialog Box; Repeating a Command

Use options in the Effects section of the Font dialog box to apply a variety of effects to documents. For example, you can create superscript and subscript text, change selected text to small caps or all caps, strikethrough selected text, and apply a shadow, outline, emboss, or engraving style to text. You can also add animation effects such as a blinking background, a shimmer, or sparkle. Animation effects added to text display on the screen but do not print. If you apply formatting to text in a document and then want to apply the same formatting to other text, use the Repeat command. Repeat a command by pressing the F4 function key.

**PROJECT:** Continuing with your design work on the First Choice Travel fact sheet, you will apply small caps and shadow effects and add animation effects to selected text in the document.

### STEPS

1. With Word S2-01 open, press Ctrl + End to move the insertion point to the end of the document.
2. Select the sentence *All tours by boat and coach depart from Pier 3 in front of the Oslo City Hall.*
3. Click Format and then Font.
4. At the Font dialog box, click Small caps in the Effects section.

   Inserting a check mark in the check box activates the feature. The Preview section of the Font dialog box displays how the effect(s) chosen affect the text.
5. Click OK to close the dialog box.

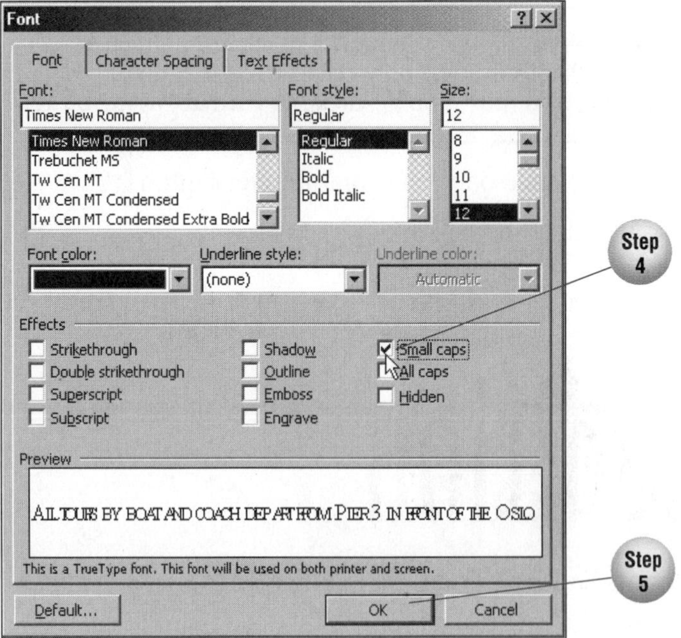


6. Click outside the selected sentence to deselect it.
7. Select the text *Tour 1: Mini Cruise.*
8. Click Format and then Font.

9 At the Font dialog box, click Shadow in the Effects section.

10 Click OK to close the dialog box.

11 Deselect the text.

12 Select the text *Tour 2: Fjord Cruise* and then press F4.

Pressing F4 repeats the previous command and applies the shadow effect to the selected text.

13 Select the text *Tour 3: Fjord Cruise with Dinner* and then press F4.

14 Select the text *Tour 4: Selected Oslo Sightseeing* and then press F4.

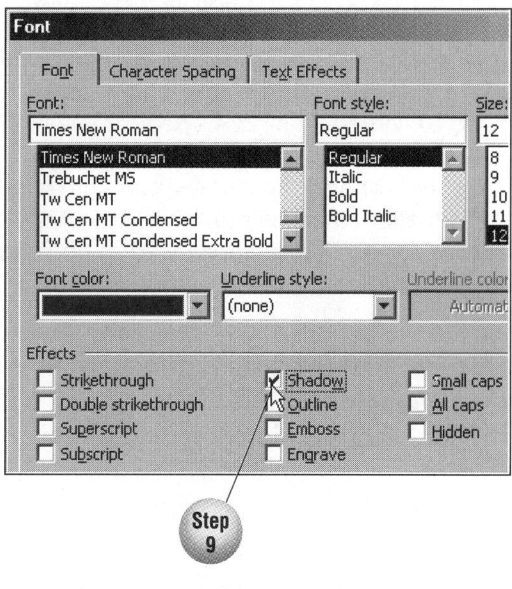


15 Deselect the text.

16 Select the title *OLSO FACT SHEET,* and then display the Font dialog box by clicking Format.

17 Click the Text Effects tab, click *Sparkle Text* in the Animations list box, and then click OK.

Animation effects such as Sparkle Text do not print and are used primarily for documents that are viewed in a Web browser.

18 Save Word S2-01.

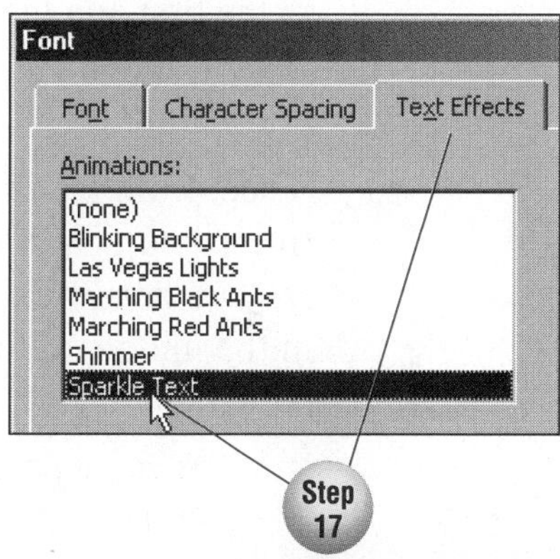


# In Addition

## Applying a Superscript and Subscript Effect

Use the Superscript option in the Effects section of the Font dialog box to create text that is raised slightly above the text line and create subscript text that is lowered slightly below the text line. Use the superscript effect to create a mathematical equation such as four to the second power (written as $4^2$). Use the subscript effect to create a chemical formula such as $H_2O$. The shortcut key to create superscript text is Ctrl + Shift + = and the shortcut key to create subscript text is Ctrl + =.

## In Brief

**Apply Font Effects**
1 Select text.
2 Click Format, Font.
3 Click desired effect check box to insert a check mark.
4 Click OK.

**Apply Animation Effect**
1 Select text.
2 Click Format, Font.
3 Click Text Effects tab.
4 Click desired animation effect in Animations list box.
5 Click OK.

## 2.4 Aligning Text in Paragraphs

Paragraphs of text in a document are aligned at the left margin by default. This default alignment can be changed to center alignment (used for titles, headings, or other text you want centered), right alignment (used for addresses, date, time, or other text you want aligned at the right margin), and justified (used for text you want aligned at both the left and right margins such as text in a report or book). Change paragraph alignment with buttons on the Formatting toolbar; with the Alignment option at the Paragraph dialog box; or with shortcut keys.

**PROJECT:** You will improve the appearance of the First Choice Travel fact sheet by changing text alignment.

## STEPS

1. With Word S2-01 open, select the title *OSLO FACT SHEET*, change the font to Arial and the font size to 14, remove the Sparkle Text effect (do this at the Font dialog box with the Text Effects tab selected), and then deselect the title.

2. Center the title *OSLO FACT SHEET* by positioning the insertion point on any character in the title and then clicking the Center button on the Formatting toolbar.

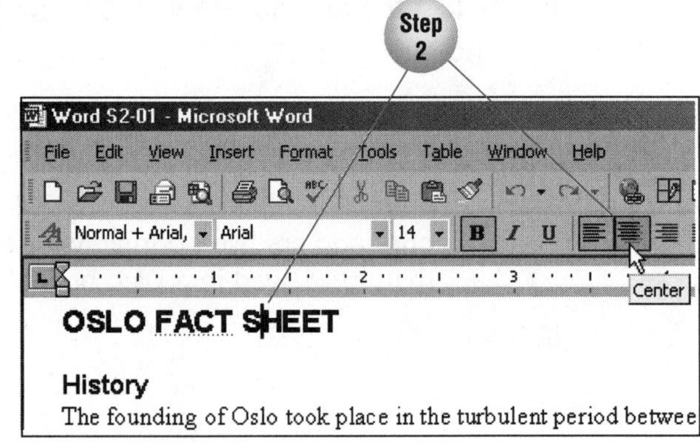


3. Select from the middle of the first paragraph of text below the *History* heading to somewhere in the middle of the third paragraph of text.

   The entire paragraphs do not have to be selected, only a portion of each paragraph.

4. Click the Justify button on the Formatting toolbar.

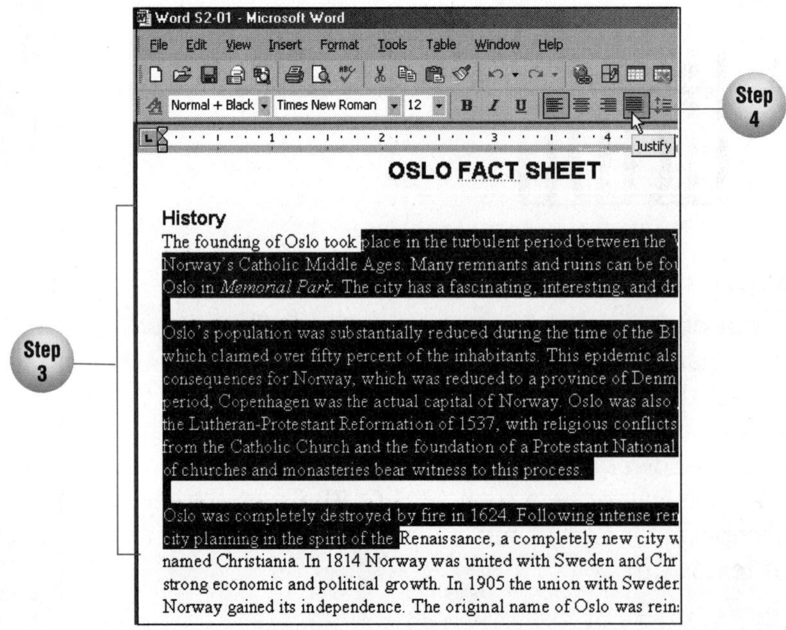

5. Click outside the selected text to deselect it.
6. Click anywhere in the paragraph below the *Population* heading and then press F4.

   Pressing F4 repeats the justification command.

PROBLEM?

If the paragraph alignment does not change, you may have executed a command after the Justify command. If this happens, click anywhere in the paragraph and then click the Justify button on the Formatting toolbar.

7. Click anywhere in the paragraph below the *Commerce and Industry* heading and then press F4.
8. Click anywhere in the paragraph below the *Climate* heading and then press F4.
9. Click anywhere in the paragraph below the *Holiday, Sport, and Leisure* heading and then press F4.
10. Press Ctrl + End to move the insertion point to the end of the document and then press the Enter key.
11. Click the Align Right button on the Formatting toolbar.
12. Key your first and last name and then press the Enter key.
13. Key **Date:**, press the spacebar once, and then press Alt + Shift + D.

    Alt + Shift + D is the shortcut key to insert the current date.
14. Press the Enter key and then click the Align Left button on the Formatting toolbar.

    This step returns the paragraph alignment back to left.
15. Save Word S2-01.

# In Addition

## Options for Changing Alignment

Paragraph alignment can be changed with the Alignment option at the Paragraph dialog box shown at the right. Display the Paragraph dialog box by clicking Format and then Paragraph. At the Paragraph dialog box, click the down-pointing triangle at the right side of the Alignment option, and then click the desired alignment at the drop-down list. Alignment can also be changed with the following shortcut keys:

| Alignment | Shortcut Key |
|---|---|
| Left | Ctrl + L |
| Center | Ctrl + E |
| Right | Ctrl + R |
| Justified | Ctrl + J |

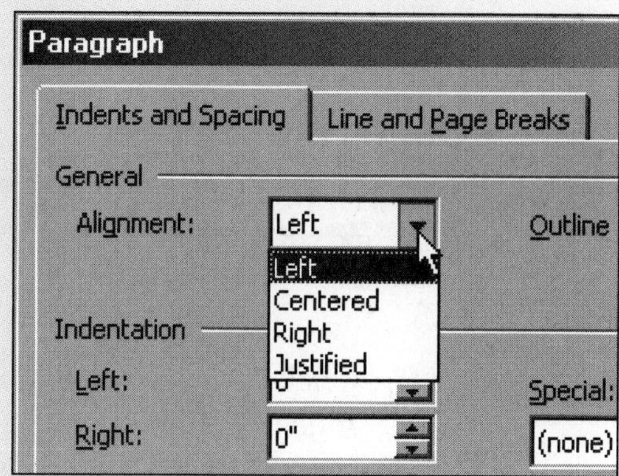

## 2.5 Indenting Text

To draw attention to specific text in a document, consider indenting the text. Indenting might include indenting the first line of text in a paragraph, indenting all lines of text in a paragraph, and indenting the second and subsequent lines of a paragraph (called a hanging indent). Several methods are available for indenting text including buttons on the Formatting toolbar, markers on the Ruler, options at the Paragraph dialog box with the Indents and Spacing tab selected, and shortcut keys.

**PROJECT:** You have decided to visually highlight certain paragraphs of information in the First Choice Travel fact sheet document. Indenting seems preferable to other formatting choices such as changing the font.

### STEPS

1. With Word S2-01 open, select the three paragraphs below the *History* heading.
2. Position the mouse pointer on the Left Indent marker on the Ruler, shown in Figure W2.1, hold down the left mouse button, drag the marker to the 0.5-inch mark on the Ruler, and then release the mouse button.

   When you position the mouse pointer on the Left Indent marker, a ScreenTip displays with *Left Indent* in a yellow box. To precisely position a marker on the Ruler, hold down the Alt key while dragging the marker.
3. Position the mouse pointer on the First Line Indent marker on the Ruler, hold down the left mouse button, drag the marker to the 1-inch mark on the Ruler, and then release the mouse button.
4. Position the mouse pointer on the Right Indent marker on the Ruler, hold down the left mouse button, drag the marker to the 5.5-inch mark on the Ruler, and then release the mouse button.
5. Deselect the text.

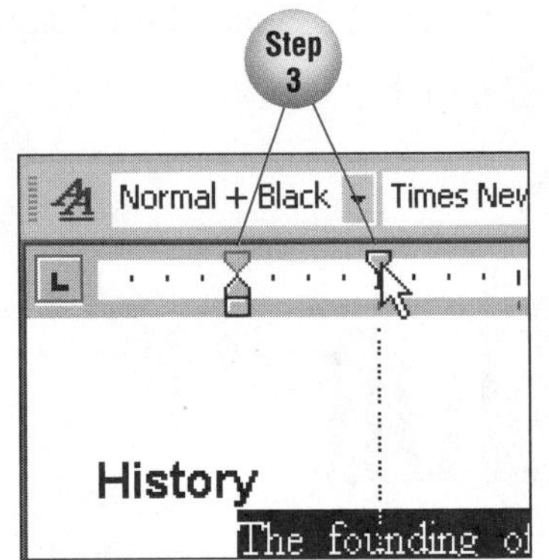


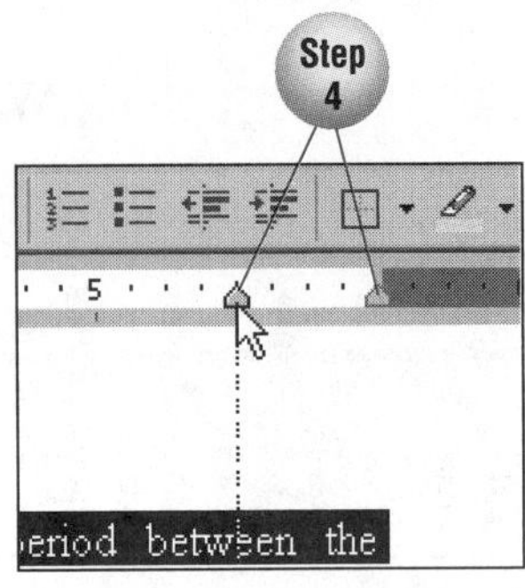


**FIGURE W2.1** Ruler Indent Markers

First Line Indent
Left Indent
Hanging Indent
Right Indent

6. Click anywhere in the paragraph below the *Population* heading. Drag the Left Indent marker on the Ruler to the 0.5-inch mark and drag the Right Indent marker on the Ruler to the 5.5-inch mark. Follow the same procedures to indent the paragraphs below the headings *Commerce and Industry*; *Climate*; and *Holiday, Sport, and Leisure*.

7. Select from the line of text beginning *Tour 1: Mini Cruise* through the three lines of text pertaining to *Tour 4: Selected Oslo Sightseeing*.
8. Click twice on the Increase Indent button on the Formatting toolbar and then deselect the text.

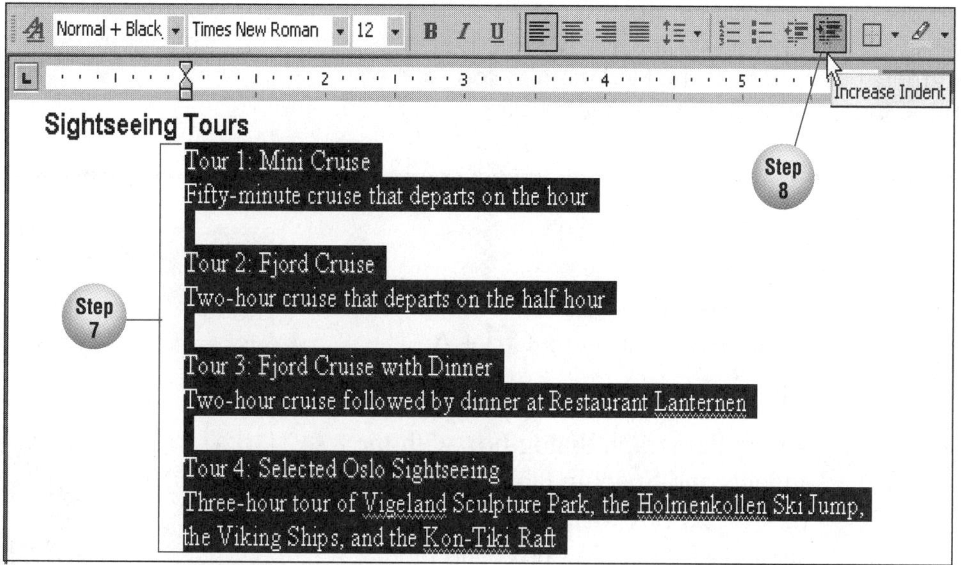


9. Select the three paragraphs below the *History* heading.
10. Drag the First Line Indent marker to the 0.5-inch mark on the Ruler and drag the Hanging Indent marker to the 1-inch mark on the Ruler.

    This creates hanging indent paragraphs.

11. Deselect the paragraph.
12. Save Word S2-01.

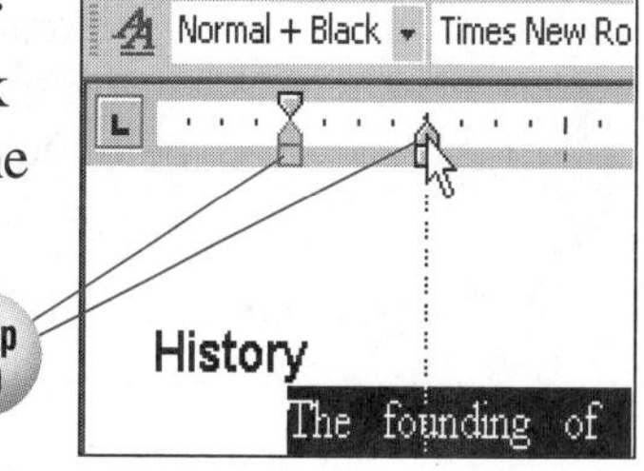


# In Addition

## Indenting Text at the Paragraph Dialog Box

Another method for indenting text is to use options at the Paragraph dialog box with the Indents and Spacing tab selected as below. Indent text from the left margin with the Left option and indent text from the right with the Right option. Create a hanging paragraph by choosing *Hanging* at the Special drop-down list. Specify the amount of indent for second and subsequent lines in the paragraph with the By option. You can also indent text with the following shortcut keys:

| Action | Shortcut Key |
|---|---|
| Indent text from left margin | Ctrl + M |
| Decrease indent from left margin | Ctrl + Shift + M |
| Create a hanging indent | Ctrl + T |
| Remove hanging indent | Ctrl + Shift + T |

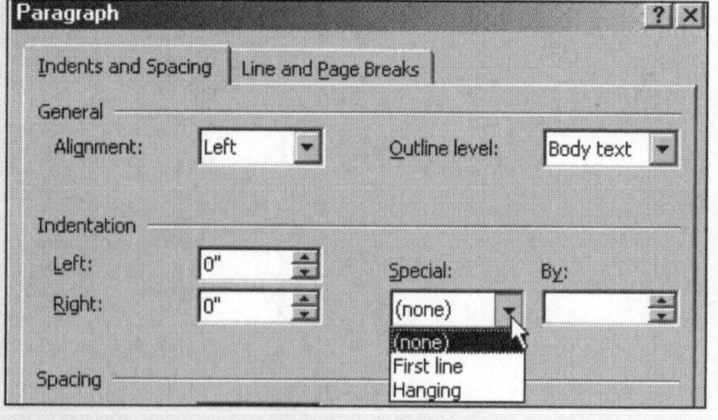

## 2.6 Changing Line and Paragraph Spacing

By default, the word wrap feature single-spaces text. This default line spacing can be changed with the Line Spacing button on the Formatting toolbar, shortcut keys, or with the Line spacing and At options at the Paragraph dialog box. Control spacing above and below paragraphs with the Before and/or After options at the Paragraph dialog box with the Indents and Spacing tab selected.

**PROJECT:** The Oslo fact sheet project deadline is at hand. However, you have time to make a few spacing changes in the document before printing the final version.

## STEPS

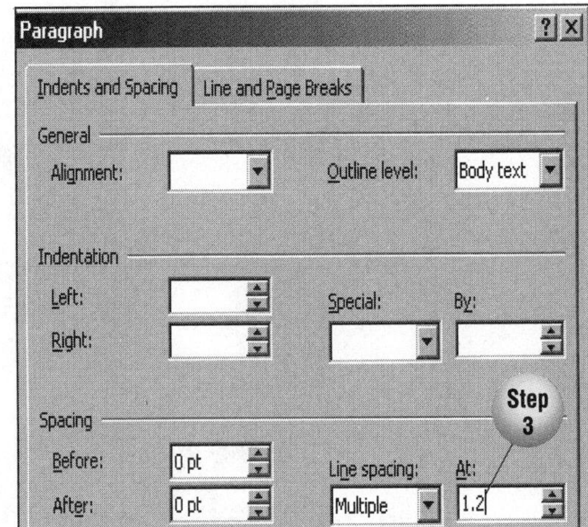


1. With Word S2-01 open, select the entire document by pressing Ctrl + A.
2. Click Format and then Paragraph.
3. At the Paragraph dialog box with the Indents and Spacing tab selected, click in the At text box located in the Spacing section of the dialog box, and then key **1.2**.

   The Paragraph dialog box also contains a Line spacing option. Click the down-pointing triangle at the right side of the option and a drop-down list displays with spacing choices.
4. Click OK to close the dialog box and then deselect the text.

PROBLEM? If line spacing seems too spread out, make sure you keyed the period in *1.2* in the At text box at the Paragraph dialog box.

5. Select from the line of text beginning *Tour 1: Mini Cruise* through the three lines of text pertaining to *Tour 4: Selected Oslo Sightseeing*.
6. Click the down-pointing triangle at the right side of the Line Spacing button and then click *1.0* at the drop-down list.

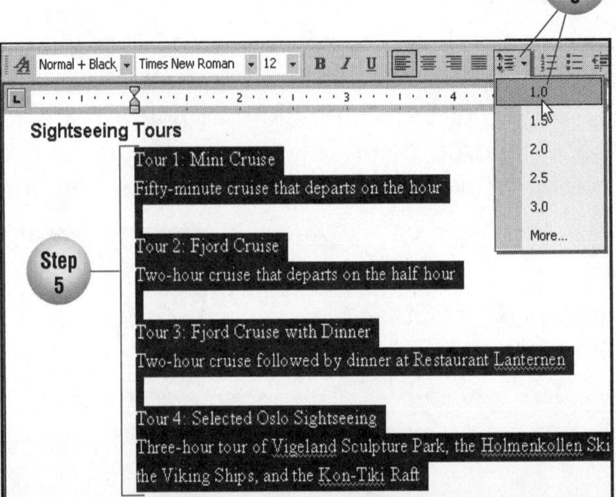

Choosing this option changes the line spacing to single for the selected paragraphs of text. You can also change line spacing with shortcut keys. Press Ctrl + 1 to change to single spacing, Ctrl + 2 to change to double spacing, and Ctrl + 5 to change to 1.5-line spacing.

7. Click anywhere in the *History* heading, click Format, and then click Paragraph.
8. At the Paragraph dialog box with the Indents and Spacing tab selected, click once on the up-pointing triangle at the right side of the After text box, and then click OK to close the dialog box.

   Clicking the up-pointing triangle at the right side of the After text box inserts *6 pt* in the text box.

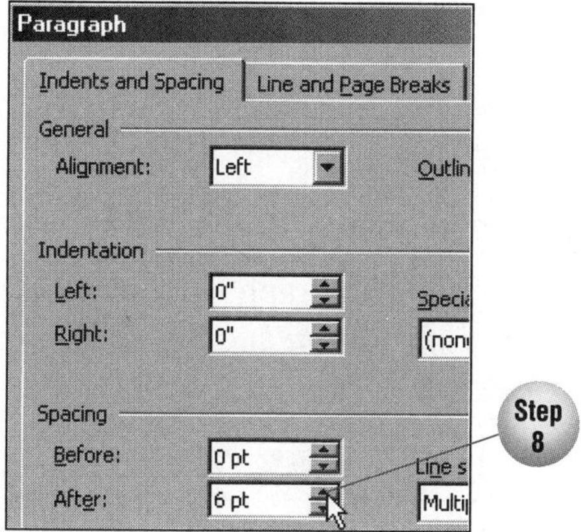


9. Click anywhere in the *Population* heading and then press F4. (You will need to scroll down the document to display the *Population* heading.)

   Pressing F4 repeats the paragraph spacing command.

10. Click individually anywhere in each of the remaining headings (*Commerce and Industry*; *Climate*; *Holiday, Sport, and Leisure*; and *Sightseeing Tours*) and then press F4.
11. Save and then print Word S2-01.
12. Close Word S2-01 by clicking File and then Close.

**Change Line Spacing**
1 Click down-pointing triangle at right side of Line Spacing button on Formatting toolbar.
2 Click desired line spacing at drop-down list.

**OR**
1 Display Paragraph dialog box.
2 Key desired line spacing in At text box.
3 Click OK.

# In Addition

## Spacing Above or Below Paragraphs

Spacing above or below paragraphs is added in points. For example, to add 9 points of spacing below selected paragraphs, display the Paragraph dialog box with the Indents and Spacing tab selected, select the current measurement in the After text box, and then key **9**. You can also click the up-pointing or down-pointing triangles to increase or decrease the amount of spacing before or after paragraphs.

## 2.7 Inserting Bullets and Numbering

If you want to draw the reader's attention to a list of items, consider inserting a bullet before each item. Insert a bullet before items in a list using the Bullets button on the Formatting toolbar or with options at the Bullets and Numbering dialog box. If a list of items is in a sequence, consider inserting numbers before each item. Insert a number before sequenced items using the Numbering button on the Formatting toolbar or with options at the Bullets and Numbering dialog box.

**PROJECT:** First Choice Travel has a new document on traveling by train in Europe. After reviewing the document, you decide to insert numbers and bullets before selected paragraphs to make the information easier to read.

### STEPS

1. Open FCT Rail Travel.
2. Save the document with Save As and name it Word S2-02.
3. Select text from the paragraph *Have your pass validated.* through the paragraph *Be at the right train station* and then click the Numbering button on the Formatting toolbar.

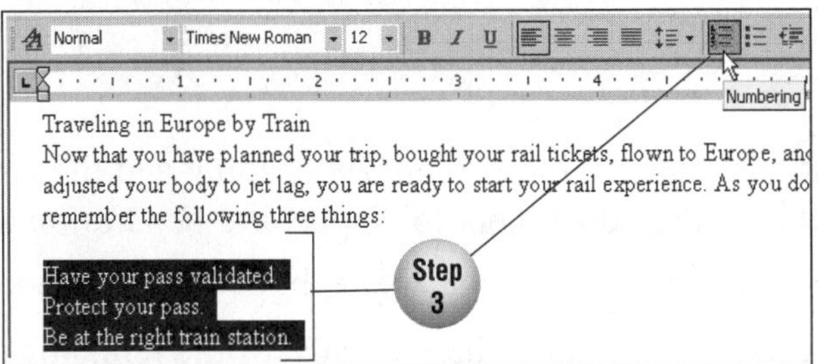


4. Deselect the text.

PROBLEM?
If you click the wrong button, immediately click the Undo button.

5. Position the insertion at the end of the second numbered paragraph (the paragraph that displays as *2. Protect your pass.*) and then press the Enter key once.

   Pressing the Enter key automatically inserts the number *3.* and renumbers the third paragraph to *4.*

6. Key **Arrive 20 minutes before train departure time.**

   Numbering before paragraphs is automatically changed when paragraphs of text are inserted and/or deleted.

1. Have your pass validated.
2. Protect your pass.
3. Arrive 20 minutes before train departure time.
4. Be at the right train station.

Step 6

7 Select text from the paragraph that begins *Free or discount transportation...* through the paragraph that begins *Reduced rental rates with...* and then click the Bullets button on the Formatting toolbar.

Clicking the Bullets button on the Formatting toolbar inserts a round bullet before each paragraph. A variety of other bullets are available at the Bullets and Numbering dialog box.

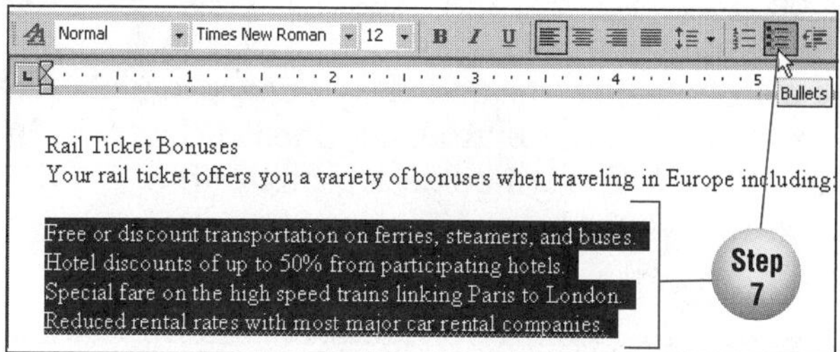


8 With the paragraphs still selected, click Format and then Bullets and Numbering.

9 At the Bullets and Numbering dialog box, make sure the Bulleted tab is selected, and then click a bullet option similar to the arrow bullet shown below. If this bullet is not available, click a similar bullet.

Bullet choices at the Bullets and Numbering dialog box vary depending on the most recent bullets selected.

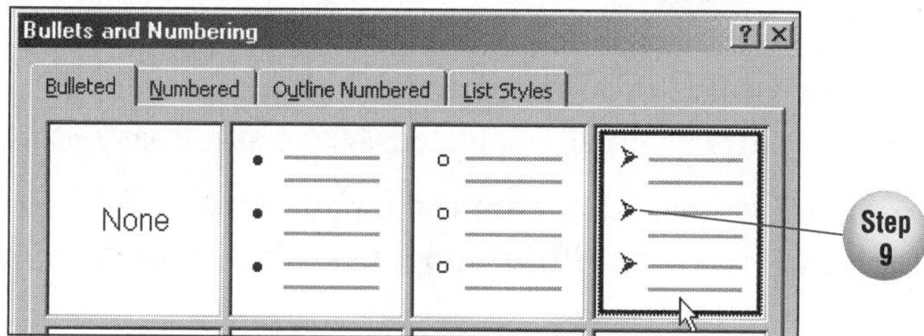


10 Click OK to close the Bullets and Numbering dialog box.

11 Deselect the text.

12 Save Word S2-02.

# In Addition

## Inserting a Picture Bullet

Customize bullets by choosing a bullet option at the Bullets and Numbering dialog box and then clicking the Customize button. This displays the Customize Bulleted List dialog box shown at the right. At this dialog box, you can choose a different bullet character and change the bullet and text positions. Click the Picture button and the Picture Bullet dialog box displays with picture options for bullets.

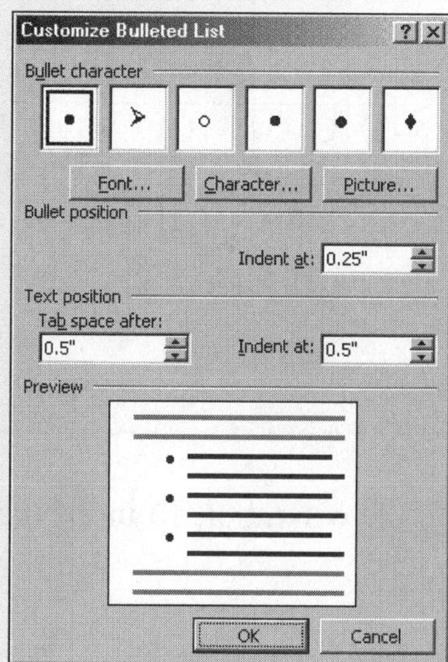


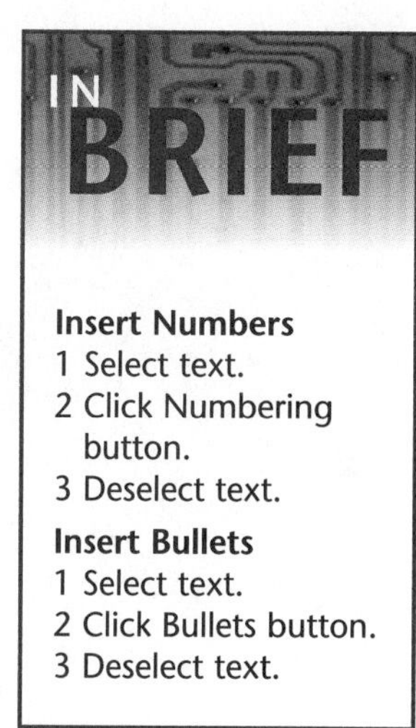


**Insert Numbers**
1 Select text.
2 Click Numbering button.
3 Deselect text.

**Insert Bullets**
1 Select text.
2 Click Bullets button.
3 Deselect text.

## 2.8 Inserting Symbols

Many of the fonts include special symbols such as bullets, publishing symbols, and letters with special punctuation (such as é, ö, and Ã). To insert a symbol, click Insert and then Symbol to display the Symbol dialog box. Click the desired symbol at the dialog box, click the Insert button, and then click the Close button. At the Symbol dialog box with the Symbols tab selected, you can change the font and display different symbols. Change the font by clicking the down-pointing triangle at the right of the Font list box, and then click the desired font at the drop-down list.

**PROJECT:** You have identified a few city names in the train travel document that need special letters in their spellings.

## STEPS

1. With Word S2-02 open, move the insertion point to the end of the document.
2. Key the text shown in Figure W2.2 up to the Å in Århus. To insert the Å symbol, click Insert and then Symbol.
3. At the Symbol dialog box with the Symbols tab selected, click the down-pointing triangle at the right side of the Font list box, and then click *(normal text)* at the drop-down list. (You may need to scroll up to see this option. Skip this step if *(normal text)* is already selected. Make sure that *Latin-1* is the Subset option.)
4. Scroll down the list box until the ninth row is visible and then click the Å symbol (approximately the fifth symbol from the left in the ninth row).

PROBLEM? If you do not see the Å symbol, make sure *(normal text)* is selected at the Font text box.

5. Click the Insert button and then click the Close button.

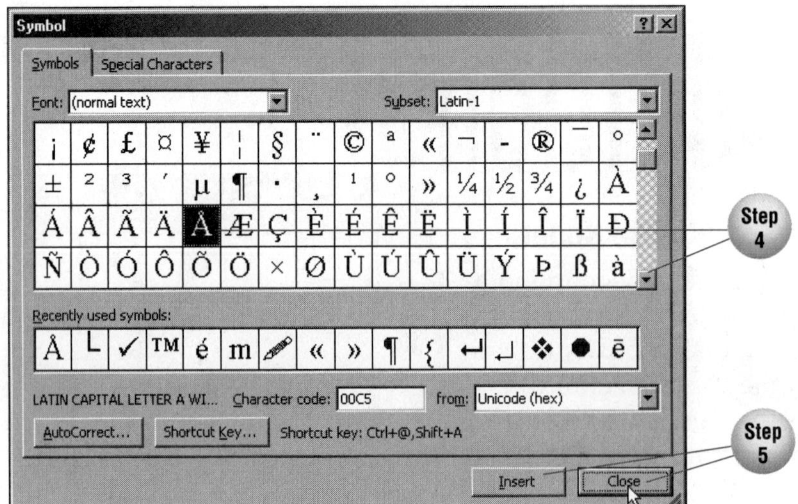


6. Key text up to the ø symbol. To insert the ø symbol, click Insert and then Symbol.

7. At the Symbol dialog box, click the ø symbol (approximately the eighth symbol from the left in the twelfth row).
8. Click the Insert button and then click the Close button.

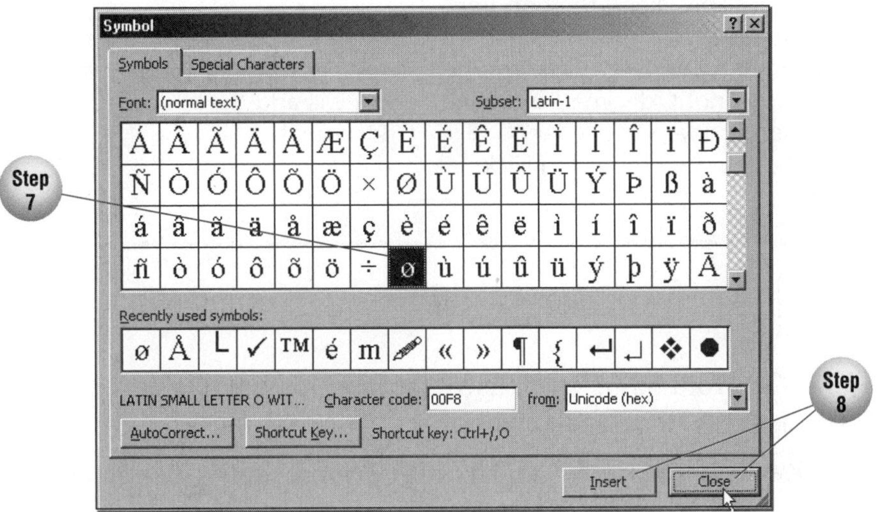


9. Key the remaining text shown in Figure W2.2.
10. Save Word S2-02.

**FIGURE W2.2**

> Some companies offer outstanding reductions on transportation. For example, you can travel on the ferry in Denmark between Århus and Kalundborg and between Nyborg and Korsør at a 75% discount!

# In Addition

## Inserting a Symbol with a Shortcut Key

Another method for inserting symbols in a document is to use a shortcut key. The shortcut key for a symbol displays at the Symbol dialog box. Click a symbol at the Symbol dialog box and the shortcut keys display toward the bottom of the dialog box. For example, click the ø symbol and the shortcut key *Ctrl+/,O* displays toward the bottom of the dialog box. To insert the ø symbol in a document using the shortcut key, hold down the Ctrl key and then press the / key. Release the Ctrl key and then press the o key. Not all symbols contain a shortcut key.

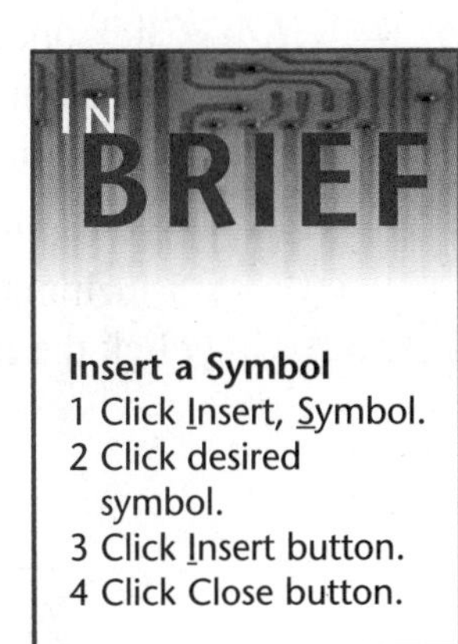

**IN BRIEF**

**Insert a Symbol**
1 Click Insert, Symbol.
2 Click desired symbol.
3 Click Insert button.
4 Click Close button.

## 2.9 Setting Tabs

Word offers a variety of default settings including left tabs set every 0.5 inch. You can set your own tabs using the Ruler or at the Tabs dialog box. Use the Ruler to set, move, and delete tabs. The default tabs display as tiny vertical lines along the bottom of the Ruler. With a left tab, text aligns at the left edge of the tab. The other types of tabs that can be set on the Ruler are center, right, decimal, and bar. The small button at the left side of the Ruler is called the Alignment button. Each time you click the Alignment button, a different tab or paragraph alignment symbol displays. To set a tab, display the desired alignment button on the Ruler and then click on the Ruler at the desired position.

**PROJECT:** You have done some additional research on train travel in Europe with train connections. You will add the airport names to the train travel document.

## STEPS

1. With Word S2-02 open, move the insertion point to the end of the document and then press the Enter key twice.
2. Key **International Airports with Train Connections** and then press the Enter key once.
3. Make sure the left tab symbol displays in the Alignment button at the left side of the Ruler.

   If the Ruler is not displayed, turn it on by clicking View and then Ruler.

4. Position the arrow pointer below the 1-inch mark on the Ruler and then click the left mouse button.
5. Click once on the Alignment button located at the left side of the Ruler to display the center tab symbol.
6. Position the arrow pointer below the 3-inch mark on the Ruler and then click the left mouse button.
7. Click once on the Alignment button located at the left side of the Ruler to display the right tab symbol.
8. Position the arrow pointer below the 5-inch marker on the Ruler and then click the left mouse button.

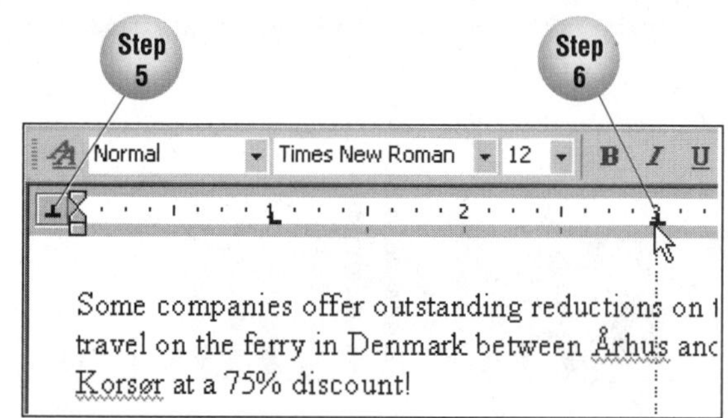


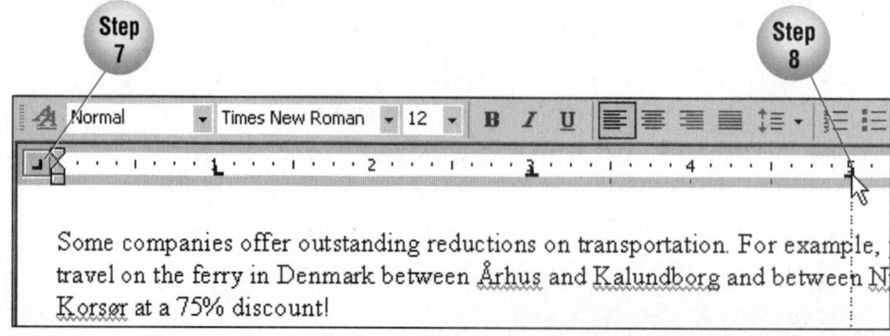

9. Key the text shown in Figure W2.3, pressing the Tab key before keying each tabbed entry. Make sure you press the Tab key before keying the entry in the first column.

PROBLEM?

If your columns of text do not look similar to those in Figure W2.3, check to make sure you inserted the tab symbols at the correct locations on the Ruler and that you pressed Tab before keying each entry in the first column.

10. After keying the last entry in the third column *(Fiumicino)*, press the Enter key twice, and then press Ctrl + Q, the shortcut key to move paragraph formatting.

    Pressing Ctrl + Q removes the tabs you set from the Ruler.

11. Save Word S2-02.

**FIGURE W2.3**

| **Country** | **City** | **Airport** |
|---|---|---|
| Austria | Vienna (Wein) | Schwechat |
| Belgium | Brussels | Nationaal |
| Britain | London | Heathrow |
| France | Paris | Orly |
| Germany | Berlin | Schoenefeld |
| Italy | Rome | Fiumicino |

# In Addition

## Moving a Tab

Move a tab on the Ruler by positioning the mouse pointer on the tab symbol on the Ruler. Hold down the left mouse button, drag the symbol to the new location on the Ruler, and then release the mouse button.

## Deleting a Tab

Delete a tab from the Ruler by positioning the arrow pointer on the tab symbol, holding down the left mouse button, dragging the symbol down onto the document screen, and then releasing the mouse button.

## Setting a Decimal Tab

Set a decimal tab for column entries you want aligned at the decimal point. To set a decimal tab, click the Alignment button located at the left side of the Ruler until the decimal tab symbol displays, and then click on the desired position on the Ruler.

**Set Tab on Ruler**
1. Display desired alignment symbol on Alignment button.
2. Click on Ruler at desired position.

## 2.10 Setting Tabs with Leaders

The four types of tabs can be set with leaders. Leaders are useful for material where you want to direct the reader's eyes across the page. Leaders can be periods, hyphens, or underlines. Tabs with leaders are set with options at the Tab dialog box. To display this dialog box, click Format and then Tabs. At the Tabs dialog box, choose the type of tabs, the type of leader, and then enter a tab position measurement.

**PROJECT:** The information you found listing airports with train connections also includes schedule times. You will add this data to the train travel document.

STEPS

1. With Word S2-02 open, move the insertion point to the end of the document.
2. Click the Alignment button at the left side of the Ruler until the left tab symbol displays.
3. Position the arrow pointer below the 1-inch mark on the Ruler and then click the left mouse button.
4. Click the Alignment button at the left side of the Ruler until the right tab symbol displays.
5. Position the arrow pointer below the 5-inch mark on the Ruler and then click the left mouse button.
6. To key the headings shown in Figure W2.4, press the Tab key, click the Bold button on the Formatting toolbar, and then key **Airport**.
7. Press the Tab key, key **Service**, and then click the Bold button to turn off Bold.
8. Press the Enter key twice and then press Ctrl + Q to remove the paragraph tab formatting.
9. Set a left tab and a right tab with leaders by clicking Format and then Tabs.
10. At the Tabs dialog box, make sure Left is selected in the Alignment section of the dialog box. (If it is not, click Left.) With the insertion point positioned in the Tab stop position text box, key **1**, and then click the Set button.

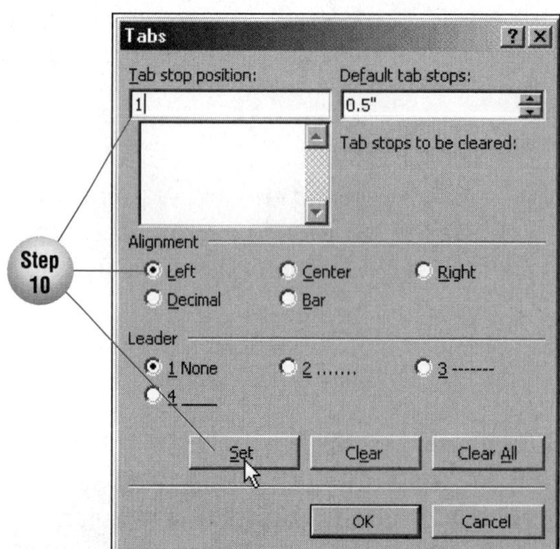

11. Key **5** in the Tab stop position text box. Click Right in the Alignment section of the dialog box. Click 2….. in the Leader section of the dialog box. Click the Set button and then click OK to close the dialog box.

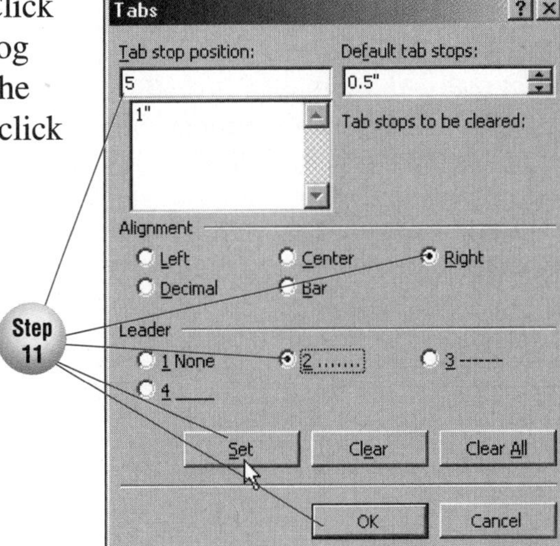


12. Key the remaining text shown in Figure W2.4, making sure you press the Tab key before keying the first text entry.

PROBLEM ?

If your columns of text do not look similar to those in Figure W2.4, check to make sure you inserted the tab symbols at the correct measurements and that you pressed Tab before keying each entry in the first column.

13. Save Word S2-02.

**FIGURE W2.4**

| **Airport** | **Service** |
|---|---|
| Schwechat........................................ | Train every 30 minutes |
| Nationaal.......................................... | Train every 20 minutes |
| Heathrow ..................................... | LT train every 10 minutes |
| Orly .......................................... | RER train every 20 minutes |
| Schoenefeld .......................... | S-Bahn train every 20 minutes |
| Fiumicino ................................ | Train every 10 to 20 minutes |

# In Addition

## Clearing Tabs at the Tabs Dialog Box

At the Tabs dialog box, you can clear an individual tab or all tabs. To clear all tabs, click the Clear All button. To clear an individual tab, specify the tab position, and then click the Clear button.

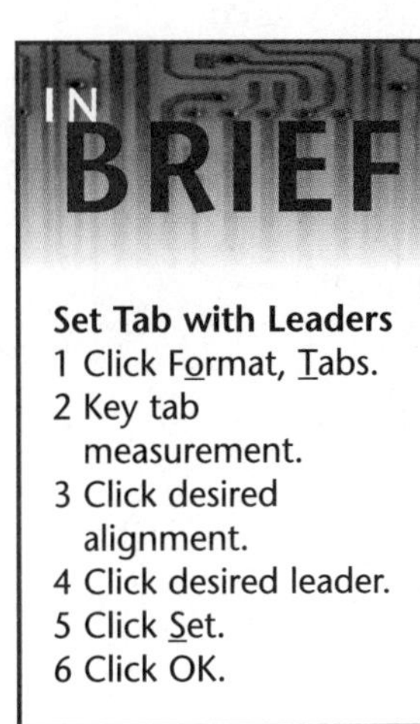


**Set Tab with Leaders**

1 Click Format, Tabs.
2 Key tab measurement.
3 Click desired alignment.
4 Click desired leader.
5 Click Set.
6 Click OK.

## 2.11 Adding Borders and Shading

Insert a border around text in a paragraph or selected text with the Border button on the Formatting toolbar or with options at the Borders and Shading dialog box. To display this dialog box, click Format and then Borders and Shading. At the Borders and Shading dialog box with the Borders tab selected, you can specify the border type, style, color, and width. Click the Shading tab and the dialog box contains options for choosing a fill color and pattern style.

**PROJECT:** To highlight certain information in First Choice Travel's train travel document, you will apply a border to selected text. You will also apply border and shading formatting to the column text.

## STEPS

1. With Word S2-02 open, select the numbered paragraphs.
2. Click the Outside Border button on the Formatting toolbar.

   The name of the button changes depending on the border choice that was previously selected at the button drop-down palette. When Word is first opened, the button displays as Outside Border. Clicking this button inserts a border around the numbered paragraphs.

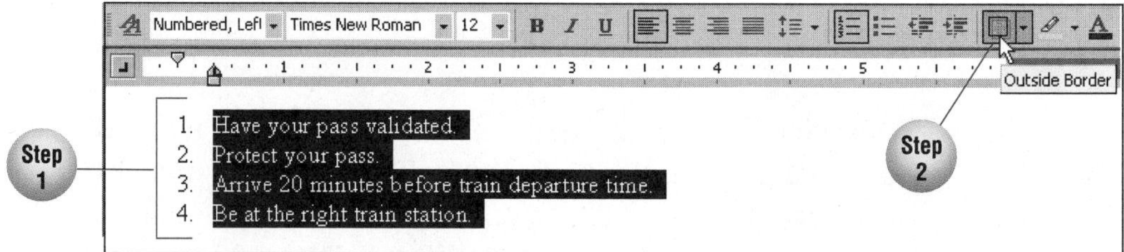


3. Select the bulleted paragraphs and then click the Outside Border button on the Formatting toolbar.
4. Select from the line of text containing the column headings *Country*, *City*, and *Airport* through the line of text containing the column entries *Italy*, *Rome*, and *Fiumicino*.
5. Click Format and then Borders and Shading. At the Borders and Shading dialog box, make sure the Borders tab is selected.
6. Click the down-pointing triangle at the right side of the Style list box until the first double-line option displays and then click the double-line option.

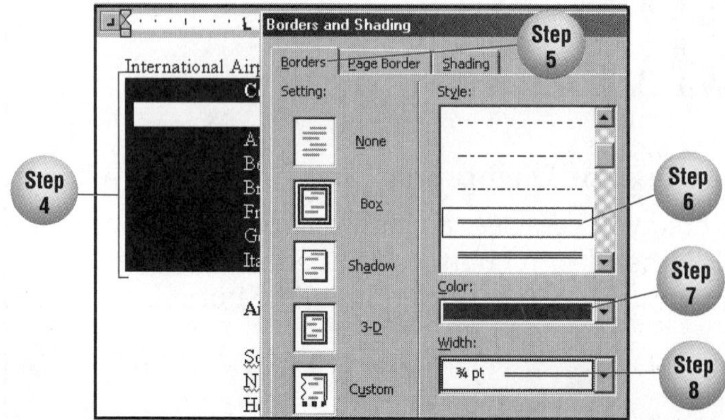

7. Click the down-pointing triangle at the right side of the Color list box and then click the Dark Blue option (sixth color from the left in the top row).
8. Click the down-pointing triangle at the right side of the Width list box and then click *¾ pt* at the pop-up list.
9. Click the Shading tab and then click the fifth color (Light Turquoise) from the left in the bottom row of the Fill palette.

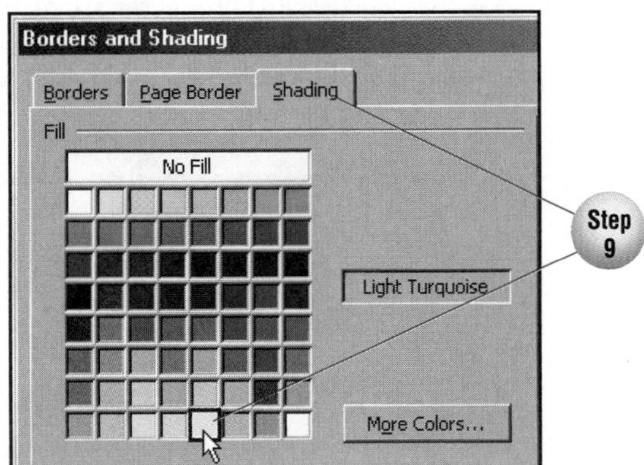


10. Click OK to close the dialog box.

PROBLEM ?

If the border does not appear around all sides of the column text, display the Borders and Shading dialog box with the Borders tab selected, and then click the Box option in the Setting section.

11. Add the same border and shading to the other columns of text by selecting from the line of text containing the column headings *Airport* and *Service* through the line of text containing the column entries *Fiumicino* and *Train every 10 to 20 minutes* and then pressing F4.
12. Save Word S2-02.

# In Addition

## Inserting Borders with the Border Button

Click the Border button on the Formatting toolbar and a border is inserted around the paragraph of text where the insertion point is positioned. Click the down-pointing triangle at the right side of the button and a palette of border choices displays as shown at the right. Click the option at the palette that will insert the desired border. Position the arrow pointer on an option at the palette and a ScreenTip displays with the name of the option.

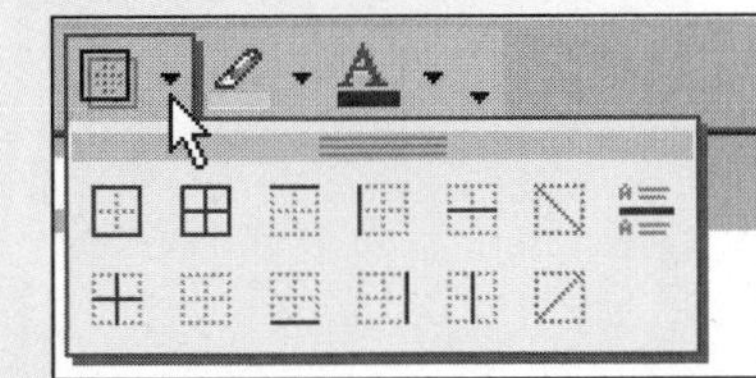

## In Brief

**Insert Border and Shading**

1. Select text.
2. Click Format, Borders and Shading.
3. Choose desired border(s).
4. Click Shading tab.
5. Choose desired shading and/or pattern.
6. Click OK.

# 2.12 Applying Styles and Creating an Outline-Style Numbered List

A Word document, by default, contains a number of styles that apply specific formatting. To display the available styles, click the down-pointing triangle at the right side of the Style button on the Formatting toolbar or click the Styles and Formatting button to display the Styles and Formatting Task Pane. This task pane contains a list of styles available with the current document. You can also display all available styles. An outline-style numbered list can be created in a document if a Heading style is applied to text.

Certain options at the Bullets and Numbering dialog box with the Outline Numbered tab selected are available only when heading styles have been applied to text.

**PROJECT:** To further enhance the train travel document, you decide to apply paragraph and character styles to specific text and then apply outline numbering to the headings.

## STEPS

1. With Word S2-02 open, position the insertion point on any character in the heading *Traveling in Europe by Train* and then apply a style by clicking the down-pointing triangle at the right side of the Style button on the Formatting toolbar and then clicking *Heading 2* at the drop-down list.

   The Heading 2 style applies 14-point Arial bold italic with 12 points of space above the heading and 3 points of space below the heading.

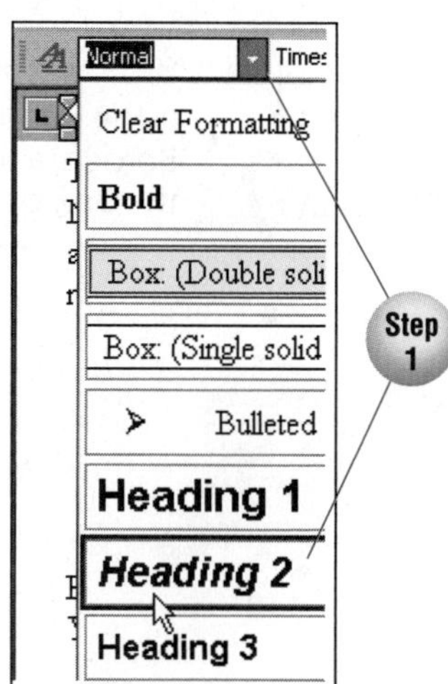


2. Click anywhere in the heading *Rail Ticket Bonuses* and then apply the Heading 2 style by completing directions similar to those in step 1.
3. Click anywhere in the heading *International Airports with Train Connections* and then apply the Heading 2 style.
4. Click the Styles and Formatting button on the Formatting toolbar.

   Clicking this button display the Styles and Formatting Task Pane at the right side of the screen. This task pane contains styles available with the current document including styles for applying the bullet and borders and shading formatting you applied to text in the document.

5. Select the numbered paragraphs inside the border.
6. Click the Box style (containing the light turquoise background) in the Styles and Formatting Task Pane and then click the Bulleted style.

   This applies the border and shading formatting and inserts arrow bullets to the selected text.

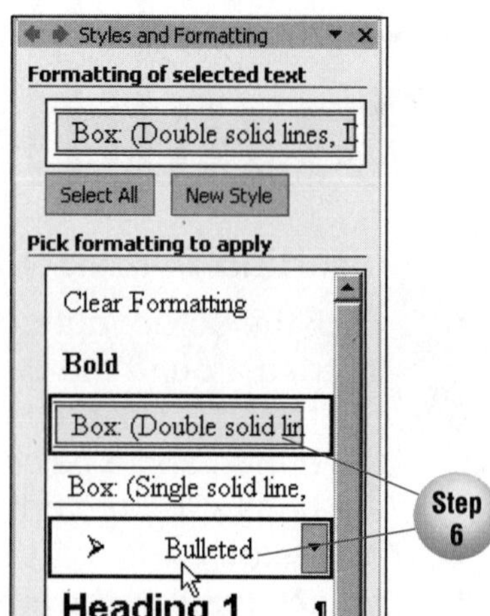

7 Select the four bulleted items that begin with *Free or discount transportation...*, click the Box style (containing light turquoise background) in the Styles and Formatting Task Pane, and then click the Bulleted style.

8 Display all available styles by clicking the down-pointing triangle at the right of the Show option located toward the bottom of the Styles and Formatting Task Pane and then click *All styles* at the drop-down list.

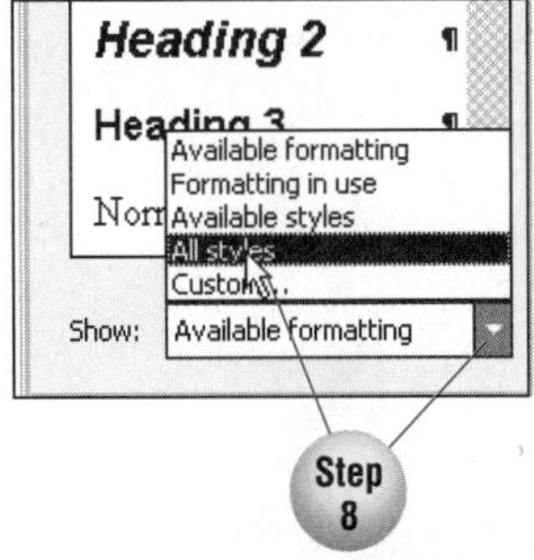


Paragraph styles display in the Styles and Formatting Task Pane followed by a paragraph symbol (¶) and character styles display followed by a character symbol (a). To apply a paragraph style, position the insertion point anywhere in the paragraph and then click the style. To apply a character style, select the text first, and then click the desired style.

9 With the four bulleted items still selected, scroll through the *Pick formatting to apply* list box at the Styles and Formatting Task Pane and then click the *Strong* style.

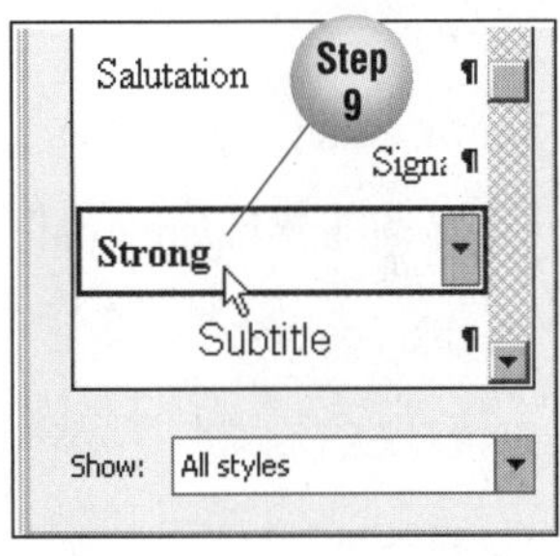


Styles are alphabetized in the task pane. The Strong style is a character style.

10 Select the other four bulleted items that begin with *Have your pass validated.* and then click the *Strong* style at the Styles and Formatting Task Pane.

11 Click the Styles and Formatting button on the Formatting toolbar to turn off the display of the Styles and Formatting Task Pane.

12 Press Ctrl + Home to move the insertion point to the beginning of the document.

13 Apply outline-style numbering by clicking Format and then Bullets and Numbering. At the Bullets and Numbering dialog box, click the Outline Numbered tab.

14 Click the third option from the left in the bottom row and then click OK to close the dialog box.

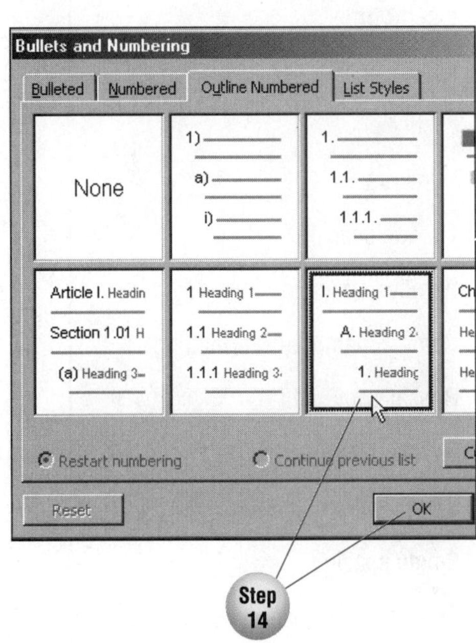


The numbering style applies the letters *A, B,* and *C* before the three headings.

15 Save, print, and then close Word S2-02.

# FEATURES SUMMARY

| Feature | Button | Menu | Keyboard |
|---|---|---|---|
| Align Center | | | Ctrl + E |
| Align Left | | | Ctrl + L |
| Align Right | | | Ctrl + R |
| Apply style | Normal | | |
| Bold | B | | Ctrl + B |
| Borders and Shading dialog box | | Format, Borders and Shading | |
| Bullets | | Format, Bullets and Numbering | |
| Create a hanging indent | | | Ctrl + T |
| Decrease text indent from left margin | | | Ctrl + Shift + M |
| Double spacing | | | Ctrl + 2 |
| Font Color palette | A | | |
| Font dialog box | | Format, Font | Ctrl + D |
| Font drop-down list | Times New Roman | | |
| Font Size drop-down list | 12 | | |
| Format Painter | | | |
| Indent text from left margin | | | Ctrl + M |
| Insert border | | | |
| Italics | I | | Ctrl + I |
| Justify | | | Ctrl + J |
| Numbers | | Format, Bullets and Numbering | |
| 1.5-line spacing | | | Ctrl + 5 |
| Remove a hanging indent | | | Ctrl + Shift + T |
| Remove paragraph formatting | | | Ctrl + Q |
| Repeat command | | Edit, Repeat | F4 or Ctrl + Y |
| Save a document | | File, Save | Ctrl + S |
| Select entire document | | Edit, Select All | Ctrl + A |
| Single spacing | | | Ctrl + 1 |
| Styles and Formatting Task Pane | | | |

| Function | Button | Menu | Keyboard |
|---|---|---|---|
| Symbol dialog box | | Insert, Symbol | |
| Tabs dialog box | | Format, Tabs | |
| Underline | U | | Ctrl + U |

# PROCEDURES CHECK

**Completion:** In the space provided at the right, indicate the correct term, symbol, button, or command.

1. Press these keys on the keyboard to italicize selected text. ________________
2. Click these options to display the Paragraph dialog box. ________________
3. Click this button to indent text from the left margin. ________________
4. Click these options to select the entire document. ________________
5. Press this function key to repeat a command. ________________
6. Press these keys on the keyboard to underline selected text. ________________
7. Click this button on the Formatting toolbar to display a palette of font colors. ________________
8. Click this button on the Formatting toolbar to right align text. ________________
9. Click this button on the Formatting toolbar to number selected paragraphs. ________________
10. Change line spacing with this button on the Formatting toolbar. ________________
11. Click these options to display the Bullets and Numbering dialog box. ________________
12. Set tabs at the Tabs dialog box or using this. ________________
13. Click these options to display the Borders and Shading dialog box. ________________
14. Apply an outline-style numbered list with options at this dialog box with the Outline Numbered tab selected. ________________

# SKILLS REVIEW

### Activity 1: APPLYING FONTS; USING THE FORMAT PAINTER

1 Open FCT Petersburg.
2 Save the document with Save As and name it Word S2-R1.
3 Select the entire document and then make the following changes:
   a Change the font to Bookman Old Style. (If this font is not available, choose a similar font such as Garamond or Century Schoolbook.)
   b Change the font size to 11 points.
4 Select the title *FACT SHEET – PETERSBURG, ALASKA*, change the font to 16-point Arial bold, and then deselect the text.
5 Select the heading *Services*, change the font to 14-point Arial bold, and then deselect the heading.

6 Using Format Painter, change the font to 14-point Arial bold for the remaining headings (*Visitor Attractions*, *Walking Tours*, *Accommodations*, and *Transportation*).
7 Save Word S2-R1.

### Activity 2: APPLYING FONT EFFECTS; USING THE REPEAT COMMAND

1 With Word S2-R1 open, select the last sentence in the document *(If you would like more information on traveling in Alaska, check with a First Choice Travel representative.)* and then apply a small caps effect.
2 Select the title *FACT SHEET – PETERSBURG, ALASKA* and then apply a shadow effect.
3 Use the Repeat command to apply the shadow effect to the headings in the document (*Services*, *Visitor Attractions*, *Walking Tours*, *Accommodations*, and *Transportation*).
4 Save Word S2-R1.

### Activity 3: ALIGNING AND INDENTING TEXT

1 With Word S2-R1 open, position the insertion point anywhere in the paragraph below the title *FACT SHEET – PETERSBURG, ALASKA* and then change the paragraph alignment to justified.
2 Position the insertion point anywhere in the last sentence of the document *(If you would like more information on traveling in Alaska, check with a First Choice Travel representative.)* and then change the paragraph alignment to centered.
3 Select the two paragraphs below the *Services* heading and then make the following changes:
   a Change the paragraph alignment to justified.
   b Indent the paragraphs 0.5 inch from the left margin using the Increase Indent button.
   c Deselect the paragraphs.
4 Change the paragraph alignment to justified and indent paragraphs 0.5 inch from the left margin using the Increase Indent button for the following paragraphs:
   - Four paragraphs below the *Visitor Attractions* heading
   - One paragraph below the *Walking Tours* heading
   - Two paragraphs below the *Accommodations* heading
   - Two paragraphs below the *Transportation* heading
5 Move the insertion point to the end of the document and then make the following changes:
   a Press the Enter key twice.
   b Change the alignment to right and then insert the current date.
   c Press the Enter key once and then insert the current time.
6 Save Word S2-R1.

### Activity 4: CHANGING LINE AND PARAGRAPH SPACING

1 With Word S2-R1 open, select the entire document, change the line spacing to 1.2, and then deselect the document.
2 Click anywhere in the heading *Services* and then change the paragraph spacing after to 6 points.
3 Use the Repeat command to insert 6 points of spacing after the remaining headings (*Visitor Attractions*, *Walking Tours*, *Accommodations*, and *Transportation*).
4 Save, print, and then close Word S2-R1.

## Activity 5: INSERTING BULLETS AND SYMBOLS

1 Open FCT Packages.
2 Save the document with Save As and name it Word S2-R2.
3 Select the five paragraphs of text below *Fast Facts* in the OREGON section of the document and then insert bullets.
4 Select the six paragraphs of text below *Fast Facts* in the NEVADA section of the document and then insert bullets.
5 Deselect the text.
6 Move the insertion point to the end of the document, press the Enter key twice, and then key the text shown in Figure W2.5. Insert the é, è, and ñ symbols using the Symbol dialog box.
7 Save Word S2-R2.

**FIGURE W2.5** Activity 5

Additional accommodations are available at the Ste. Thérèse Chateau and Silver Creek Resort. For information, please contact Carlos Nuñez.

## Activity 6: SETTING TABS

1 With Word S2-R2 open, move the insertion point a double space below the heading *Rates and Packages* in the OREGON section and then create the tabbed text shown in Figure W2.6 with the following specifications (key the text as shown in the figure):
   a Set a left tab at the 1-inch mark on the Ruler.
   b Set a center tab at the 3.25-inch mark on the Ruler.
   c Set a right tab at the 5-inch mark on the Ruler.
2 Move the insertion point a double space below the heading *Rates and Packages* in the NEVADA section and then create the tabbed text shown in Figure W2.7. Use the same tab settings you set for the text in the OREGON section.
3 Save Word S2-R2.

**FIGURE W2.6** Activity 6

| **Accommodation** | **No. Persons** | **Daily Price** |
|---|---|---|
| Studio/one bedroom | 2–4 | $75–125 |
| Two bedrooms | 4–6 | $95–225 |
| Three bedrooms | 6–8 | $135–300 |
| Four bedrooms | 8–12 | $160–400 |
| Five/six bedrooms | 10–16 | $250–500 |

**FIGURE W2.7** Activity 6

| **Package** | **Length** | **Price** |
|---|---|---|
| Tuck and Roll | 3 days/2 nights | $269 |
| Ski Sneak | 4 days/3 nights | $409 |
| Take a Break | 6 days/5 nights | $649 |
| Ultimate | 8 days/7 nights | $1,009 |

### Activity 7: ADDING BORDERS AND SHADING

1 With Word S2-R2 open, select the tabbed text below the *Rates and Packages* heading in the OREGON section, insert a border and shading of your choosing, and then deselect the text.
2 Select the tabbed text below the *Rates and Packages* heading in the NEVADA section, insert a border and shading of your choosing, and then deselect the text.
3 Save Word S2-R2.

### Activity 8: APPLYING STYLES; CREATING AN OUTLINE-STYLE NUMBERED LIST

1 With Word S2-R2 open, apply the Heading 1 style to the headings *OREGON* and *NEVADA*.
2 Apply the Heading 2 style to the *Fast Facts* and *Rates and Packages* headings in the OREGON section and the NEVADA section.
3 Move the insertion point to the beginning of the document and then apply outline-style numbering to the document. (Apply the third option from the left in the bottom row of the Bullets and Numbering dialog box with the Outline Numbered tab selected.)
4 Save, print, and then close Word S2-R2.

## PERFORMANCE PLUS

### Activity 1: CHANGING FONTS; ALIGNING AND INDENTING TEXT; CHANGING PARAGRAPH SPACING

1 Open FCT CC Skiing.
2 Save the document with Save As and name it Word S2-P1.
3 Make the following changes to the document:
   a Set the entire document in Century Schoolbook. (If this typeface is not available, choose a similar typeface such as Bookman Old Style or Garamond.)
   b Set the title in 14-point Tahoma bold. (If Tahoma is not available, choose Arial.)
   c Set the names of the cross-country resorts in 12-point Tahoma bold and add a shadow effect.
   d Change the line spacing for the entire document to 1.3.
   e Insert 6 points of space after each of the names of the cross-country resorts.
   f Center align the title.
   g Indent the paragraph of text below each cross-country resort name 0.5 inch from the left margin and change the alignment to justified.
4 Save, print, and then close Word S2-P1.

### Activity 2: PREPARING AND FORMATTING A LETTER

1 Open MP Letterhead.
2 Save the letterhead document with Save As and name it Word S2-P2.
3 You are Neva Smith-Wilder, educational liaison for Marquee Productions. Write a letter using the date April 17, 2003, to Cal Rubine, Chair, Theatre Arts Division, Niagara Peninsula College, 2199 Victoria Street, Niagara-on-the-Lake, ON L0S 1J0 and include the following information:

- Marquee Productions will be filming in and around the city of Toronto during the summer of 2003.
- Marquee Productions would like to use approximately 20 theatre interns to assist in the shoot.
- Interns will perform a variety of tasks including acting as extras, assisting the camera crew, working with set designers on set construction, and providing support to the production team.
- Interns can work approximately 15 to 30 hours per week and will be compensated at minimum wage.
- Close your letter by asking Mr. Rubine to screen interested students and then send approximately 20 names to you.
- If Mr. Rubine has any questions, he may contact you at (612) 555-2005, or send the names to you by e-mail at NevaSW@emcp.net/marquee.

4 After keying the letter, apply the following formatting:
   a Select the letter text (do not select the letterhead image or text) and then change to a font other than Times New Roman.
   b Change the paragraph alignment to justified for the paragraph(s) in the body of the letter.

5 Save, print, and then close Word S2-P2.

### Activity 3: SETTING LEADER TABS

1 At a clear document screen, key the text shown in Figure W2.8 with the following specifications:
   a Center, bold, and italicize the text as shown.
   b Set the tabbed text as shown using a left tab for the first column and a right tab with leaders for the second column.
   c After keying the text, select the entire document, and then change to a typeface of your choosing (other than Times New Roman).

2 Save the document and name it Word S2-P3.

3 Print and then close Word S2-P3.

**FIGURE W2.8** Activity 3

**WORLDWIDE ENTERPRISES**
Distribution Schedule
*Two by Two*

United States..........................................................May 10
Canada ...................................................................June 7
Japan......................................................................July 26
Australia/New Zealand...........................................August 2
Mexico ........................................................September 20

## Activity 4: FINDING INFORMATION ON THE WIDOW/ORPHAN FEATURE; KEEPING TEXT TOGETHER

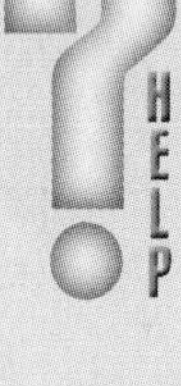


1 Use Word's Help feature to learn about the widow/orphan feature and how to keep paragraphs of text together on the same page.
2 Create a document containing information on these two features with the following specifications:
   a Create a title for the document that is centered and bolded.
   b Write a paragraph discussing the widow/orphan feature.
   c Write a paragraph discussing how to keep paragraphs of text together on the same page.
3 Save the completed document and name it Word S2-P4A.
4 Print and then close Word S2-P4A.
5 Open FCT Vacation Specials.
6 Save the document with Save As and name it Word S2-P4B.
7 Select all of the lines of indented text containing information on various categories (begins with *Category H* and continues through all lines pertaining to *Category S1*).
8 Insert a command to keep all lines of text together with the next line. *(Hint: Make sure you check the Keep with next option.)*
9 Save the document and then print only page 2 of Word S2-P4B.
10 Close Word S2-P4B.

## Activity 5: HYPHENATING WORDS IN A DOCUMENT

1 In some Word documents, the right margin may appear ragged. If the paragraph alignment is changed to justified, the right margin will appear even, but there will be extra space added throughout the line. In these situations, hyphenating long words that fall at the end of the text line provides the document with a more balanced look. Use Word's Help feature to learn how to automatically hyphenate words in a document.
2 Open FCT Petersburg.
3 Save the document with Save As and name it Word S2-P5.
4 Automatically hyphenate words in the document, limiting the consecutive hyphens to 2. (*Hint: Specify the number of consecutive hyphens at the Hyphenation dialog box.*)
5 Save, print, and then close Word S2-P5.

## Activity 6: LOCATING INFORMATION AND WRITING A LETTER

1 You are a travel consultant for First Choice Travel and have been asked by Camille Matsui, production assistant for Marquee Productions, to find information on art galleries and museums in Toronto, Ontario, Canada. Connect to the Internet and search for information on at least three art galleries and/or museums in the Toronto area.
2 Using the information you find on the Internet, write a letter to Camille Matsui, Production Assistant, Marquee Productions, 955 South Alameda Street, Los Angeles, CA 90037, and tell her about three galleries and/or museums providing a brief description of each one.
3 Use your name in the complimentary close and include the title, Travel Consultant.
4 Save the completed letter and name it Word S2-P6.
5 Print and then close Word S2-P6.

# WORD SECTION 3

# Formatting and Enhancing a Document

Use formatting features to rearrange text in a document, add special elements, or change the appearance of text. With the find and replace feature you can find specific text and replace with other text. Use buttons on the Standard toolbar to move, copy, and paste text in a document or use the Clipboard Task Pane to collect up to 24 different items and then paste them in various locations in the document. Additional document formatting includes inserting page numbering; changing margins, orientation, and views; and changing vertical alignment. Add visual appeal to documents by inserting images and WordArt, and by drawing and customizing shapes and text boxes. Use the Envelopes and Labels feature to easily create and format envelopes and labels. In this section you will learn the skills and complete the projects described here.

*Note: Before beginning this section, delete the* Word S2 *folder on your disk. Next, copy to your disk the* Word S3 *subfolder from the* Word *folder on the CD that accompanies this textbook, and then make* Word S3 *the active folder.*

## Skills

- Find and replace text
- Cut, copy, and paste text
- Use the Clipboard Task Pane to copy and paste items
- Insert a page break
- Insert and modify page numbers
- Change margins
- Change page orientation
- Change views
- Use the Click and Type feature
- Vertically align text
- Insert, size, and move a clip art image
- Insert, size, and move WordArt
- Use buttons on the Drawing toolbar
- Prepare an envelope
- Prepare labels

## Projects

Edit and format fact sheets on Petersburg and Juneau, Alaska; prepare an announcement about a workshop on traveling on a budget; prepare a document on special vacation activities in Hawaii; prepare envelopes and labels for mailing fact sheets and announcements.

Prepare an announcement about internship positions available at Marquee Productions; prepare an envelope and labels for the Theatre Arts Division.

Create an announcement for a stockholders' meeting; prepare an envelope.

Format a costume rental agreement.

Prepare an announcement about a workshop on employment opportunities in the movie industry; prepare a banner with information on the Royal Ontario Museum.

## 3.1 Finding and Replacing Text

Use the find and replace feature to find specific text and replace with other text. For example, you can use abbreviations for common phrases when entering text and then replace the abbreviations with the actual text later, or you can set up standard documents with generic names and replace the names with other names to make a personalized document. You can also find and replace some formatting. These options are available at the Find and Replace dialog box with the Replace tab selected.

**PROJECT:** You are working on a First Choice Travel document containing information on Petersburg, Alaska. Your quick review identifies some spelling and capitalization errors that you will correct using the Find and Replace feature.

## STEPS

1. Open the FCT Petersburg document.
2. Save the document with Save As and name it Word S3-01.
3. After looking over the document, you realize that *Mitkoff* is spelled incorrectly. Display the Find and Replace dialog box by clicking Edit and then Replace.
4. At the Find and Replace dialog box with the Replace tab selected, key **Mitkoff** in the Find what text box and then press the Tab key.

   Pressing the Tab key moves the insertion point to the Replace with text box.

5. Key **Mitkof** in the Replace with text box and then click the Replace All button located toward the bottom of the dialog box.

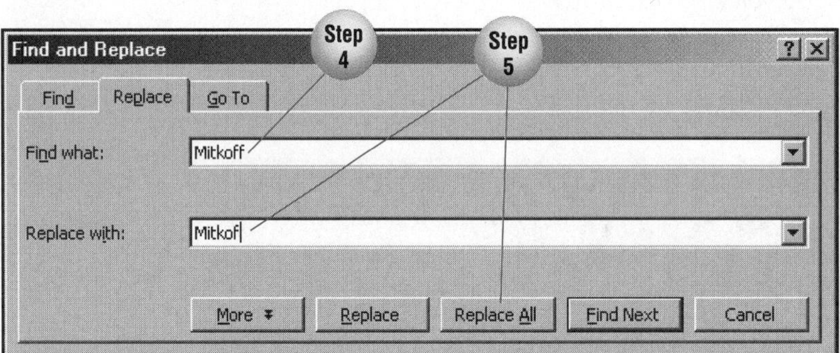


   Clicking the Replace All button replaces all occurrences of the text in the document. If you want control over what is replaced in a document, click the Replace button to replace text or click the Find Next button to move to the next occurrence of the text.

PROBLEM ? If the Replace with text box does not display, click the Replace tab.

6. At the message telling you that two replacements were made, click the OK button.
7. Click the Close button to close the Find and Replace dialog box.
8. Looking at the document, you determine that Alaska Marine Highway is a proper name and should display in the document with the first letter of each word capitalized. Click Edit and then Replace.

9. At the Find and Replace dialog box with the Replace tab selected, key **Alaska marine highway**.
10. Press Tab, key **Alaska Marine Highway** in the Replace with text box, and then click the Replace All button.

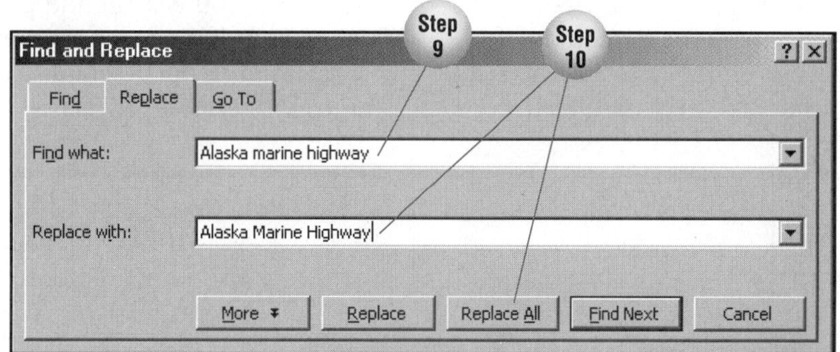


11. At the message telling you that two replacements were made, click the OK button.
12. Click the Close button to close the Find and Replace dialog box.
13. Save Word S3-01.

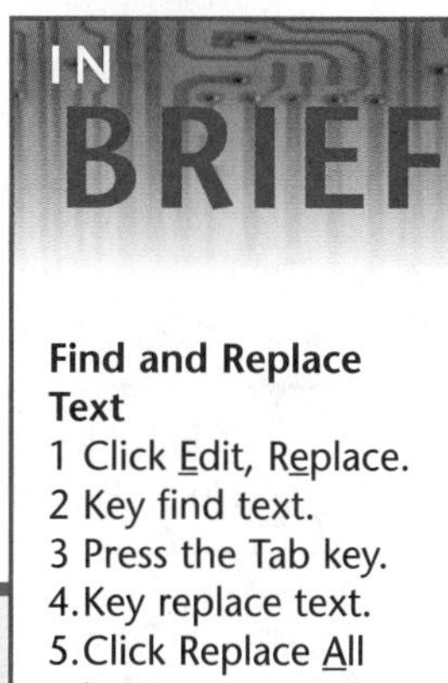


**Find and Replace Text**
1 Click Edit, Replace.
2 Key find text.
3 Press the Tab key.
4. Key replace text.
5. Click Replace All button.

# In Addition

## Options at the Expanded Find and Replace Dialog Box

The Find and Replace dialog box contains a variety of check boxes with options you can choose for completing a find and replace. To display these options, click the More button located at the bottom of the dialog box. This causes the Find and Replace dialog box to expand as shown at the right. The options are described below.

| Option | Action |
|---|---|
| Match case | Exactly match the case of the search text. For example, if you search for *Book*, Word will stop at Book but not *book* or *BOOK*. |
| Find whole words only | Find a whole word, not a part of a word. For example, if you search for *her* and *did not* select Find whole words only, Word would stop at t*here*, *her*e, *her*s, etc. |
| Use wildcards | Search for wildcards, special characters, or special search operators. |
| Sounds like | Match words that sound alike but are spelled differently such as *know* and *no*. |
| Find all word forms | Find all forms of the word entered in the Find what text box. For example, if you enter *hold*, Word will stop at *held* and *holding*. |

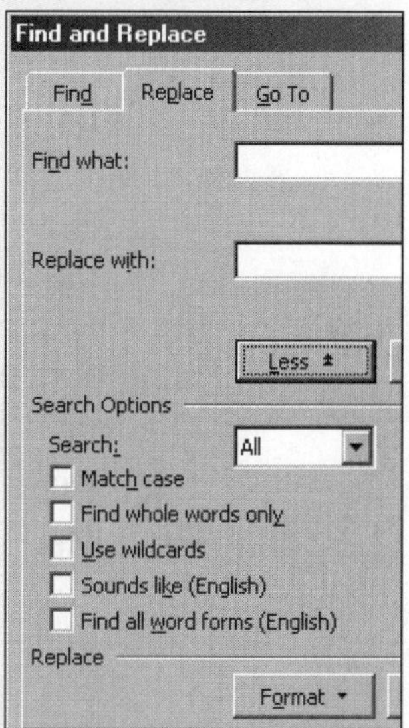

## 3.2 Cutting, Copying, and Pasting Text; Using Paste Special

With the Cut, Copy, and Paste buttons on the Standard toolbar, you can quickly move and/or copy words, sentences, or entire sections of text to other locations in a document. Text can be cut and pasted or copied and pasted within the same document or between documents. Specify the formatting of pasted text with options at the Paste Special dialog box. Display this dialog box by clicking Edit and then Paste Special. Choose how you want the text pasted with options in the As list box and then click OK to close the dialog box and paste the text.

**PROJECT:** You will cut and paste text in the Petersburg fact sheet document and also copy text from another document and paste it into the fact sheet document.

## STEPS

1. With the Word S3-01 document open, move the Services section below the Walking Tours section by selecting the *Services* heading, the two paragraphs of text below it, and the blank line below the second paragraph.
2. Click the Cut button on the Standard toolbar.

   This places the text in a special location within Word called the "clipboard."

PROBLEM? If you click the wrong button, immediately click the Undo button.

3. Move the insertion point to the beginning of the *Accommodations* heading and then click the Paste button on the Standard toolbar.

   A Paste Options button displays below the pasted text. Click this button and options display for specifying the formatting of the pasted text. The default setting keeps source formatting for the pasted text. You can choose to match the destination formatting, keep only the text and not the formatting, or display the Styles and Formatting Task Pane where you can choose the desired formatting.

4. Copy text from another document and paste it in the Petersburg fact sheet. To do this, open FCT PA 01.
5. Select the *Points of Interest* heading, the four lines of text below the heading and the blank line below the lines of text, and then click the Copy button on the Standard toolbar.
6. Click the button on the Taskbar representing Word S3-01.

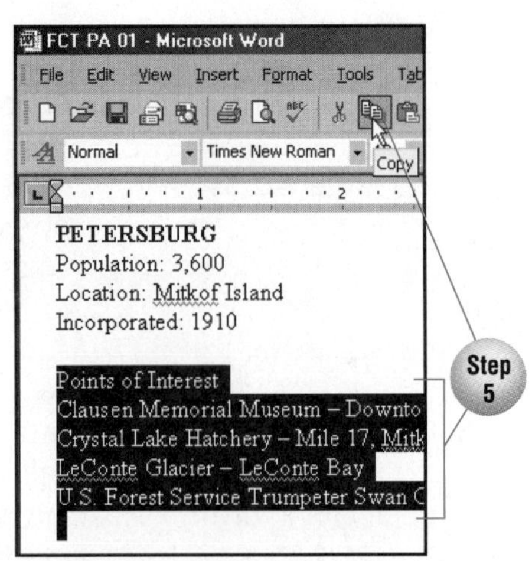

7 Position the insertion point at the beginning of the sentence *If you would like more information…* located toward the end of the document and then click the Paste button.

8 Click the button on the Taskbar representing FCT PA 01.

9 Select the text *Resources:* and the three lines below it and then click the Copy button.

10 Click the button on the Taskbar representing Word S3-01.

11 Move the insertion point to the end of the document (a double space below the last sentence) and then paste the copied text into the document without the formatting by clicking Edit and then Paste Special.

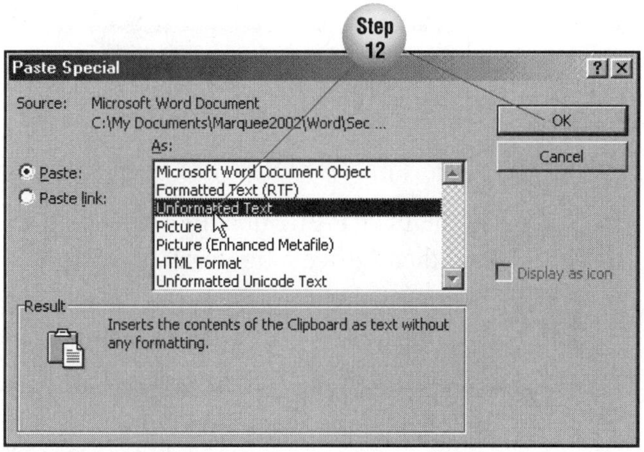

12 At the Paste Special dialog box, click *Unformatted Text* in the As list box and then click OK.

Step 12

Paste Special

Source: Microsoft Word Document
C:\My Documents\Marquee2002\Word\Sec ...

As:

Paste:
Paste link:

Microsoft Word Document Object
Formatted Text (RTF)
Unformatted Text
Picture
Picture (Enhanced Metafile)
HTML Format
Unformatted Unicode Text

OK
Cancel
Display as icon

Result
Inserts the contents of the Clipboard as text without any formatting.

13 Save Word S3-01.

14 Click the button on the Taskbar representing the FCT PA 01 document and then close the document.

Closing the FCT PA 01 document displays the Word S3-01 document.

# In Addition

## Moving and Copying Text with the Mouse

Selected text can be moved using the mouse. To do this, select the text with the mouse and then move the I-beam pointer inside the selected text until the I-beam pointer turns into an arrow pointer. Hold down the left mouse button, drag the arrow pointer (displays with a gray box attached) to the location where you want the selected text inserted, and then release the button. You can copy and move selected text by following similar steps. The difference is that you need to hold down the Ctrl key while dragging with the mouse. With the Ctrl key down, a box containing a plus symbol displays near the gray box by the arrow pointer.

## IN BRIEF

**Cut and Paste Text**
1 Select text.
2 Click Cut button.
3 Move insertion point to desired position.
4 Click Paste button.

**Copy and Paste Text**
1 Select text.
2 Click Copy button.
3 Move insertion point to desired position.
4 Click Paste button.

**Display Paste Special Dialog Box**
1 Cut or copy text.
2 Click Edit, Paste Special.
3 Click desired format in As list box.
4 Click OK.

## 3.3 Using the Clipboard Task Pane

Using the Clipboard Task Pane, you can collect up to 24 different items and then paste them in various locations in a document. Display the Clipboard Task Pane by clicking Edit and then Office Clipboard or by pressing Ctrl + C twice. Cut or copy an item and the item displays in the Clipboard Task Pane. If the item is text, the first 50 characters display. Paste an item by positioning the insertion point at the desired location and then clicking the item in the Clipboard Task Pane. When all desired items are inserted, click the Clear All button located in the upper right corner of the task pane.

**PROJECT:** You will open another fact sheet document, copy items in the document, and then paste the items into the Petersburg fact sheet document.

### STEPS

1. Make sure Word S3-01 is open and then open the FCT PA 02 document.
2. In the FCT PA 02 document, display the Clipboard Task Pane by clicking Edit and then Office Clipboard.

   If any items display in the Clipboard Task Pane, click the Clear All button located in the upper right corner of the task pane.
3. Select the *Sightseeing* heading, the two paragraphs of text below it, and the blank line below the second paragraph, and then click the Copy button.

   Notice how the copied item is represented in the Clipboard Task Pane.
4. Select the *Little Norway Festival* heading, the two paragraphs of text below it and the blank line below the second paragraph, and then click the Copy button.
5. Select the *Salmon Derby* heading, the paragraph of text below it and the blank line below the paragraph, and then click the Copy button.
6. Click the button on the Taskbar representing Word S3-01.
7. Press Ctrl + C twice to display the Clipboard Task Pane.
8. Move the insertion point to the beginning of the *Walking Tours* heading.
9. Click the item in the Clipboard Task Pane representing Salmon Derby.
10. Move the insertion point to the beginning of the *Points of Interest* heading.

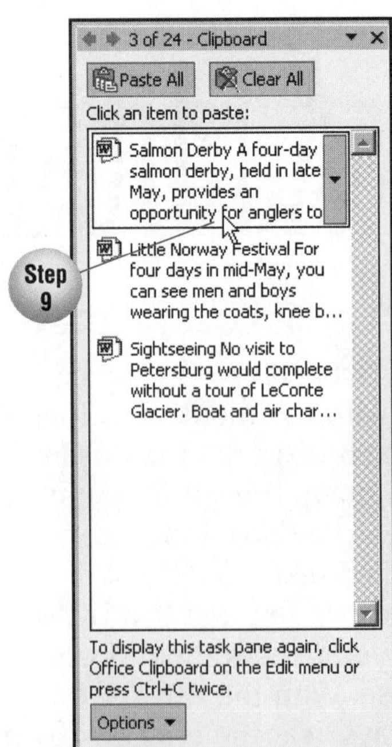

11 Click the item in the Clipboard Task Pane representing Sightseeing.

12 Click the Clear All button located in the upper right corner of the Clipboard Task Pane.

13 Click the Close button ☒ in the upper right corner of the Clipboard Task Pane to close the task pane.

14 Save Word S3-01.

15 Click the button on the Taskbar representing FCT PA 02 and then close the document.

The Word S3-01 document displays when you close FCT PA 02.

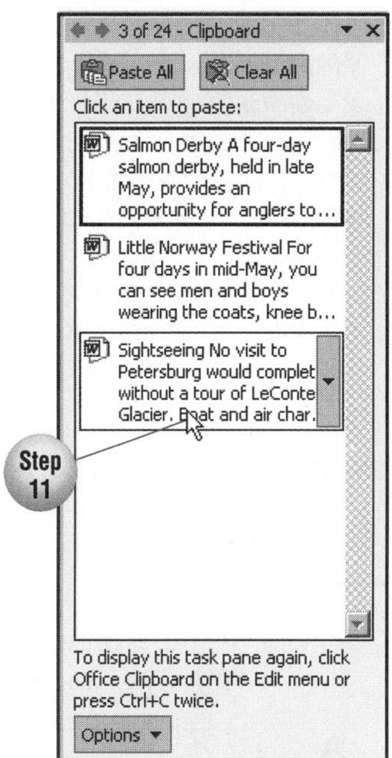


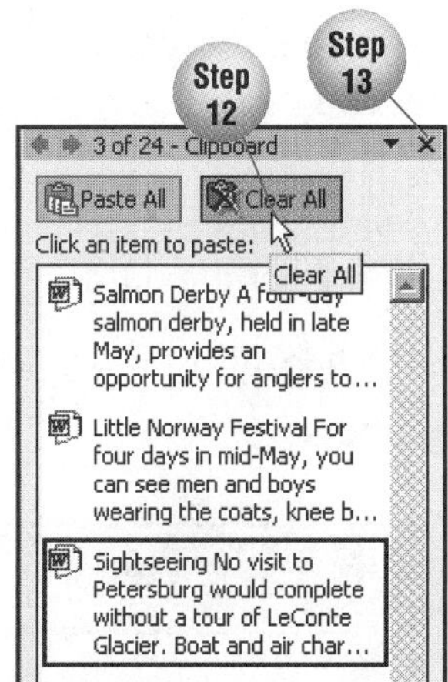


# In Addition

## Clipboard Task Pane Options

Click the Options button located toward the bottom of the Clipboard Task Pane and a pop-up menu displays with four options as shown at the right. Insert a check mark before those options that you want active. For example, you can choose to display the Clipboard Task Pane automatically when you cut or copy text, cut and copy text without displaying the Clipboard Task Pane, display the Office Clipboard icon near the Taskbar when the clipboard is active, and display the item message when copying items to the Clipboard.

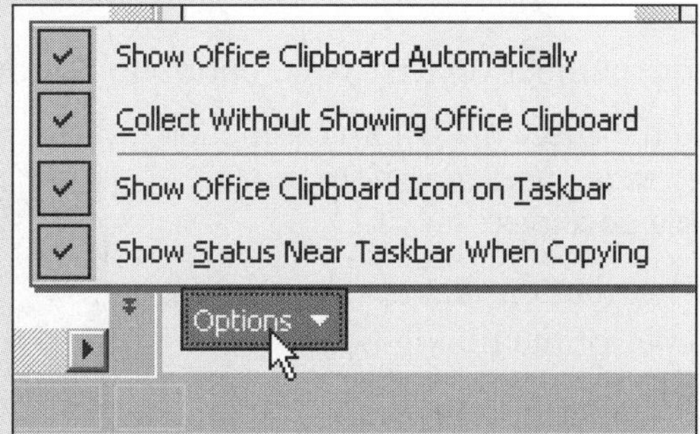


## In Brief

**Use the Clipboard Task Pane**

1 Click Edit, Office Clipboard.
2 Select text.
3 Click Copy button.
4 Select and copy any additional items.
5 Move insertion point to desired position.
6 Click item in Clipboard Task Pane representing desired item.
7 Paste any other desired items from the Clipboard Task Pane.
8 Click Clear All button.

## 3.4 Inserting a Page Break; Inserting and Modifying Page Numbers

By default, Word will insert a page break in a document at approximately 10 inches or approximately line 45 (this number may vary). If you want to control where a page breaks, insert your own page break by pressing Ctrl + Enter. Add page numbering to a document with options at the Page Numbers dialog box where you specify whether page numbering appears at the top or bottom of the page and specify the alignment. Click the Format button at the Page Numbers dialog box and the Page Number Format dialog box displays. Use options at this dialog box to change numbering format and specify where you want page numbering to begin.

**PROJECT:** The Petersburg fact sheet is one of several fact sheets produced by First Choice Travel. You will insert a page break in the document, insert page numbering, and begin page numbering with page 12.

### STEPS

1. With Word S3-01 open, move the insertion point to the beginning of the heading *Points of Interest* (located toward the end of the document) and then insert a page break by pressing Ctrl + Enter.

   A page break appears in Normal view as a line of dots across the screen with the words *Page Break* displayed in the middle of the dots.

2. Press Ctrl + Home to move the insertion point to the beginning of the document.
3. Click Insert and then click Page Numbers.
4. At the Page Numbers dialog box, click the down-pointing triangle at the right side of the Position text box, and then click *Top of page (Header)*.

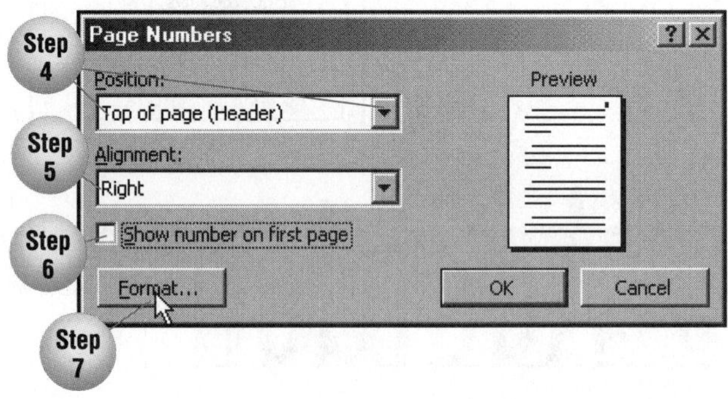


5. Make sure the Alignment option displays as *Right*. (If not, click the down-pointing triangle at the right of the Alignment text box, and then click *Right* at the drop-down list.)
6. Click the Show number on first page option to remove the check mark.

   Removing the check mark from this option eliminates page numbering from the first page of the document.

7. Click the Format button that displays in the lower left corner of the dialog box.
8. At the Page Number Format dialog box, click Start at and then key **12** in the Start at text box.

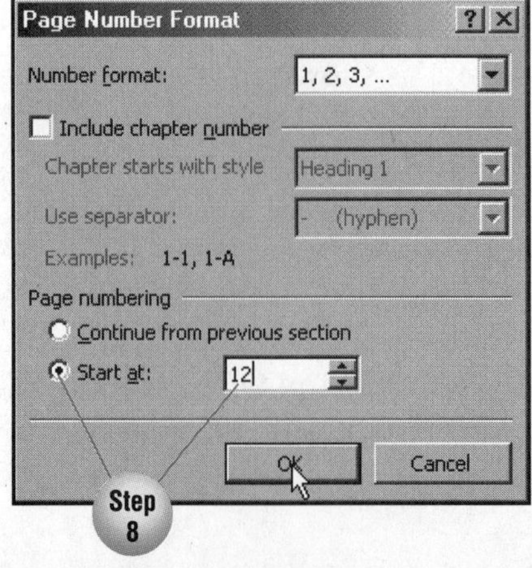

9. Click OK to close the Page Number Format dialog box and then click OK to close the Page Numbers dialog box.
10. Select the title *FACT SHEET – PETERSBURG, ALASKA*, change the font to 16-point Arial bold, and change the alignment to center.
11. Select the heading *Visitor Attractions* and then change the font to 12-point Arial bold and add 6 points of space after the paragraph. *(Hint: Add the 6 points of space at the Paragraph dialog box with the Indents and Spacing tab selected.)*
12. Use Format Painter to format the remaining headings (*Salmon Derby*, *Walking Tours*, *Services*, *Accommodations*, *Transportation*, *Sightseeing*, and *Points of Interest*) with 12-point Arial bold and 6 points of space after the paragraph.

PROBLEM?

If Format Painter does not apply the proper formatting, check to make sure you position the insertion point on any character in the *Visitor Attractions* heading and then double-click the Format Painter button.

13. Preview the document by clicking the Print Preview button on the Standard toolbar. Scroll through the document to see how the page numbering appears (page numbering will not appear on the first page).

    If you cannot see the page number in Print Preview, increase the Zoom size.

14. Click the Close button to close Print Preview.
15. Save Word S3-01.

# In Addition

## Deleting Page Numbering

A page number is created in a document as a header or footer. To delete page numbering, click View and then Header and Footer. Display the header or footer pane containing the page numbering, select the page numbering, and then press the Delete key. Click the Close button on the Header and Footer toolbar.

## IN BRIEF

**Insert Page Break**

1 Move insertion point to desired position.
2 Press Ctrl + Enter.

**Insert Page Numbering**

1 Click Insert, Page Numbers.
2 Specify position and alignment of page numbering.
3 Click OK.

## 3.5 Changing Margins and Page Orientation

A Word document, by default, contains 1-inch top and bottom margins and 1.25-inch left and right margins. These default margins can be changed with options at the Page Setup dialog box. Along with these defaults, Word assumes you are using standard-sized stationery, which is 8.5 inches by 11 inches. Word provides two orientations for paper sizes—portrait and landscape. Portrait is the default and prints the document so the short edge of the paper is the top of the page. This can be changed to landscape, which prints the document so the long edge of the paper is the top of the page.

**PROJECT:** You have decided that the Petersburg fact sheet will look better if printed with a landscape orientation. You will change the margins and orientation for the document and then print it.

### STEPS

1. With Word S3-01 open, click File and then Page Setup.
2. At the Page Setup dialog box, make sure the Margins tab is selected. If it is not, click the Margins tab.
3. Click the up-pointing triangle at the right side of the Top option until *1.5″* displays.

   You can also change a margin measurement by selecting the measurement and then keying the new measurement.

4. Click the up-pointing triangle at the right side of the Bottom option until *1.5″* displays.
5. Click the up-pointing triangle at the right side of the Left option until *1.5″* displays.
6. Click the up-pointing triangle at the right side of the Right option until *1.5″* displays.
7. Click the Landscape option in the Orientation section of the dialog box.

   Refer to Figure W3.1 for a display of the portrait and landscape orientations.

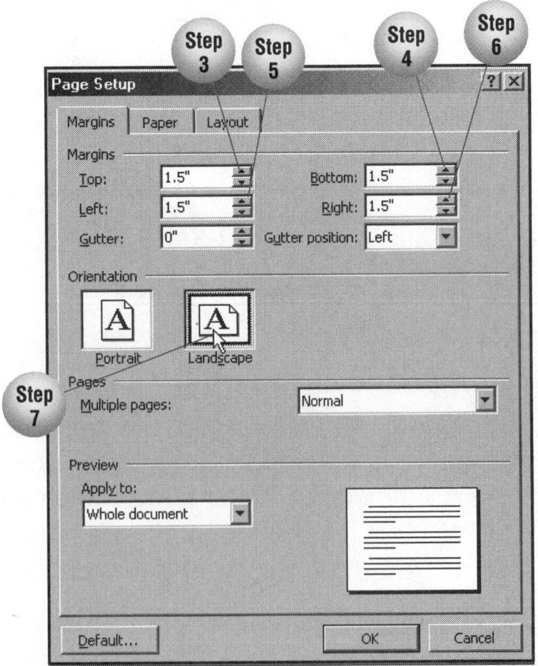

**FIGURE W3.1** Orientations

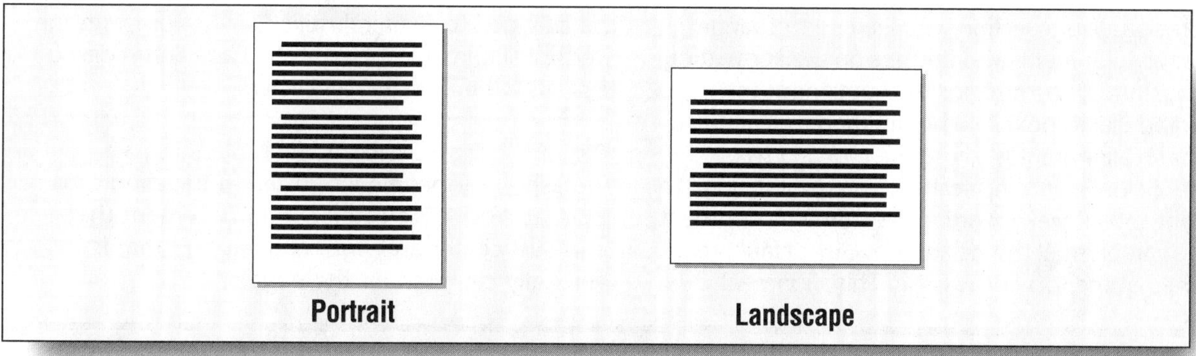


8. Click Click OK to close the dialog box.
9. Click Save Word S3-01.
10. Print and then close Word S3-01.

# In Addition

## Changing Margins with the Ruler

At the Page Setup dialog box, you can specify margin measurements. Using the Ruler, you can visually set margins. To set margins using the Ruler, change to the Print Layout view. At this view, the horizontal ruler displays below the Formatting toolbar and a vertical ruler displays along the left side of the screen as shown below. The horizontal and vertical rulers each contain a gray area and a white area. The gray area indicates the margin while the white area indicates the space between margins. The edge between the gray and white is called the *margin boundary*. To change margins, position the mouse pointer on the margin boundary. This causes the mouse pointer to turn into a double-headed arrow. Hold down the left mouse button, drag the margin boundary to the desired location, and then release the mouse button.

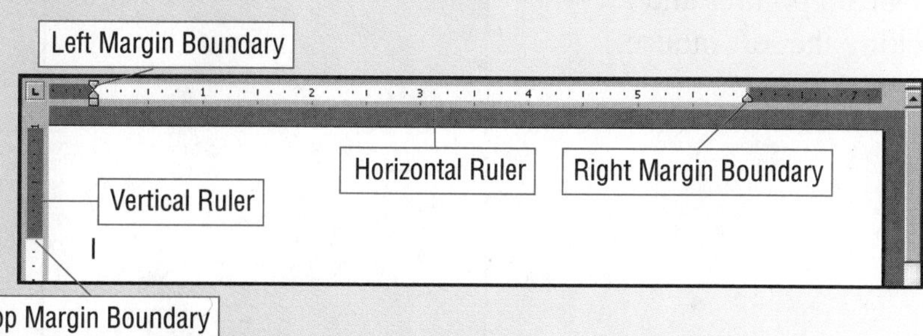


## IN BRIEF

**Change Margins**
1 Click File, Page Setup.
2 Click Margins tab.
3 Specify margin measurements.
4 Click OK.

**Change Page Orientation**
1 Click File, Page Setup.
2 Click Margins tab.
3 Click desired orientation.
4 Click OK.

## 3.6 Changing Views; Using Click and Type; Vertically Aligning Text

In a previous Word section, you learned to change paragraph alignment with buttons on the Formatting toolbar, shortcut commands, and options at the Paragraph dialog box. Another method for changing paragraph alignment is to use the *click and type* feature. Before using this feature, you must change to the Print Layout view. Word offers different document views, with Normal the default view. By default, text is aligned at the top of the page. This alignment can be changed to Center, Justified, or Bottom with the Vertical alignment option at the Page Setup dialog box with the Layout tab selected.

**PROJECT:** First Choice Travel is planning a workshop for people interested in traveling on a budget. You will create an announcement that contains center and right aligned text that is vertically centered on the page.

### STEPS

1. Make sure a clear document screen displays (this is a screen with a white background). If a clear document screen is not displayed, click the New Blank Document button on the Standard toolbar.
2. Change to the Print Layout view by clicking View and then Print Layout.

   When you change to the Print Layout view, a horizontal and vertical ruler display and the insertion point appears 1 inch from the top of the screen. Print Layout offers a visual representation of the actual paper.
3. Position the I-beam pointer between the left and right margins at about the 3-inch mark on the horizontal ruler and the top of the vertical ruler. When the center alignment lines display below the I-beam pointer, double-click the left mouse button.

PROBLEM? If the alignment lines are not displayed near the I-beam pointer when you double-click the left mouse button, a left tab is set at the position of the insertion point.

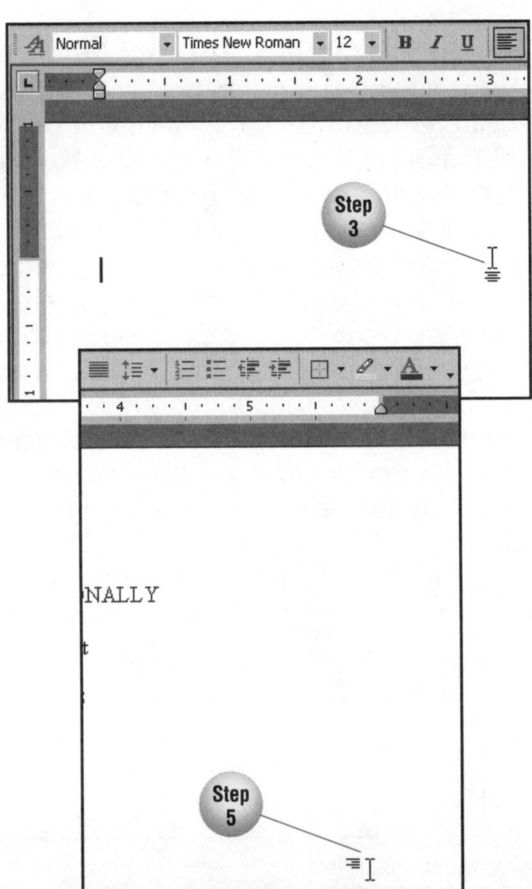


4. Key the centered text shown in Figure W3.2, pressing the Enter key twice between each line of text.
5. Change to right alignment by positioning the I-beam pointer near the right margin at approximately the 2-inch mark on the vertical ruler until the right alignment lines display at the left side of the I-beam pointer and then double-clicking the left mouse button.

6 Key the right aligned text shown in Figure W3.2.

7 Select the centered text and then change the font to 14-point Arial bold.

8 Select the right-aligned text, change the font to 8-point Arial bold, and then deselect the text.

9 Vertically align the text by clicking File and then Page Setup.

10 At the Page Setup dialog box, click the Layout tab.

11 Click the down-pointing triangle at the right side of the Vertical alignment option and then click *Center* at the drop-down list.

12 Click OK to close the Page Setup dialog box.

13 Save the document and name it Word S3-02.

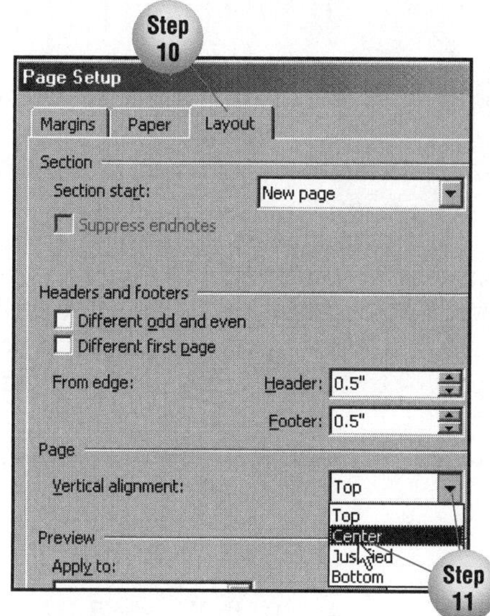


**FIGURE W3.2**

TRAVELING INTERNATIONALLY

Traveling on a Budget

Friday, May 16, 2003

3:30 - 5:00 p.m.

Sponsored by
First Choice Travel

# In Addition

## Changing the View

Change the view by clicking View on the Menu bar and then clicking the desired view at the drop-down menu. Another method for changing the view is to click the desired button on the View toolbar shown at the right. The View toolbar is located in the lower left corner of the screen immediately above the Status bar. For example, to change to the Print Layout view, click the Print Layout View button.

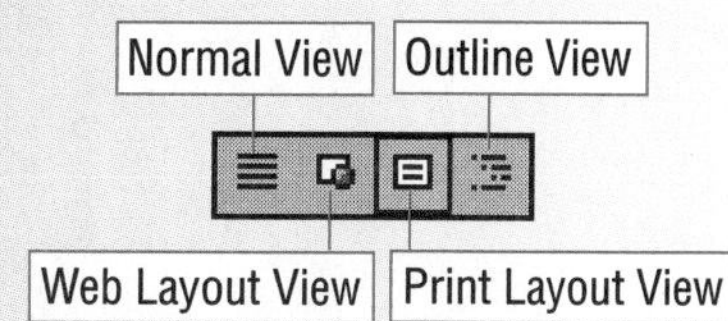


## In Brief

**Change to Print Layout View**
Click View, Print Layout.

**Vertically Align Text**
1 Click File, Page Setup.
2 Click Layout tab.
3 Click Vertical alignment option.
4 Click *Center* at drop-down list.
5 Click OK.

## 3.7 Inserting, Sizing, and Moving Images in a Document

Office XP includes a gallery of media images you can insert in a document such as clip art, photographs, and movie images, as well as sound clips. Specify and insert images in a document with options at the Insert Clip Art Task Pane. You can also insert a picture or image from a specific file location with options at the Insert Picture dialog box. You can move, size, and customize an inserted image or picture with buttons on the Picture toolbar. With options from the Zoom button on the Standard toolbar, you can increase or decrease the display of text and also display the whole page, which is useful for positioning images.

**PROJECT:** You have decided to insert a travel clip art image and the First Choice Travel logo to enhance the visual interest of the announcement.

### STEPS

1. With Word S3-02 open, return the vertical alignment to *Top*. To do this, click File and then Page Setup. At the Page Setup dialog box, click the Layout tab. Click the down-pointing triangle at the right side of the Vertical alignment option and then click *Top* at the drop-down list. Click OK to close the dialog box.
2. Press Ctrl + End to move the insertion point to the end of the document.
3. Display the Drawing toolbar by clicking the Drawing button on the Standard toolbar.

   The Drawing toolbar displays toward the bottom of the screen, above the Status bar. When you click the Drawing button, the view automatically changes to Print Layout.
4. Click the Insert Clip Art button on the Drawing toolbar.

   This displays the Insert Clip Art Task Pane at the right side of the screen.
5. Key **travel** in the Search text: text box and then click the Search button.

   If text displays in the Search text: text box, select the text first, and then key **travel**.
6. When the clip art images display, click the image shown below and at the right. (If this image is not available, choose another image related to *travel*.)
7. Close the Insert Clip Art Task pane by clicking the Close button located in the upper right corner of the task pane.

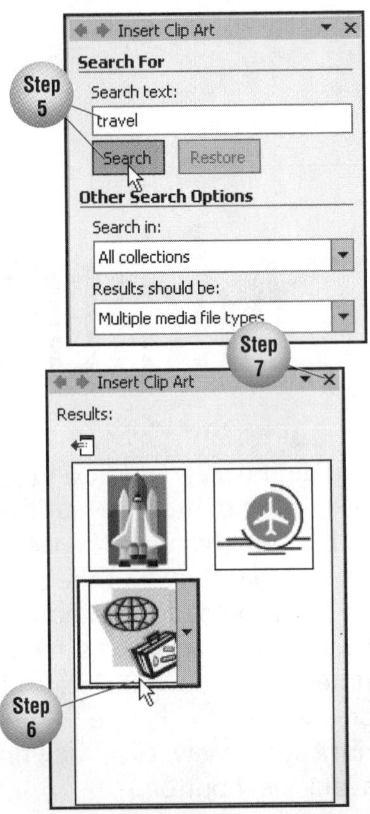

8 Click the image in the document to select it.

The selected image displays surrounded by black squares called *sizing handles* and the Picture toolbar displays. Refer to Figure W3.3 for the names of the Picture toolbar buttons. If the Picture toolbar is not displayed, right-click the image, and then click Show Picture Toolbar at the shortcut menu.

**FIGURE W3.3** Picture Toolbar Buttons

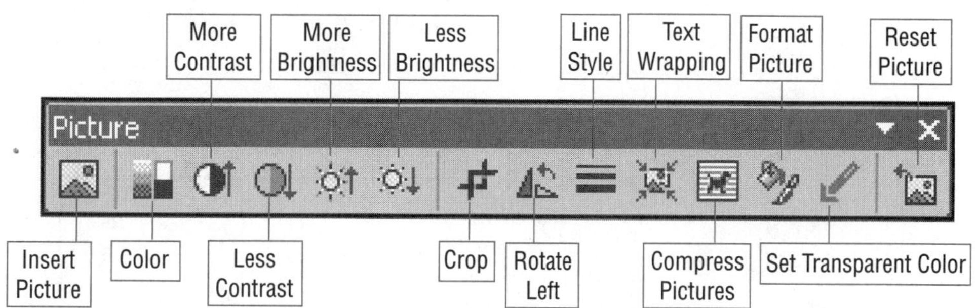


9 Click the Text Wrapping button on the Picture toolbar, and then click *Square* at the drop-down list.

When you choose a text wrapping option, all of the sizing handles change to white circles.

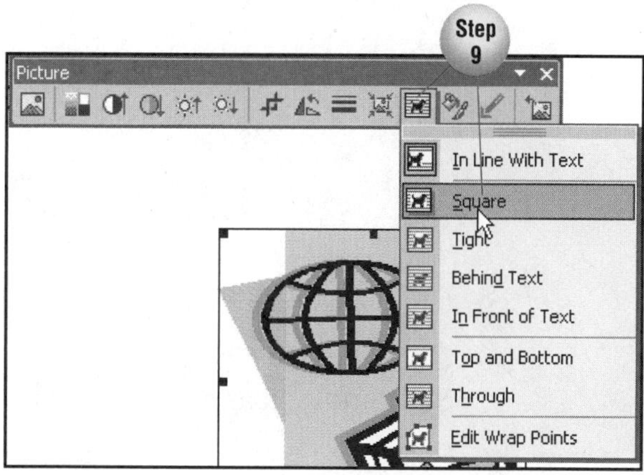


PROBLEM? If the sizing handles do not change to white, choose the wrapping style again.

10 Click the Format Picture button on the Picture toolbar.

11 At the Format Picture dialog box, click the Size tab.

12 Select the current measurement in the Height spin box (in the Size and rotate section), key **1.7**, and then click OK.

When you change the height measurement, the width measurement is automatically changed to maintain the proportions of the image.

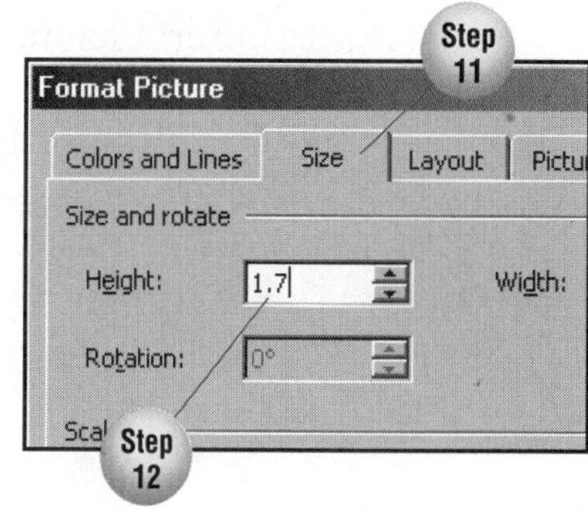


*(continued)*

13. Click the down-pointing triangle at the right side of the Zoom button on the Standard toolbar. At the drop-down list that displays, click the *Whole Page* option.

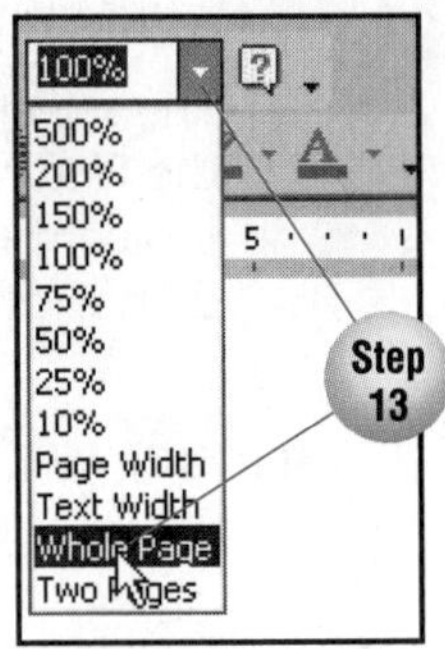


14. Move the image by positioning the arrow pointer on the image until the pointer turns into a four-headed arrow, holding down the left mouse button, dragging the image up and to the left (as shown below), and then releasing the mouse button.

    Position the image as shown in Figure W3.4.

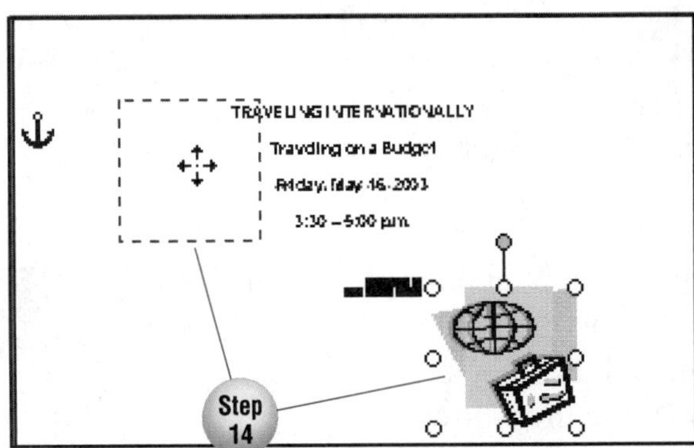


15. Click outside the image to deselect it.
16. Click the down-pointing triangle at the right side of the Zoom button on the Standard toolbar and then click *100%* at the drop-down list.
17. Select and then delete the text *First Choice Travel* that displays in small font size at the right side of the screen.
18. Press Ctrl + End to move the insertion point to the end of the document and then press the Enter key.
19. Insert the First Choice Logo below *Sponsored by* by clicking Insert, pointing to Picture, and then clicking From File.
20. At the Insert Picture dialog box, display the folder where your data documents are located and then double-click *FCT Logo*.

    The First Choice Travel logo is inserted in the document. Your document should display similar to the document shown in Figure W3.4.

21. Save, print, and then close Word S3-02.

**FIGURE W3.4** Completed Word 3-02 Document

# In Addition

## Downloading Clip Art

The Microsoft Design Gallery Live Web site offers a gallery with hundreds of images you can download. To display the Design Gallery, you must have access to the Internet. To download an image, display the Insert Clip Art Task Pane, and then click the *Clips Online* hyperlink located toward the bottom of the Insert Clip Art Task Pane. At the Microsoft Design Gallery Live Web site, click in the Search for text box, key the desired category, and then click the Go button. Download the desired image by clicking the download button that displays below the image.

**Insert Clip Art Image**

1. Click Insert Clip Art button on Drawing toolbar.
2. Click desired image in the Insert Clip Art Task Pane.

**Insert Image**

1. Click Insert, Picture, From File.
2. Double-click desired image.

# 3.8 Inserting, Sizing, and Moving WordArt in a Document

Use the WordArt application to distort or modify text to conform to a variety of shapes. Consider using WordArt to create a company logo, letterhead, flier title, or heading. With WordArt, you can change the font, style, and alignment of text; use different fill patterns and colors; customize border lines, and add shadow and three-dimensional effects. Selected WordArt text can be sized and moved in the document.

**PROJECT:** You will add a WordArt heading to the document on Hawaiian specials to enhance the visual appeal of the document.

## STEPS

1. Open FCT Hawaiian Specials and then save the document with Save As and name it Word S3-03.
2. Complete a spelling and grammar check on the document. You determine what to correct and what to ignore. (The name *Molokini* is spelled correctly in the document.)
3. Select and then delete the title *HAWAIIAN SPECIALS*.
4. Insert WordArt by clicking Insert, pointing to Picture, and then clicking WordArt.

   You can also display the WordArt Gallery by clicking the Insert WordArt button on the Drawing toolbar.

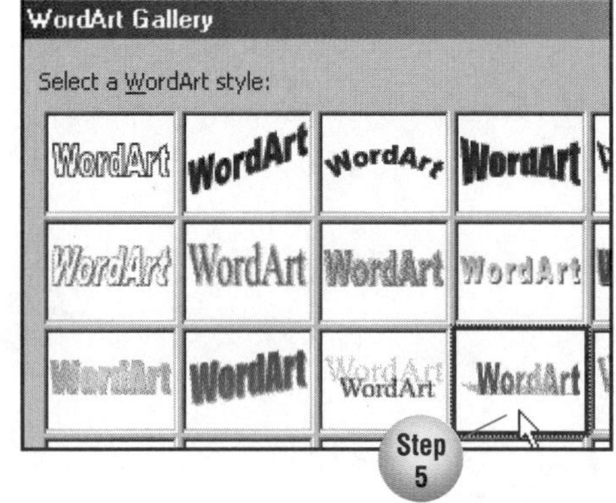


5. At the WordArt Gallery dialog box, double-click the fourth option from the left in the third row.
6. At the Edit WordArt Text dialog box, key **Hawaiian Specials** and then click OK to close the dialog box.

   The text will wrap inside the text box.

7. Increase the height of the WordArt text by positioning the mouse pointer on the bottom, middle sizing handle until the pointer turns into an arrow pointing up and down. Hold down the left mouse button, drag down approximately 0.5 inch, and then release the mouse button.

PROBLEM? If you do not like the size of the WordArt, click the Undo button, and then size it again.

8 Click the Text Wrapping button and then click *Square* at the drop-down list.

Choosing a text wrapping style changes the black sizing handles to white sizing handles. Customize WordArt with buttons on the WordArt toolbar shown in Figure W3.5.

9 Drag the WordArt text so it is positioned centered between the left and right margins. To do this, position the mouse pointer on the WordArt text until the pointer displays with a four-headed arrow attached. Hold down the left mouse button, drag the WordArt text to the desired position, and then release the mouse button.

Make sure that the heading *White Sands Charters* and the following text display below the WordArt text and not at the right side.

10 Click outside the WordArt text box to deselect it.

11 Apply the Heading 1 style to the following headings: *White Sands Charters*, *Air Adventures*, *Deep Sea Submarines*, *Snorkeling Fantasies*, and *Bicycle Safari*.

12 Press Ctrl + A to select the entire document and then change the font color to dark blue. To do this, click the down-pointing triangle at the right side of the Font Color button on the Formatting toolbar and then click *Dark Blue* (sixth color from the left in the top row).

13 Click outside the selected text to deselect it.

14 Save Word S3-03.

**FIGURE W3.5** WordArt Toolbar Buttons

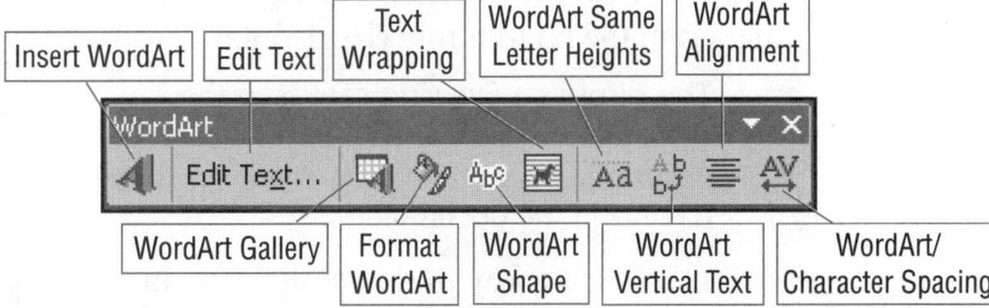


# In Addition

## Changing the Font and Font Size

The font for WordArt text will vary depending on the choice you make at the WordArt Gallery. You can change the font at the Edit WordArt Text dialog box by clicking the down-pointing triangle at the right side of the Font option and then clicking the desired font at the drop-down list. Change the font size by clicking the down-pointing triangle at the right side of the Size text box. The Edit WordArt Text dialog box also contains a Bold button and an Italic button you can click to apply the specific formatting.

## 3.9 Using the Drawing Toolbar

With buttons on the Drawing toolbar, you can draw a variety of shapes and lines and then customize the shapes or lines by changing line color, adding fill, adding a shadow, including a border, and so on. With options from the AutoShapes button, you can choose from a variety of predesigned shapes to draw shapes in a document. Use the Text Box button to draw a box and then key text inside the box. This box, like a shape, can be customized. A drawn object can be sized and moved in the same manner as an image or WordArt text.

**PROJECT:** You will add an autoshape containing text as a visual element to the end of the Hawaiian specials document.

## STEPS

1. With Word S3-03 open, press Ctrl + End to move the insertion point to the end of the document, and then press the Enter key twice.
2. Click the Drawing button on the Standard toolbar to turn on the display of the Drawing toolbar.

   Skip this step if the Drawing toolbar is already displayed. Refer to Figure W3.6 for the names and descriptions of the Drawing toolbar buttons.

**FIGURE W3.6** Drawing Toolbar Buttons

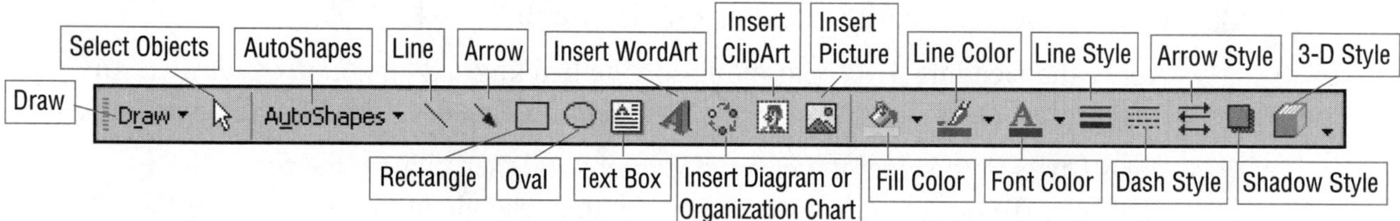


3. Draw the banner autoshape shown in Figure W3.7. To do this, click the AutoShapes button on the Drawing toolbar, point to Stars and Banners, and then click the second banner from the left in the bottom row (Horizontal Scroll).

   This displays a Drawing canvas in the document. Draw a shape in this canvas or delete the canvas and then draw the shape directly in the document.

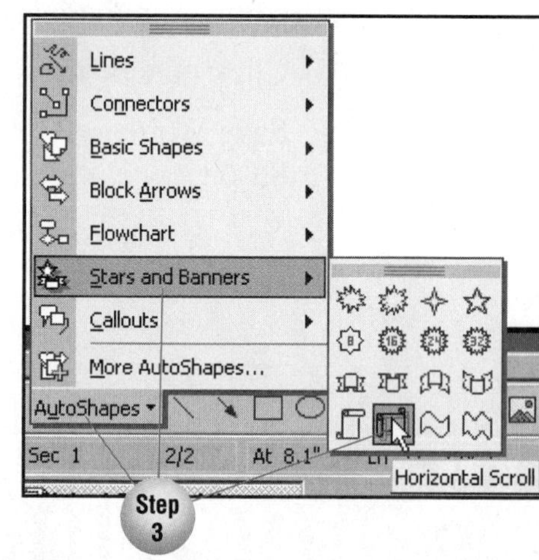


4. Press the Delete key to delete the drawing canvas.
5. Position the mouse pointer (displays as crosshairs) below the text at approximately the 1.5-inch mark on the horizontal ruler and the 7.5-inch mark on the vertical ruler. Hold down the left mouse button, drag down and to the right until the banner is approximately 3 inches wide and 1.25 inches high, and then release the mouse button.

**FIGURE W3.7**

**Sign up today for your Hawaiian adventure!**

6 Fill the banner with light green color by clicking the down-pointing triangle at the right side of the Fill Color button on the Drawing toolbar, and then clicking Light Green (fourth color from the left in the bottom row) at the pop-up menu.

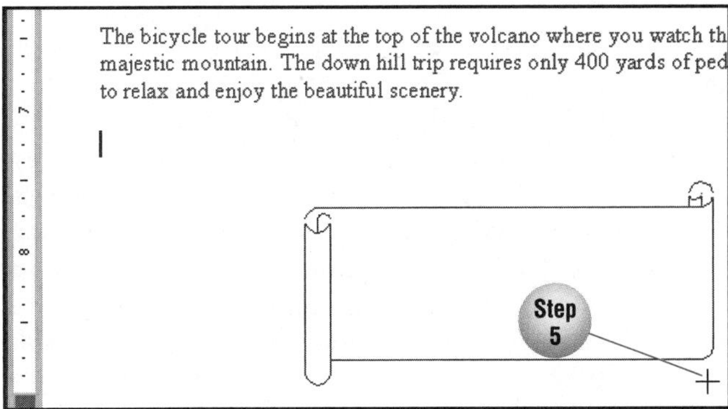


7 Draw a text box inside the image by clicking the Text Box button on the Drawing toolbar.

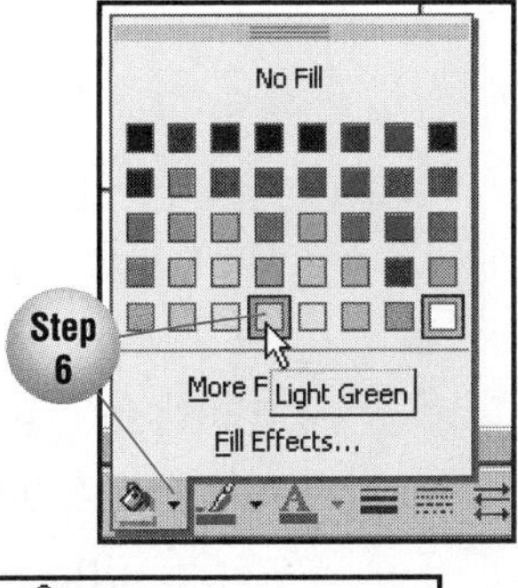


8 Position the mouse pointer (displays as crosshairs) inside the banner, hold down the left mouse button, drag to create a text box similar to the one shown at the right, and then release the mouse button.

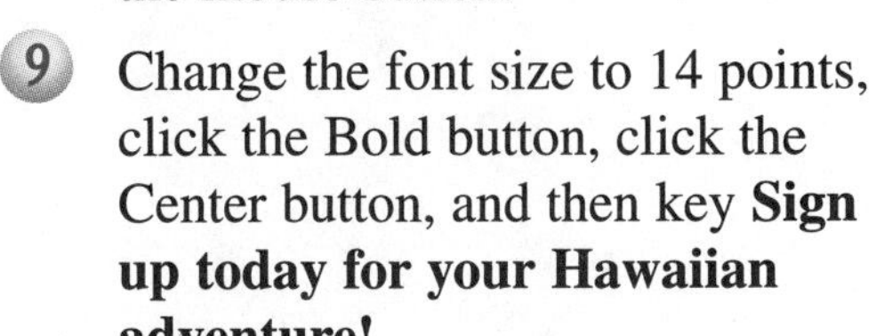

9 Change the font size to 14 points, click the Bold button, click the Center button, and then key **Sign up today for your Hawaiian adventure!**

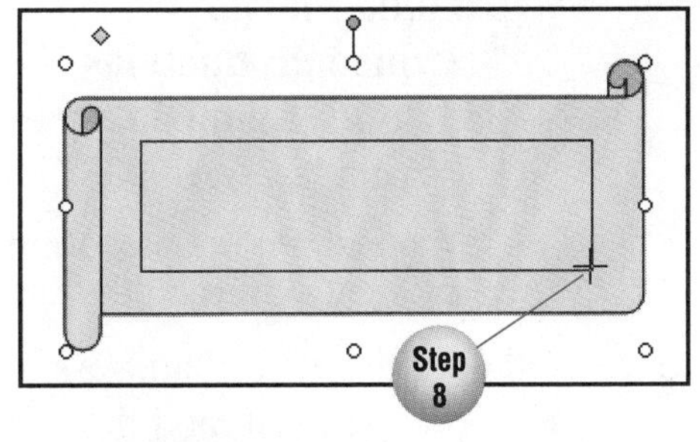


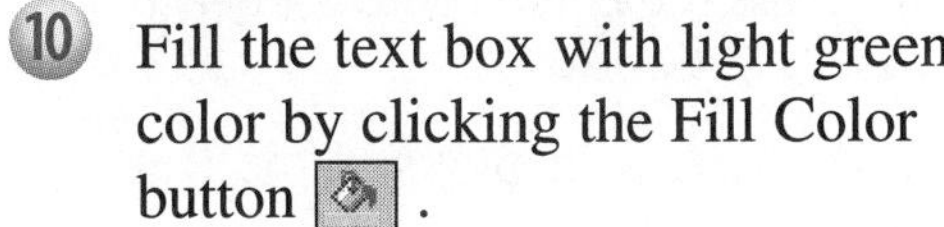

10 Fill the text box with light green color by clicking the Fill Color button .

The Fill Color button retains the color previously selected.

11 Remove the border around the text box by clicking the down-pointing triangle at the right side of the Line Color button on the Drawing toolbar and then clicking *No Line* that displays at the top of the pop-up menu.

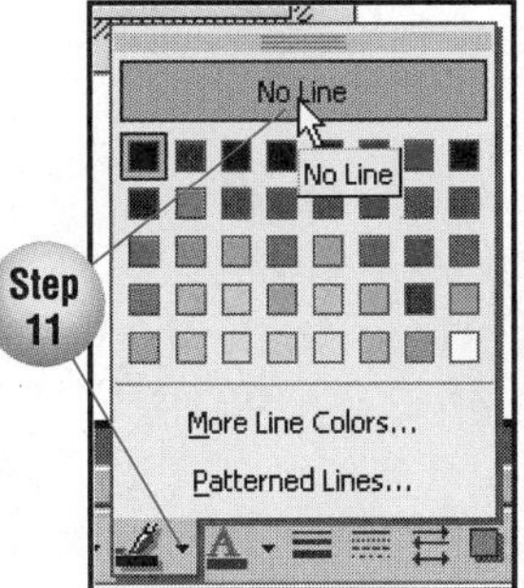


12 Deselect the text box by clicking outside the banner and text box.

13 Save, print, and then close Word S3-03.

**Draw an Autoshape**
1 Click AutoShapes button on Drawing toolbar.
2 Point to desired category and then click desired shape.
3 Drag with mouse to draw shape.

**Draw a Text Box**
1 Click Text Box button on Drawing toolbar.
2 Drag with mouse to draw text box.

# 3.10 Preparing an Envelope

Word automates the creation of envelopes with options at the Envelopes and Labels dialog box with the Envelopes tab selected. At this dialog box, key a delivery address and a return address. If you open the Envelopes and Labels dialog box in a document containing a name and address, the name and address are automatically inserted as the delivery address. If you enter a return address, Word will ask you before printing if you want to save the new return address as the default return address. Answer yes if you want to use the return address for future envelopes, or answer no if you will use a different return address for future envelopes.

**PROJECT:** You will create an envelope for sending the Hawaiian specials document to Camille Matsui at Marquee Productions.

## STEPS

1. At a clear document screen, click Tools, point to Letters and Mailings, and then click Envelopes and Labels. At the Envelopes and Labels dialog box, make sure the Envelopes tab is selected. (If not, click the Envelopes tab.)

2. With the insertion point positioned inside the Delivery address text box, key the following name and address:

   **Camille Matsui**
   **Marquee Productions**
   **955 South Alameda Street**
   **Los Angeles, CA 90037**

   When keying the name and address, press the Enter key to end each line *except* the last line (containing the city, state, and Zip Code).

3. Click in the Return address text box. If any text displays in the Return address text box, select it, and then delete it.

4. With the insertion point positioned in the Return address text box, key the following name and address:

   **First Choice Travel**
   **Los Angeles Office**
   **3588 Ventura Boulevard**
   **Los Angeles, CA 90102**

5. Click the Add to Document button.

   Click the Add to Document button and the envelope is inserted in the clear document screen. You can also send the envelope directly to the printer by clicking the Print button.

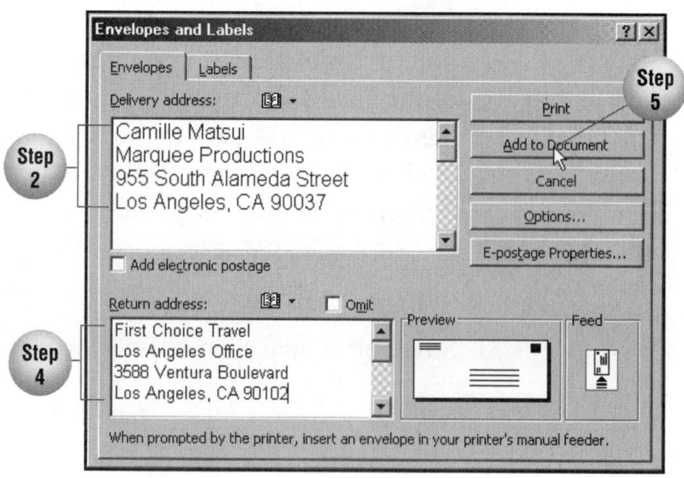

6 At the message asking if you want to save the new return address as the default address, click the No button.

7 Save the document and name it Word S3-04.

8 Print Word S3-04. *(Note: Manual feed of the envelope may be required. Please check with your instructor.)*

9 Close Word S3-04.

PROBLEM ?

If a blank envelope prints after the first envelope, this means that you pressed the Enter key after the city, state, and Zip Code in the Delivery address text box.

# In Addition

## Customizing Envelopes

With options at the Envelopes Options dialog box you can customize an envelope. Display this dialog box by clicking the Options button at the Envelopes and Labels dialog box. At the Envelope Options dialog box, you can change the envelope size, insert a delivery point bar code, change the font for the delivery and return addresses, and specify the positioning of the addresses in relation to the left and top of the envelope. Insert a check mark in the Delivery point barcode check box and Word prints a POSTNET (POSTal Numeric Encoding Technique) bar code. This bar code is a machine-readable representation of the U.S. Zip Code and delivery address.

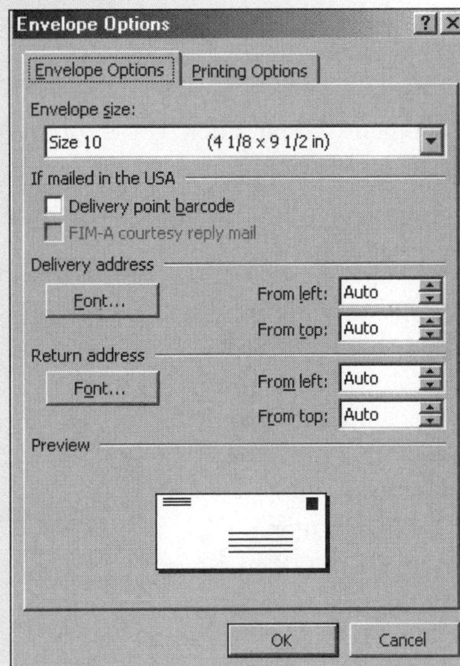

**Prepare an Envelope**

1. Click Tools, Letters and Mailings, Envelopes and Labels.
2. Click Envelopes tab.
3. Key delivery address.
4. Key return address.
5. Click either Add to Document button or Print button.

## 3.11 Preparing Labels

Use Word's labels feature to print text on mailing labels, file labels, disk labels, or other types of labels. You can create labels for printing on a variety of predefined labels that can be purchased at an office supply store. With the labels feature, you can create a sheet of mailing labels with the same name and address or enter a different name and address on each label. Create a label with options at the Envelopes and Labels dialog box with the Labels tab selected.

**PROJECT:** You will create a sheet of mailing labels containing the First Choice Travel name and address and then create mailing labels for sending the Hawaiian specials document to several First Choice Travel customers.

### STEPS

1. At a clear document screen, click Tools, point to Letters and Mailings, and then click Envelopes and Labels. At the Envelopes and Labels dialog box, click the Labels tab.
2. Key the following information in the Address text box. (Press Enter at the end of each line, except the last line containing the city name, state, and Zip Code.)

   **First Choice Travel**
   **Los Angeles Office**
   **3588 Ventura Boulevard**
   **Los Angeles, CA 90102**

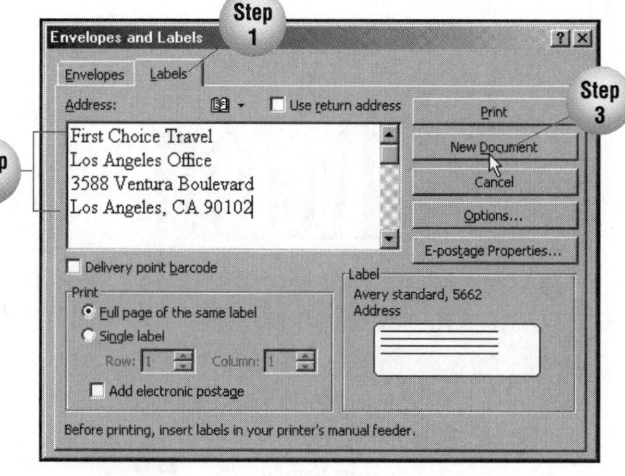


3. Click the New Document button.
4. Save the mailing label document and name it Word S3-05.
5. Print and then close Word S3-05.

   The number of labels printed on the page varies depending on the label selected at the Envelopes and Labels dialog box.

6. At a clear document screen, click Tools, point to Letters and Mailings, and then click Envelopes and Labels.
7. At the Envelopes and Labels dialog box with the Labels tab selected, click the Options button.
8. At the Label Options dialog box, make sure *Avery standard* displays in the Label products text box. Click the down-pointing triangle at the right side of the Product number list box until *5662 – Address* is visible and then click *5662 – Address*. Click OK to close the Label Options dialog box.

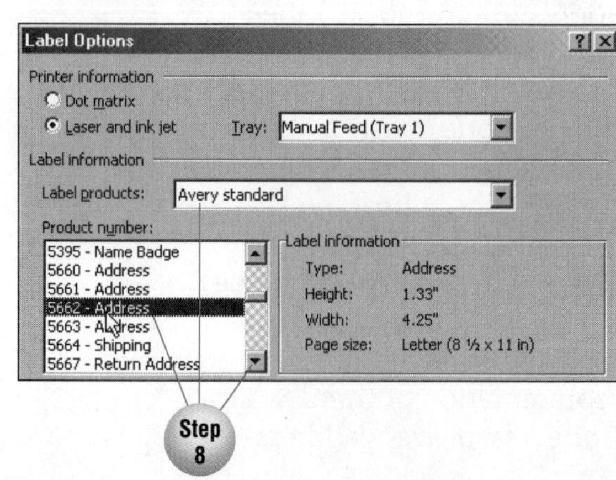

9. At the Envelopes and Labels dialog box, click the New Document button.
10. At the document screen, key the first name and address shown in Figure W3.8 in the first label. Press the Tab key to move the insertion point to the next label and then key the second name and address shown in Figure W3.8. Continue in this manner until all names and addresses have been keyed.
11. Save the document and name it Word S3-06.
12. Print and then close Word S3-06.
13. At the clear document screen, close the document screen without saving the changes.

**FIGURE W3.8**

| | |
|---|---|
| Moreno Products<br>350 Mission Boulevard<br>Pomona, CA 91767 | Mr. Miguel Santos<br>12120 Barranca Parkway<br>Irvine, CA 92612 |
| Dr. Esther Riggins<br>9077 Walnut Street<br>Los Angeles, CA 90097 | Automated Services, Inc.<br>4394 Seventh Street<br>Long Beach, CA 92602 |

# In Addition

## Customizing Labels

Click the Options button at the Envelopes and Labels dialog box with the Labels tab selected and the Label Options dialog box displays as shown below. At this dialog box, choose the type of printer, the desired label product, and the product number. This dialog box also displays information about the selected label such as type height, width, and paper size. When you select a label, Word automatically determines label margins. If, however, you want to customize these default settings, click the Details button at the Label Options dialog box.

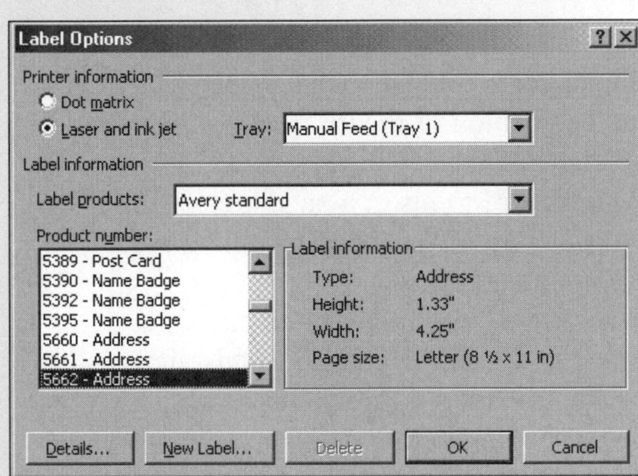


## IN BRIEF

**Prepare Mailing Labels with Same Name and Address**

1. Click Tools, Letters and Mailings, Envelopes and Labels.
2. Click Labels tab.
3. Key name and address in Address text box.
4. Click either New Document button or Print button.

**Prepare Mailing Labels with Different Names and Addresses**

1. Click Tools, Letters and Mailings, Envelopes and Labels.
2. Click Labels tab.
3. Click New Document button.
4. At document screen key names and addresses.

# FEATURES SUMMARY

| Feature | Button | Menu | Keyboard |
|---|---|---|---|
| Clipboard Task Pane | | Edit, Office Clipboard | Ctrl + C, Ctrl + C |
| Copy selected text | | Edit, Copy | Ctrl + C |
| Cut selected text | | Edit, Cut | Ctrl + X |
| Envelopes and Labels dialog box | | Tools, Letters and Mailings, Envelopes and Labels | |
| Find and Replace dialog box | | Edit, Replace | Ctrl + H |
| Insert Clip Art Task Pane | | Insert, Picture, Clip Art | |
| Insert a page break | | | Ctrl + Enter |
| Insert Picture dialog box | | Insert, Picture, From File | |
| Normal view | | View, Normal | |
| Page Numbers dialog box | | Insert, Page Numbers | |
| Page Setup dialog box | | File, Page Setup | |
| Paste selected text | | Edit, Paste | Ctrl + V |
| Paste Special dialog box | | Edit, Paste Special | |
| Print Layout view | | View, Print Layout | |
| WordArt Gallery | | Insert, Picture, WordArt | |

# PROCEDURES CHECK

**Completion:** In the space provided at the right, indicate the correct term, symbol, or command.

1. Click this button at the Find and Replace dialog box to replace all occurrences of text. ____________
2. Click this button on the Standard toolbar to cut selected text. ____________
3. Click this button on the Standard toolbar to insert selected text in the document at the position of the insertion point. ____________
4. Press Ctrl + C twice to display this task pane. ____________
5. Press these keys on the keyboard to insert a page break. ____________
6. Click these options to display the Page Numbers dialog box. ____________
7. This is the default page orientation. ____________
8. This is the default left and right margin measurement. ____________
9. Before using the click and type feature, change to this view. ____________
10. One method for displaying the Insert Clip Art Task Pane is clicking the Insert Clip Art button on this toolbar. ____________

11. Display the WordArt Gallery by clicking this option on the Menu bar, pointing to Picture, and then clicking WordArt. _______________
12. Click this button on the Picture toolbar to choose a wrapping style. _______________
13. Use options from this button on the Drawing toolbar to draw a variety of predesigned shapes. _______________
14. To display the Envelopes and Labels dialog box, click Tools, point to this option, and then click Envelopes and Labels. _______________

# SKILLS REVIEW

## Activity 1: FINDING AND REPLACING TEXT; CUTTING AND PASTING TEXT

1 Open FCT Juneau.
2 Save the document with Save As and name it Word S3-R1.
3 Find every occurrence of *Mendanhall* and replace it with *Mendenhall.*
4 Find every occurrence of *Treadwill* and replace it with *Treadwell.*
5 Select the heading *Visitor Centers*, the three paragraphs of text below it, and the blank line below the three paragraphs, and then move the selected text before the heading *Visitor Attractions*.
6 Select the heading *Museums*, the three paragraphs of text below it, and the blank line below the three paragraphs, and then move the selected text before the heading *Visitor Attractions*.
7 Save Word S3-R1.

## Activity 2: COLLECTING AND PASTING TEXT

1 With Word S3-R1 open, open the document named FCT JA 01.
2 Press Ctrl + C twice to turn on the display of the Clipboard Task Pane. Make sure the Clipboard Task Pane is empty.
3 In the FCT JA 01 document, select and then copy from the heading *Visitor Services* through the two paragraphs of text below the heading and the blank line below the two paragraphs.
4 Select and then copy from the heading *Transportation* through the paragraph of text below the heading and the blank line below the paragraph.
5 Select and then copy from the heading *Points of Interest* through the columns of text below the heading and the blank line below the columns of text.
6 Make Word S3-R1 the active document.
7 Turn on the display of the Clipboard Task Pane.
8 Move the insertion point to the end of the document and then paste the text that begins with the heading *Points of Interest*.
9 Move the insertion point to the beginning of the heading *Museums* and then paste the text that begins with the heading *Transportation*.

10 Move the insertion point to the beginning of the heading *Points of Interest* and then paste the text that begins with the heading *Visitor Services.*
11 Clear the contents of the Clipboard Task Pane and then close the Clipboard Task Pane.
12 Save Word S3-R1.
13 Make FCT JA 01 the active document and then close it.

### Activity 3: INSERTING PAGE NUMBERS; CHANGING MARGINS; CHANGING PAGE ORIENTATION

1 With Word S3-R1 open, insert page numbers that print centered at the bottom of each page and change the starting page number to 7.
2 Change the left and right margins to 1 inch and the top and bottom margins to 1.5 inches.
3 Select the title *FACT SHEET – JUNEAU, ALASKA* and then change the font to 14-point Arial bold and center the title.
4 Set the headings in the document in 12-point Arial bold. (The headings include *History, Visitor Centers, Transportation, Museums, Visitor Attractions, Visitor Services,* and *Points of Interest.*)
5 Change the page orientation to landscape.
6 Save Word S3-R1.
7 Print Word S3-R1.

### Activity 4: INSERTING WORDART AND DRAWING SHAPES

1 With Word S3-R1 open, change the page orientation to portrait.
2 Select and then delete the title *FACT SHEET – JUNEAU, ALASKA.*
3 Insert a WordArt of your choosing at the beginning of the document that contains the words *Juneau, Alaska.*
4 Size and move the WordArt text so it spans the margins.
5 Move the insertion point to the end of the document and then press Enter twice.
6 Using the buttons on the Drawing toolbar, draw and format the shape and draw and format the text box as shown in Figure W3.9.
7 Save, print, and then close Word S3-R1.

**FIGURE W3.9** Activity 4

### Activity 5: CHANGING VIEWS; USING CLICK AND TYPE; VERTICALLY ALIGNING TEXT

1 At a clear document screen, change to the Print Layout view.
2 Using the click and type feature, key the text shown in Figure W3.10.
3 Select the centered text you just keyed and then change the font to 14-point Arial bold.
4 Select the right aligned text you just keyed and then change the font to 10-point Arial bold.
5 Change the vertical alignment of the text on the page to *Center*.
6 Save the document and name it Word S3-R2.
7 Print Word S3-R2.

**FIGURE W3.10** Activity 5

EMPLOYMENT OPPORTUNITIES

Working in the Movie Industry

Wednesday, March 20, 2003

7:00 – 8:30 p.m.

Sponsored by
Marquee Productions

### Activity 6: INSERTING IMAGES

1 With Word S3-R2 open, change the vertical alignment of the text on the page back to *Top*.
2 Insert a clip art image of your choosing related to the announcement. (You determine the clip art image as well as the size and position of the image.)
3 Deselect the text *Marquee Productions* from the document and then insert the Marquee Productions logo image named M_Prod.tif below the text *Sponsored by. (Hint: Do this at the Insert Picture dialog box.)*
4 Save, print, and then close Word S3-R2.

### Activity 7: PREPARING AN ENVELOPE

1 At a clear document screen, prepare an envelope with the return and delivery addresses shown in Figure W3.11, and add the envelope to the document.
2 Save the document and name it Word S3-R3.
3 Print and then close Word S3-R3. (Manual feed may be required.)

**FIGURE W3.11** Activity 7

First Choice Travel
Los Angeles Office
3588 Ventura Boulevard
Los Angeles, CA 90102

Chris Greenbaum
Marquee Productions
955 South Alameda Street
Los Angeles, CA 90037

### Activity 8: PREPARING MAILING LABELS

1 At a clear document screen, prepare a sheet of mailing labels for the following name and address using the Avery standard 5662 – Address form.
First Choice Travel
Toronto Office
4277 Yonge Street
Toronto, ON M4P 2E6
2 Save the mailing label document and name it Word S3-R4.
3 Print and then close Word S3-R4.

## PERFORMANCE PLUS

### Activity 1: FORMATTING A COSTUME RENTAL AGREEMENT

1 Open PT Agreement.
2 Save the agreement with Save As and name it Word S3-P1.
3 Search for all occurrences of *Customer* and replace with *Marquee Productions*.
4 Move the *4. Alterations* section above the *3. Customer Agrees* section. Renumber the two sections.
5 Select the entire document, change the font to 12-point Bookman Old Style, and then deselect the document. (If this typeface is not available, choose another typeface.)
6 Change the top, left, and right margins to 1.5 inches.
7 Insert page numbering at the bottom right side of each page.
8 Save Word S3-P1.
9 Print and then close Word S3-P1.

### Activity 2: CREATING AN ANNOUNCEMENT

1 At a clear document screen, create an announcement for Niagara Peninsula College by keying the text shown in Figure W3.12.
2 After keying the text, change the horizontal alignment to center for the entire document.
3 Change the font for the entire document to a decorative font and size of your choosing and change the text color to Dark Blue.
4 Change the line spacing to double for the entire document.
5 Insert, size, and move a clip art image of your choosing in the document. Choose a clip art image related to the subject of the announcement.
6 Save the document and name it Word S3-P2.
7 Print and then close Word S3-P2.

**FIGURE W3.12** Activity 2

NIAGARA PENINSULA COLLEGE
Internship Opportunities
Marquee Productions, Toronto Office
June 16 through August 29, 2003
Contact Cal Rubine, Theatre Arts Division

### Activity 3: PREPARING AN ENVELOPE

1 Create an envelope to send the Niagara Peninsula College announcement to Camille Matsui, Marquee Productions, 955 South Alameda Street, Los Angeles, CA 90037. Include the following name and address as the return address: Niagara Peninsula College, Theatre Arts Division, 2199 Victoria Street, Niagara-on-the-Lake, ON L0S 1J0.
2 Save the envelope document and name it Word S3-P3.
3 Print and then close Word S3-P3.

### Activity 4: PREPARING MAILING LABELS

1 Prepare return mailing labels with the following information:
Niagara Peninsula College
Theatre Arts Division
2199 Victoria Street
Niagara-on-the-Lake, ON L0S 1J0
2 Save the labels document and name it Word S3-P4.
3 Print and then close Word S3-P4.

### Activity 5: FINDING INFORMATION ON FLIPPING AND COPYING OBJECTS

1 Use Word's Help feature to learn how to flip objects and copy objects.
2 At a clear document screen, create the document shown in Figure W3.13. Create the arrow at the left by clicking the AutoShapes button, pointing to Block Arrows, and then clicking Striped Right Arrow. Format the arrow with blue fill as shown. Copy and flip the arrow to create the arrow at the right side.
3 Save the completed document and name it Word S3-P5.
4 Print and then close Word S3-P5.

**FIGURE W3.13** Activity 5

### Activity 6: CREATING AN ENVELOPE WITH A POSTNET BAR CODE AND FIM-A

1 Use Word's Help feature to learn how to create an envelope with a POSTNET bar code and a FIM-A.
2 Create an envelope with the return and delivery addresses shown in Figure W3.14. Include a POSTNET bar code and a FIM-A for the envelope.
3 Save the envelope document and name it Word S3-P6.
4 Print and then close Word S3-P6.

**FIGURE W3.14** Activity 6

Worldwide Enterprises
1112-1583 Broadway
New York, NY 10110

Marquee Productions
955 South Alameda Street
Los Angeles, CA 90037

### Activity 7: LOCATING INFORMATION AND CREATING A BANNER

1 You are Camille Matsui, production assistant for Marquee Productions. You have been asked by Chris Greenbaum, the production manager, to find information on the Royal Ontario Museum. Marquee Productions will need to do some interior shots and would like to contact the museum as a possible site. Connect to the Internet and search for information on the Royal Ontario Museum. Find the following information: the museum address, telephone number, and hours of operation.
2 Using the information you find on the museum, create a banner using an autoshape and insert the museum information inside the banner.
3 Save the banner document and name it Word S3-P7.
4 Print and then close Word S3-P7.

# WORD SECTION 4

## Formatting with Special Features

Word contains special formatting features you can apply in a document to enhance the display of text. For example, you can use the Tables feature to create, modify, and format data in columns and rows. Improve the ease with which a person can read and understand groups of words by setting text in columns. Create a header and/or footer with text you want to appear on each printed page. A Word document can be saved as a Web page and formatting can be applied to the page. Insert a hyperlink in a document to another document or a site on the Internet. Compare an edited document with the original document using the compare and merge feature and visually display text in an organizational chart and diagram. In this section you will learn the skills and complete the projects described here.

*Note: Before beginning this section, delete the* Word S3 *folder on your disk. Next, copy to your disk the* Word S4 *subfolder from the* Word *folder on the CD that accompanies this textbook, and then make* Word S4 *the active folder.*

### Skills

- Create, modify, and format a table
- Change column widths and row heights
- Move a table
- Apply a border and shading to a table
- Apply an autoformat to a table
- Insert a section break
- Create and modify columns
- Insert and modify a header and footer
- Save a document as a Web page
- Create a hyperlink
- Preview a Web page in the default browser
- Compare and merge documents
- Create an organizational chart and a diagram

### Projects

Create, modify, and format a table containing information on scenic flights on the island of Maui; create and format newsletters with information on Petersburg, Alaska, and Hawaiian vacation specials; save the newsletters as Web pages and add hyperlinks to sites on the Internet; compare the edited newsletters with the original newsletters; prepare an organizational chart and a diagram of services.

Create, modify, and format a table with information on classes offered by the Theatre Arts Division; create and format a newsletter about the Theatre Arts Division; compare the edited newsletter with the original newsletter.

Create, modify, and format a table containing information about catered lunch options.

Create an organizational chart for the production department; create, modify, and format a table containing information on rental cars.

Create an organizational chart for the design department.

Insert a formula in a table that calculates total sales.

## 4.1 Creating a Table

Word's Table feature is useful for displaying data in columns and rows. This data may be text, values, and/or formulas. You can create a table using the Insert Table button on the Standard toolbar or with options at the Insert Table dialog box. Once you specify the desired number of rows and columns, Word displays the table and you are ready to enter information into the cells. A *cell* is the "box" created by the intersection of a row and a column. When a table is created, the insertion point is positioned in the cell in the upper left corner of the table. Cells are designated with a letter-number label representing the column and row intersection. Columns are lettered from left to right, beginning with A. Rows are numbered from top to bottom, beginning with 1. The cell in the upper left corner of the table is cell A1. The cell to the right of A1 is B1, the cell to the right of B1 is C1, and so on. The cells below A1 are A2, A3, A4, and so on.

**PROJECT:** You are developing a new First Choice Travel information document about sightseeing flights around the island of Maui. You will create a table to display the data.

### STEPS

1. Open FCT Island Flights. Save the document with Save As and name it Word S4-01.
2. Press Ctrl + End to move the insertion point to the end of the document.
3. Position the mouse pointer on the Insert Table button on the Standard toolbar and then hold down the left mouse button. (This displays a grid below the button.) Drag the mouse pointer down and to the right until the number below the grid displays as *6 X 3*, and then release the mouse button.

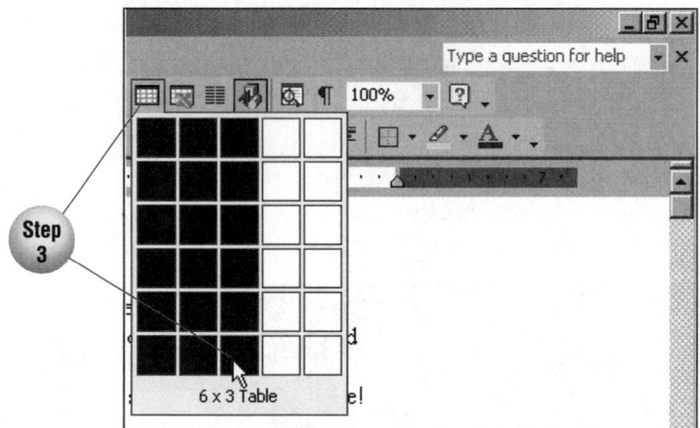


4. Key the text in the cells as shown in Figure W4.1. Press the Tab key to move the insertion point to the next cell or press Shift + Tab to move the insertion point to the previous cell. When keying text in the cells in the second column, do not press the Enter key to end a line. Key the text and let the word wrap feature wrap the text within the cell. After keying text in the last cell, do not press the Tab key. This will insert another row. If you press the Tab key accidentally, immediately click the Undo button.

   To move the insertion point to different cells within the table using the mouse, click in the desired cell.

5. Save Word S4-01.

**FIGURE W4.1**

| Adventure | Destination | Price |
|---|---|---|
| Special West Maui | Waterfalls, lush tropical valleys | $49 |
| West Maui Tropical | West Maui mountains, Hawaii's highest waterfalls | $79 |
| Haleakala-Keanae | Haleakala crater, tropical rain forest, waterfalls | $89 |
| Special Circle Island | Hana, Haleakala, west Maui mountains, tropical rain forest, waterfalls, seven sacred pools | $169 |
| Molokai-West Maui | West Maui mountains, waterfalls, sea cliffs, Kalaupapa colony | $189 |

# In Addition

## Other Methods for Creating a Table

Other methods for creating a table include using options from the Insert Table dialog box or using buttons on the Tables and Borders toolbar. Display the Insert Table dialog box by clicking Table, pointing to Insert, and then clicking Table. Specify the desired number of columns and rows and then click OK to close the dialog box. Another method for creating a table is to draw a table using buttons on the Tables and Borders toolbar. Display this toolbar, shown below, by clicking the Tables and Borders button on the Standard toolbar. Using buttons on this toolbar, you can draw, format, and customize a table.

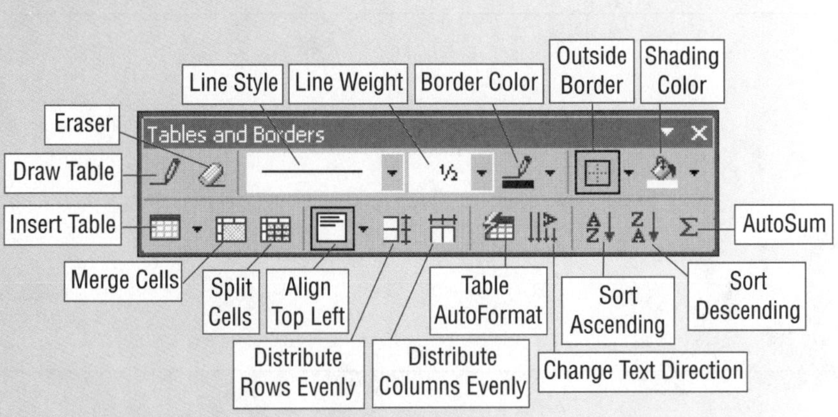


## In Brief

**Create a Table**

1. Click Insert Table button.
2. Hold down left mouse button.
3. Drag in grid to select desired number of columns and rows.
4. Release mouse button.

## 4.2 Modifying a Table

The basic structure of a table can be modified. For example, rows and/or columns can be inserted or deleted from the table and cells can be merged. Rows and columns can be inserted in a table with a button on the Standard toolbar or with options at the Table drop-down menu. Delete rows and columns with options at the Table drop-down menu. If you want text in a cell to span several columns, select and then merge the cells.

**PROJECT:** You need to add First Choice Travel discount prices to the table on Maui flights. An easy way to do this is to insert a column and enter the discount prices. You also will insert a row, delete a row, and then merge selected cells.

# STEPS

1. With Word S4-01 open, click in the cell containing the text *Price*.
2. Click Table, point to Insert, and then click Columns to the Right.

   The new column is inserted at the right side of the table and the size of the other columns is reduced.

3. Key the text shown in Figure W4.2 in the new column cells. Begin by clicking in the top cell in the new column and then key **FCT**. Press the down arrow key to move the insertion point to the empty cell below and then key **$35**. Continue pressing the down arrow key and keying the FCT prices shown in Figure W4.2.

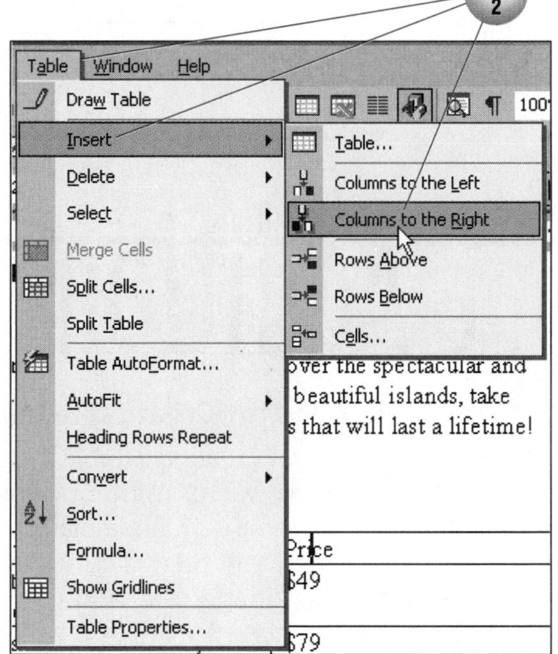

PROBLEM ? If you key the incorrect text in a cell, press Shift + Tab until the incorrect text is selected and then key the correct text.

**FIGURE W4.2**

FCT
$35
$65
$75
$155
$175

4 Click in the cell containing the text *Special Circle Island*. Click Table, point to Delete, and then click Rows. This deletes the entire row.

You can delete a column in a similar manner. Click in any cell in the column, click Table, point to Delete, and then click Columns.

5 Click in the cell containing the text *Adventure*. Click Table, point to Insert, and then click Rows Above.

6 Click in the new cell immediately above the cell containing *Adventure* and then key **MAUI FLIGHTS**.

7 With the insertion point positioned in the cell containing the text *MAUI FLIGHTS*, click Table, point to Select, and then click Row.

8 Merge the selected cells by clicking Table and then Merge Cells.

9 Click outside the table to deselect the cell.

10 Save Word S4-01.

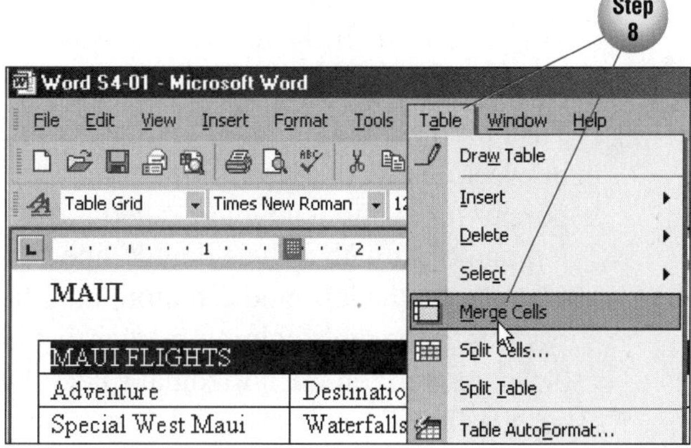


# In Addition

## Inserting Rows and Columns with Buttons on the Standard Toolbar

A button on the Standard toolbar offers another method for inserting rows and/or columns in a table. To insert rows, select a row or several rows and then click the Insert Rows button on the Standard toolbar. The Insert Table button on the Standard toolbar becomes the Insert Rows button when a row or several rows are selected. Insert a column by selecting a column or several columns and then clicking the Insert Columns button on the Standard toolbar. The Insert Table button on the Standard toolbar becomes the Insert Columns button when a column or columns are selected.

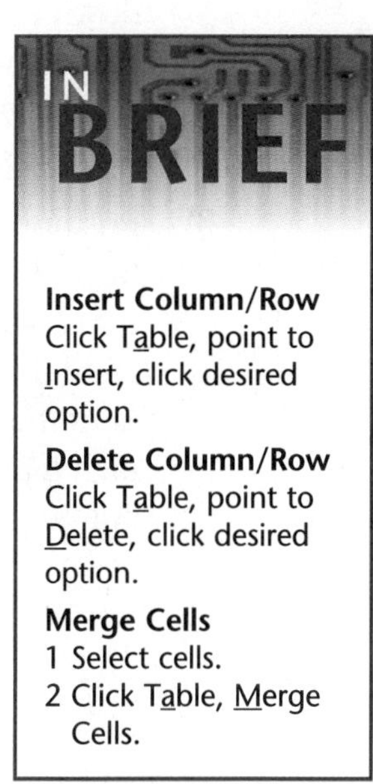

## In Brief

**Insert Column/Row**
Click Table, point to Insert, click desired option.

**Delete Column/Row**
Click Table, point to Delete, click desired option.

**Merge Cells**
1 Select cells.
2 Click Table, Merge Cells.

## 4.3 Changing Column Widths and Row Heights; Moving a Table

When a table is created, the columns are the same width and rows are the same height. The width of the columns depends on the number of columns as well as the document margins. A variety of methods are available for changing column width and row height. One of the methods for changing column width and row height is to change to the Print Layout view and then use the table gridlines. Position the mouse pointer on a gridline and the pointer turns into a double-headed arrow with a short double line in between. Drag with the mouse to increase or decrease the width or height. In the Print Layout view, move a table by dragging it using the table move handle.

**PROJECT:** The Maui Flights table needs adjustments to improve its appearance. You will increase and decrease column widths, increase the height of a row, and move the table so it is positioned between the left and right margins.

# STEPS

1. With Word S4-01 open, click View and then Print Layout. (Skip this step if the view is already Print Layout.)

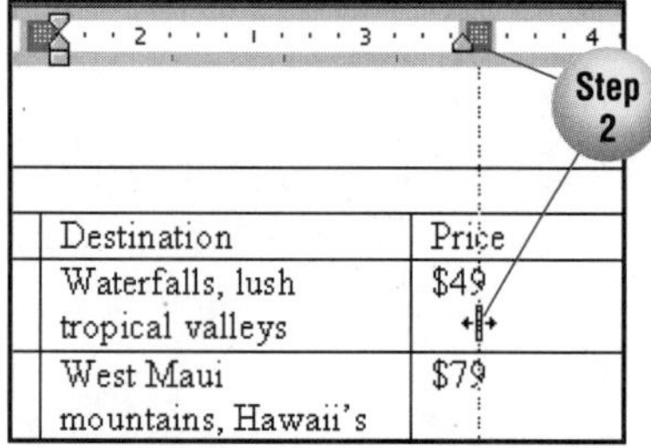


2. Position the mouse pointer on the gridline between the second and third columns until the pointer turns into a double-headed arrow pointing left and right with a short double line between. Hold down the left mouse button, drag to the right until the table column marker displays at the 3.5-inch mark on the horizontal ruler, and then release the mouse button.

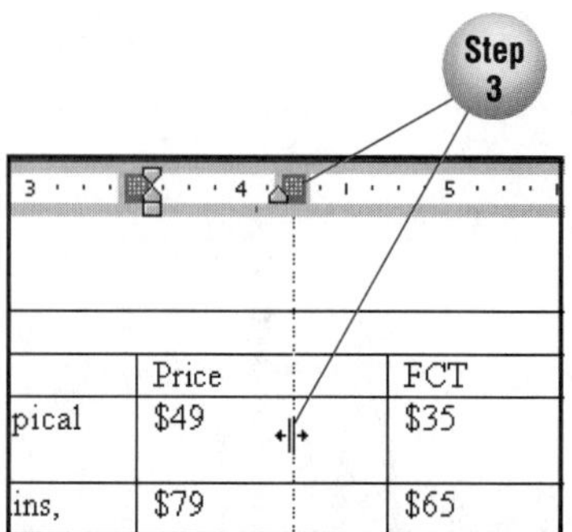


3. Following the same procedure, position the mouse pointer on the gridline between the third and fourth columns until the pointer turns into a double-headed arrow pointing left and right. Hold down the left mouse button, drag to the left until the table column marker displays on the 4.25-inch marker on the horizontal ruler, and then release the mouse button.

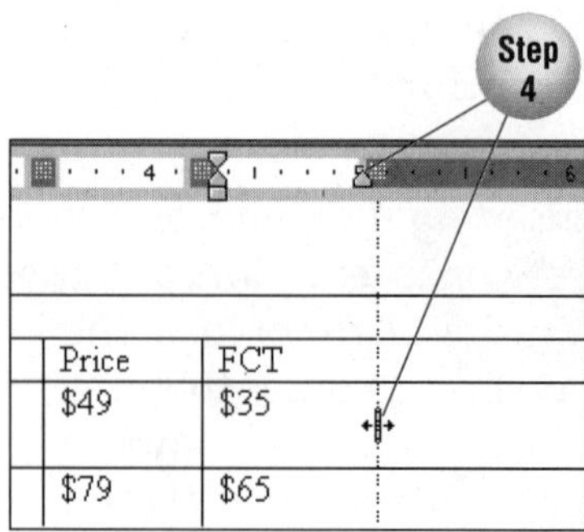


4. Position the mouse pointer on the gridline at the far right side of the table until the pointer turns into a double-headed arrow pointing left and right. Hold down the left mouse button, drag to the left until the table column marker displays on the 5-inch mark on the ruler, and then release the mouse button.

5 Position the mouse pointer on the gridline between the first and second row until the pointer turns into a double-headed arrow pointing up and down with a short double line between. Hold down the left mouse button, drag down approximately 0.25 inch on the vertical ruler, and then release the mouse button.

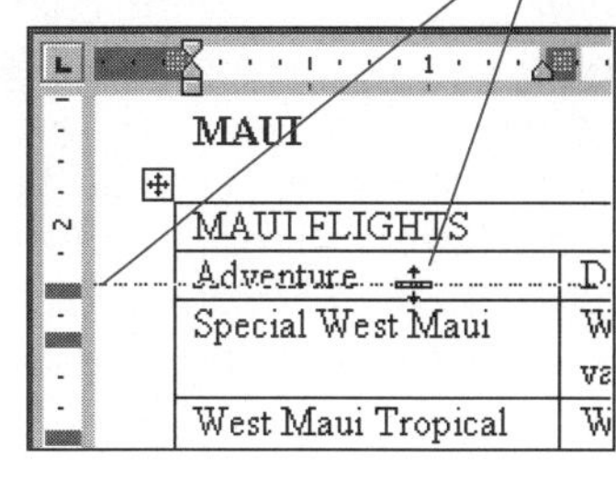


6 Position the mouse pointer inside the table.

When you position the mouse pointer inside the table, the table move handle displays in the upper left corner of the table.

7 Position the mouse pointer on the table move handle, hold down the left mouse button, drag the table to the right so it is positioned between the left and right margins, and then release the mouse button.

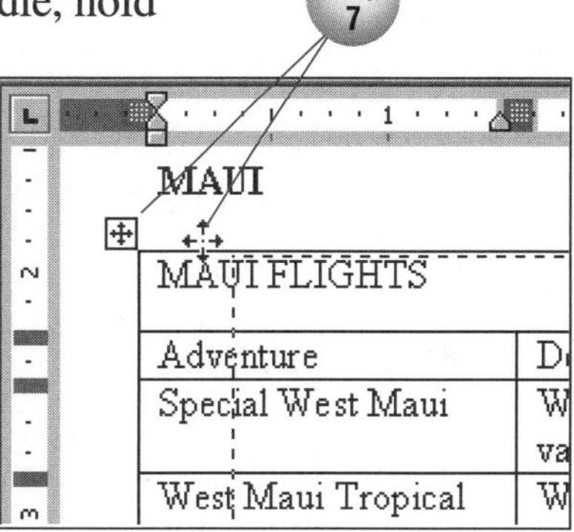


8 Save Word S4-01.

# In Addition

## Rotating Text in a Cell

You can rotate text in a cell to the left or to the right. To do this, position the insertion point in the cell, click Format, and then click Text Direction. This displays the Text Direction dialog box shown at the right. Click the desired direction in the Orientation section of the dialog box. Preview the text direction in the Preview section of the dialog box. Click OK to close the dialog box.

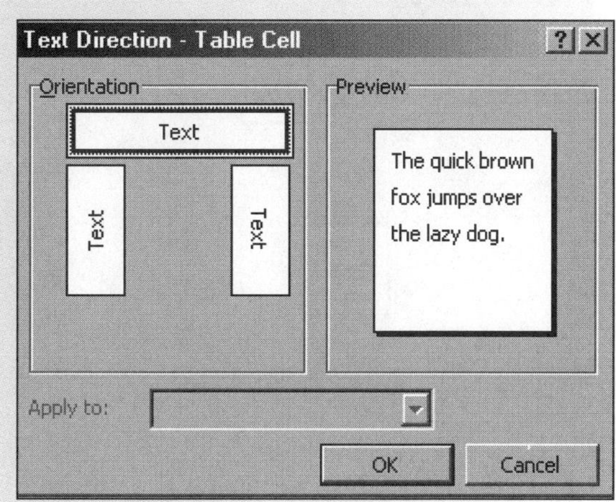


## In Brief

**Increase/Decrease Column/Row**

1 Position mouse pointer on gridline until it turns into a double-headed arrow.
2 Hold down left mouse button, drag to desired position, then release the button.

**Move Table**

1 Position insertion point in cell.
2 Position mouse pointer on table move handle, hold down left mouse button, drag to desired position, then release the mouse button.

## 4.4 Formatting a Table

Formatting can be applied to a cell or selected cells. Cell formatting might include changing the font, applying a font style, and changing text alignment within the cell. If you are applying formatting to more than one cell, select the cells using the mouse, the keyboard, or options from the Table drop-down menu. Formatting can be applied with buttons on the Formatting toolbar or with options at the Table Properties dialog box. With options at the Table Properties dialog box, you can apply formatting to the entire table, or a row, column, or cell.

**PROJECT:** You will improve the visual appeal of the Maui Flights table by applying formatting to the entire table and to specific cells.

### STEPS

1. With Word S4-01 open, click in any cell in the table.
2. Select the entire table by clicking Table, pointing to Select, and then clicking Table.
3. Click the down-pointing triangle at the right side of the Font button on the Formatting toolbar and then click *Arial* at the drop-down list.
4. Click the down-pointing triangle at the right side of the Font Size button and then click *11* at the drop-down list.
5. Click in the top cell containing the text *MAUI FLIGHTS,* click Table, point to Select, and then click Cell.
6. Click the down-pointing triangle at the right side of the Font Size button and then click *16* at the drop-down list.
7. Click the Bold button and then click the Center button on the Formatting toolbar.
8. With the cell still selected, click Table and then Table Properties.
9. At the Table Properties dialog box, click the Cell tab, and then click the Center option.

   This changes the vertical alignment to center for the text in the cell.

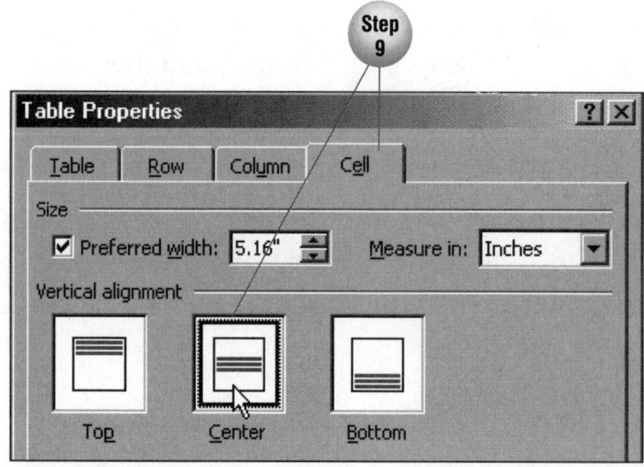

10 Click OK to close the dialog box.

11 Click in the cell containing the text *Adventure,* click Table, point to Select, and then click Row.

12 With the row selected, click the Bold button and then the Center button on the Formatting toolbar.

13 Position the mouse pointer in the cell containing the text *$49*, hold down the left mouse button, drag down and to the right to the cell containing the text *$175*, and then release the mouse button.

14 Click the Center button on the Formatting toolbar.

15 Click anywhere outside the table to deselect the cells.

16 Save Word S4-01.

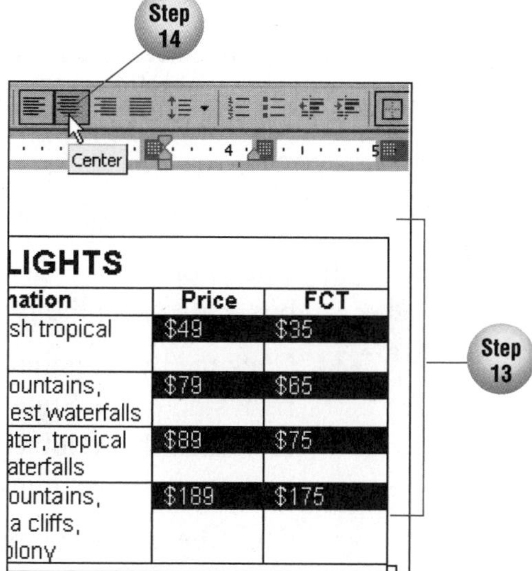


# In Addition

## Selecting Cells with the Keyboard

You have selected cells using the mouse and the Table drop-down menu. You can also select cells using the keyboard by completing the following steps:

| To select | Press |
|---|---|
| The next cell's contents | Tab |
| The preceding cell's contents | Shift + Tab |
| The entire table | Alt + 5 (on the numeric keypad with Num Lock off) |
| Adjacent cells | Hold Shift key, then press an arrow key repeatedly |
| A column | Position insertion point in top cell of column, hold down the Shift key, then press down arrow key until column is selected |

### IN BRIEF

**Display Table Properties Dialog Box**

1 Click in a cell in the table.
2 Click Table, Table Properties.

## 4.5 Applying Borders and Shading to a Table; Applying Autoformats

To enhance the visual appeal of a table, consider applying a border and/or shading to the entire table or cells within the table. Apply borders and/or shading to a table with options at the Borders and Shading dialog box. If you select specific cells in the table and then display the Borders and Shading dialog box, the choices made at the dialog box will apply only to the cells. If the insertion point is positioned in a table (with no cell selected) or if an entire table is selected, changes made to the Borders and Shading dialog box will affect the entire table. You can easily format a table with autoformats provided by Word. These autoformats do all of the formatting work for you.

**PROJECT:** You will add final formatting touches to the Maui Flights table by creating a border and adding shading to specific cells and experiment with autoformats.

### STEPS

1. With Word S4-01 open, click in any cell in the table.
2. Click Format and then Borders and Shading. At the Borders and Shading dialog box, make sure the Borders tab is selected.
3. Click the down-pointing triangle at the right side of the Style list box until the first thick/thin double-line option displays and then click the option.
4. Click the down-pointing triangle at the right side of the Color option and then click the Indigo option (seventh color from the left in the top row).
5. Click the Grid option in the Setting section of the dialog box.
6. Click the Shading tab and then click the fifth color (light turquoise) from the left in the bottom row of the Fill palette.

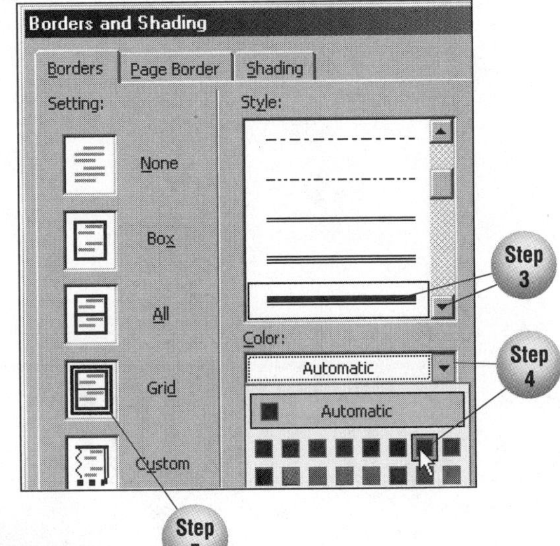


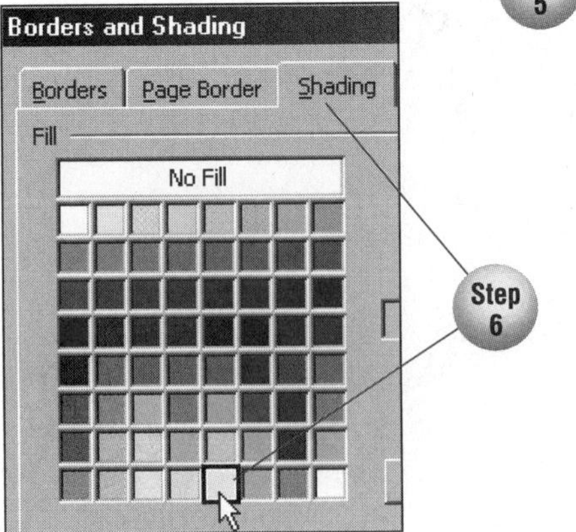


7. Click OK to close the dialog box.
8. Click in the cell containing the text *Adventure*.
9. Click Table, point to Select, and then click Row.

10. Click Format and then Borders and Shading.
11. At the Borders and Shading dialog box with the Shading tab selected, click the third color from the left in the top row (Gray-10%).

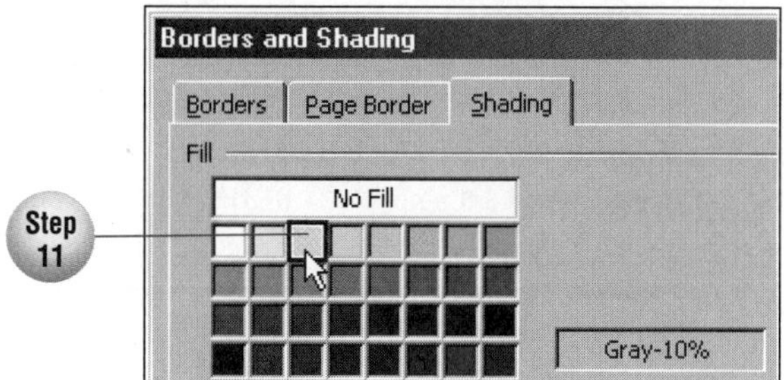


12. Click OK to close the dialog box.
13. Click anywhere outside the table to deselect the cells.

    Your table should look similar to the one shown in Figure W4.3.

14. Save and then print Word S4-01.
15. You decide to experiment with some of the autoformats provided by Word. To do this, click in any cell in the table, click Table, and then click Table AutoFormat.
16. At the Table AutoFormat dialog box, scroll up the Table styles list box, and then double-click the *Table 3D effects 2* option.

    Notice the formatting applied to the table by the autoformat feature.

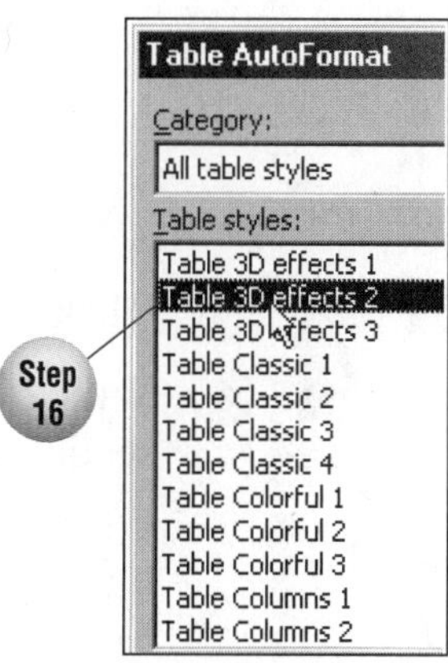


17. Click the Print button on the Standard toolbar.
18. Click the Undo button on the Standard toolbar (this removes the autoformat), click Table, and then click Table AutoFormat.
19. At the Table AutoFormat dialog box, double-click *Table Contemporary*.
20. Click the Print button on the Standard toolbar.
21. Click the Undo button on the Standard toolbar to remove the autoformat.
22. Save and then close Word S4-01.

**FIGURE W4.3**

| MAUI FLIGHTS | | | |
|---|---|---|---|
| **Adventure** | **Destination** | **Price** | **FCT** |
| Special West Maui | Waterfalls, lush tropical valleys | $49 | $35 |
| West Maui Tropical | West Maui mountains, Hawaii's highest waterfalls | $79 | $65 |
| Haleakala-Keanae | Haleakala crater, tropical rain forest, waterfalls | $89 | $75 |
| Molokai-West Maui | West Maui mountains, waterfalls, sea cliffs, Kalaupapa colony | $189 | $175 |

**Display Borders and Shading Dialog Box**

1. Click in a cell or select cells.
2. Click Format, Borders and Shading.

**Display Table AutoFormat Dialog Box**

1. Click in cell in the table.
2. Click Table, Table AutoFormat.

## 4.6 Inserting a Section Break; Creating Newspaper Columns

To increase the ease with which a person can read and understand groups of words (referred to as the *readability* of a document), consider setting text in the document in newspaper columns. Newspaper columns contain text that flows up and down on the page. Create newspaper columns with the Columns button on the Standard toolbar or with options at the Columns dialog box. If you want to apply column formatting to only a portion of a document, insert a section break in the document. Insert a section break in the document with options at the Break dialog box.

**PROJECT:** To improve the readability of the Petersburg fact sheet document, you will set the text in newspaper columns.

### STEPS

1. Open FCT Petersburg.
2. Save the document with Save As and name it Word S4-02.
3. Position the insertion point at the beginning of the first paragraph in the document (the paragraph that begins *Petersburg, Alaska, located on...*), click Insert, and then click Break.
4. At the Break dialog box, click Continuous in the Section break types section.

   In Normal view, the section break displays in the document as a double row of dots with the words *Section Break (Continuous)* in the middle. In Print Layout view, a continuous section break is not visible. A continuous section break separates the document into sections, but does not insert a page break. Click one of the other three options in the Section break types section of the Break dialog box if you want to insert a section break that begins a new page.
5. Click OK to close the Break dialog box.
6. With the insertion point positioned below the section break, format the text below the section break into three newspaper columns by clicking the Columns button on the Standard toolbar.
7. At the Columns grid, drag the mouse pointer down and to the right until three columns display with a dark background on the grid, and then click the left mouse button.

   Formatting text into columns automatically changes the view to Print Layout.

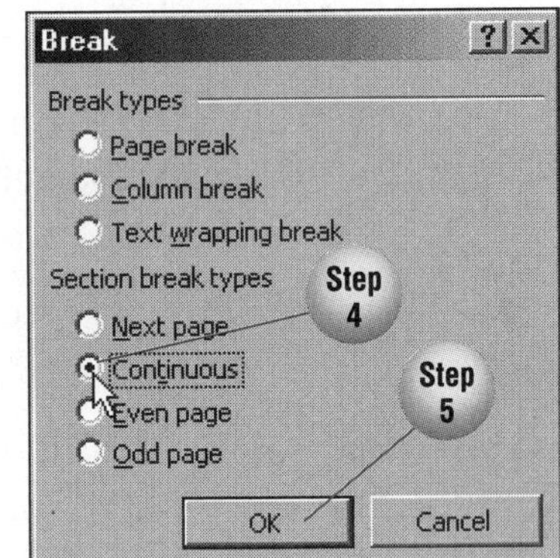


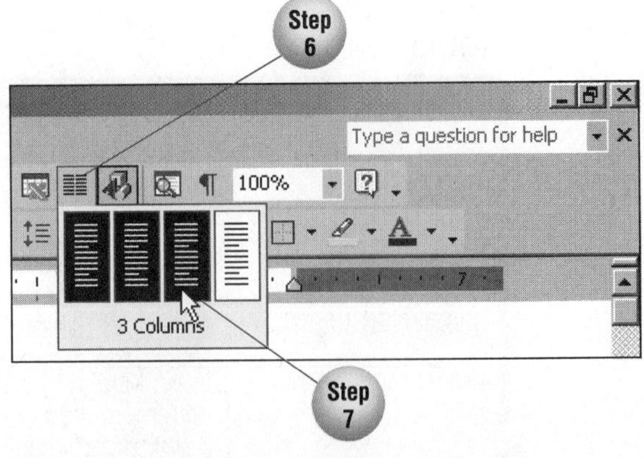


**PROBLEM?** If the second and third columns of text align with the title, click the Undo button. Make sure the insertion point is positioned at the beginning of the first paragraph of text (not the beginning of the document) and then create the columns.

8 Click Edit and then Replace to display the Find and Replace dialog box.

9 Find all occurrences of *Mitkoff* and replace with *Mitkof.*

10 Find all occurrences of *Alaska marine highway* and replace with *Alaska Marine Highway.*

11 Close the Find and Replace dialog box.

12 Select the title *FACT SHEET – PETERSBURG, ALASKA*, click the Bold button, and then click the Center button on the Formatting toolbar.

13 Select the heading *Services*, click the Bold button on the Formatting toolbar, and then add 6 points of space after the paragraph. *(Hint: Do this at the Paragraph dialog box with the Indents and Spacing tab selected.)*

14 Using Format Painter, apply bold formatting and 6 points of space after the paragraph to each of the remaining headings (*Visitor Attractions*, *Walking Tours*, *Accommodations*, and *Transportation*).

15 Save Word S4-02.

# In Addition

## Changing Column Width

One method for changing column width in a document is to drag the column marker on the horizontal ruler. The horizontal ruler displays when the Print Layout view is selected. The horizontal ruler and the column markers are identified below. To change the width (and also the spacing) of columns of text, position the arrow pointer on the left or right edge of a column marker on the horizontal ruler until it turns into a double-headed arrow pointing left and right. Hold down the left mouse button, drag the column marker to the left or right to make the column of text wider or narrower, and then release the mouse button. Hold down the Alt key while dragging the column marker and measurements display on the horizontal ruler.

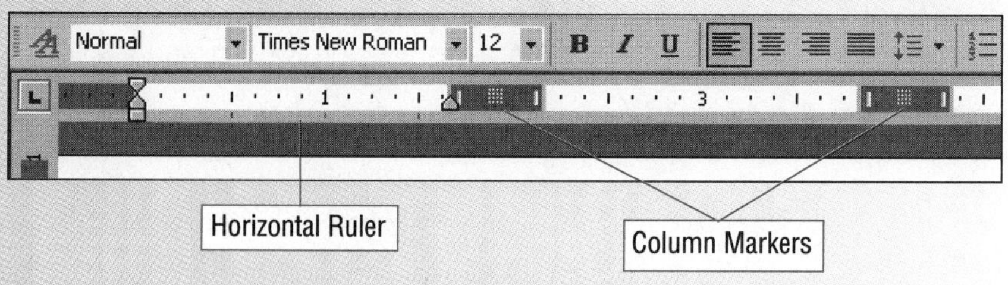


## In Brief

**Insert a Continuous Section Break**
1 Click Insert, Break.
2 Click Continuous.
3 Click OK.

**Format Text into Columns**
1 Click Columns button on Standard toolbar.
2 Drag to select desired number of columns in the Columns grid.
3 Release mouse button.

## 4.7 Revising Column Structure

The Columns button on the Standard toolbar creates columns of equal width. Use options at the Columns dialog box if you want to create columns of unequal width or if you want to specify individual column measurements, choose preset columns, or insert a line between columns. In a document containing columns, Word automatically lines up (balances) the last line of text at the bottom of each column, except on the last page. Text in the first column of the last page may flow to the end of the page, while the text in the second column may end far short of the end of the page. Balance columns on the last page by inserting a continuous section break.

**PROJECT:** After viewing the Petersburg fact sheet, you decide that the three columns are too narrow and decide to format the text into two columns. To add visual appeal to the document, you will insert a line between the two columns and balance the columns on the second page.

## STEPS

1. With Word S4-02 open, click anywhere in the first paragraph of text that displays in a column.
2. Display the Columns dialog box by clicking Format and then Columns.
3. At the Columns dialog box, click Two in the Presets section of the dialog box.
4. Increase the spacing between the two columns by clicking the up-pointing triangle at the right side of the Spacing option in the Width and spacing section until *0.7"* displays in the spin box.
5. Make sure a check mark displays in the Equal column width check box. If not, click the option to insert the check mark.

   This option, when activated, makes the two columns the same width.
6. Click the Line between option to insert a check mark.

   Activating this option inserts a line between the two columns on both pages. The Preview section of the dialog box provides a visual representation of the columns.
7. Click OK to close the Columns dialog box.

PROBLEM? If the column formatting is not applied to the text, check to make sure the insertion point is positioned at the beginning of the first paragraph (not the beginning of the document).

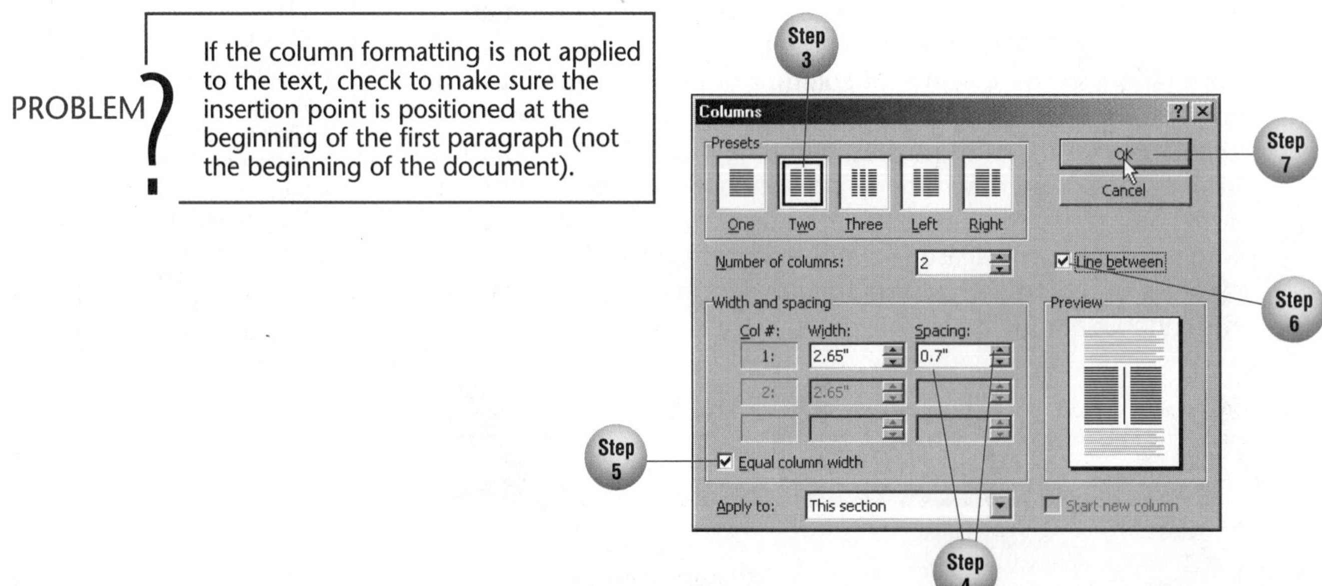

8. Balance the two columns on the second (last) page by pressing Ctrl + End to move the insertion point to the end of the document.
9. Display the Break dialog box by clicking Insert and then Break.
10. At the Break dialog box, click the Continuous option in the Section break types section of the dialog box.
11. Click OK to close the Break dialog box.
12. Save Word S4-02.

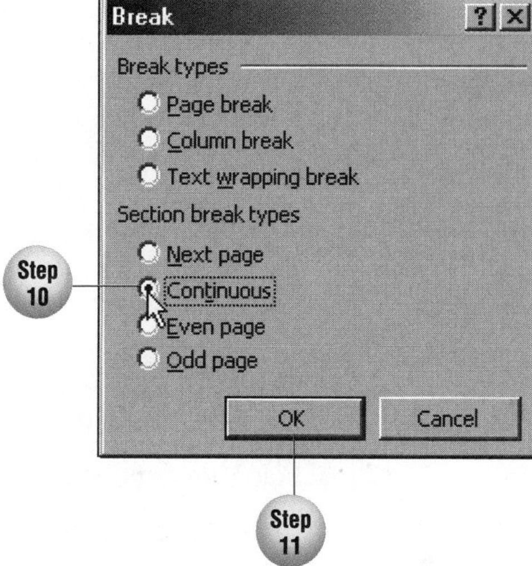


# In Addition

## Removing Column Formatting

Column formatting can be removed using the Columns button on the Standard toolbar or with an option at the Columns dialog box. To remove column formatting using the Columns button, position the insertion point in the section containing columns, click the Columns button, and then click the first column in the Column grid. To remove column formatting using the Columns dialog box, position the insertion point in the section containing columns, click Format, and then click Columns. At the Columns dialog box, click One in the Presets section, and then click OK to close the dialog box.

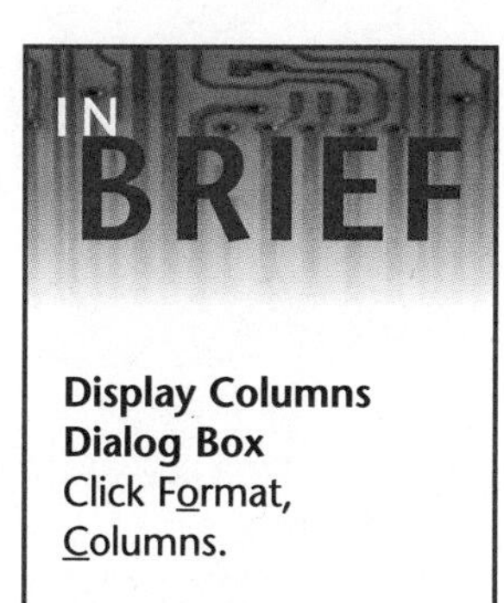


**Display Columns Dialog Box**
Click Format, Columns.

# 4.8 Inserting a Header or Footer

Insert text that you want to appear at the top of each page in a header and text you want to appear at the bottom of each page in a footer. Headers and footers are common in manuscripts, textbooks, reports, and other publications. Create a header or footer by clicking View and then Header and Footer. Word automatically changes to the Print Layout view, dims the text in the document, inserts a pane where the header or footer is entered, and displays the Header and Footer toolbar. Key the header or footer text and then click the Close button to close the Header and Footer toolbar.

**PROJECT:** You will create a header for the Petersburg fact sheet newsletter that prints the page number in the upper right corner of each page and a footer that prints *Petersburg, Alaska* at the bottom center of each page.

## STEPS

1. With Word S4-02 open, press Ctrl + Home to move the insertion point to the beginning of the document.
2. Click View and then Header and Footer.
3. At the header pane, press the Tab key twice, key the word **Page**, and then press the spacebar.

   The header pane contains tab stops at the center and the right side of the header pane.
4. Click the Insert Page Number button on the Header and Footer toolbar.

   The buttons on the Header and Footer toolbar are named in Figure W4.4.

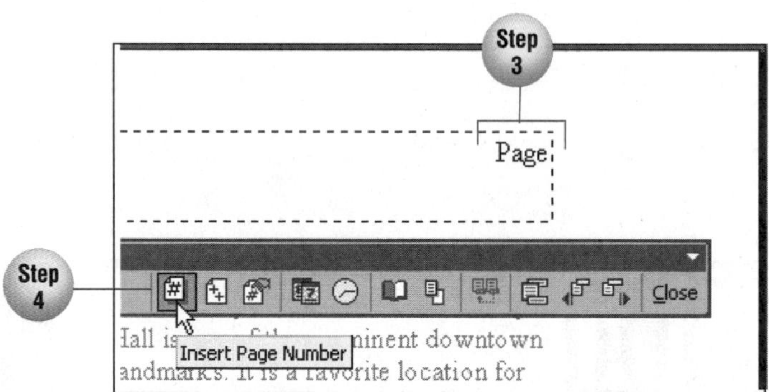


**FIGURE W4.4** Header and Footer Toolbar Buttons

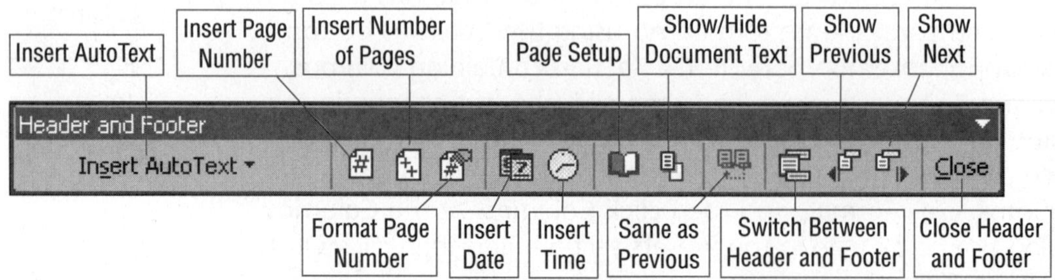

5 Click the Switch Between Header and Footer button on the Header and Footer toolbar.

Clicking this button displays the footer pane.

6 Press the Tab key once, click the Bold button, and then key **Petersburg, Alaska**.

7 Click the Close button located at the right side of the Header and Footer toolbar to close the toolbar.

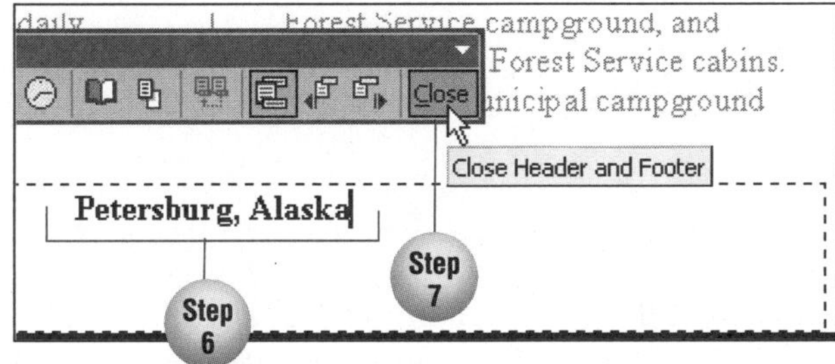


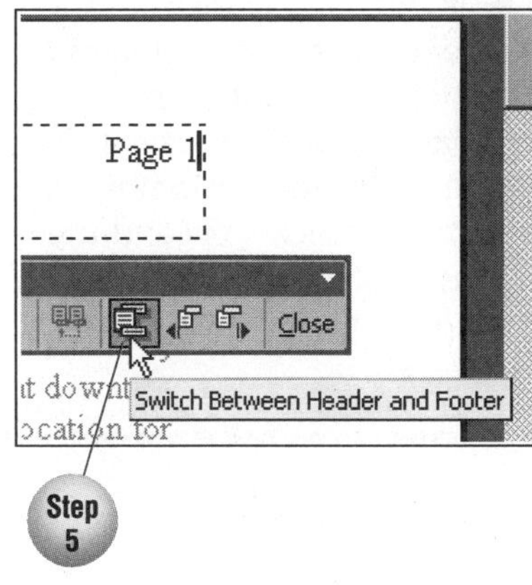


8 Scroll through the document and notice the header and footer text that displays at the top and bottom of each page.

The header and footer text displays dimmed in Print Layout view.

9 Save and then print Word S4-02.

# In Addition

## Inserting AutoText in a Header or Footer

Click the Insert AutoText button on the Header and Footer toolbar and the drop-down list shown at the right displays with a variety of options. Choose an option to automatically insert specific text. For example, choose the *Last printed* option and Word will insert the date the document was last printed; or, choose the *Filename and path* option and Word will insert the entire document name and path.

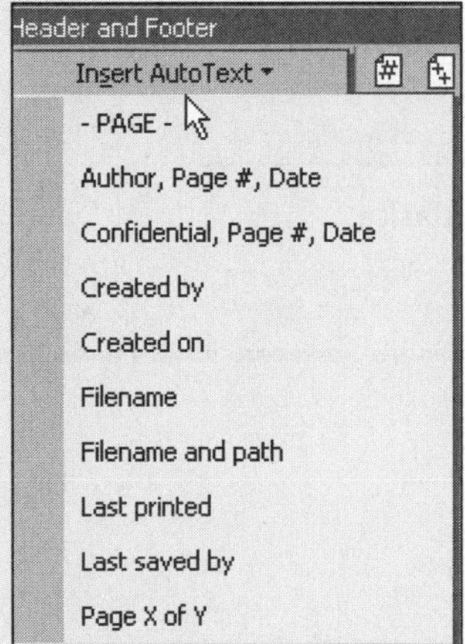


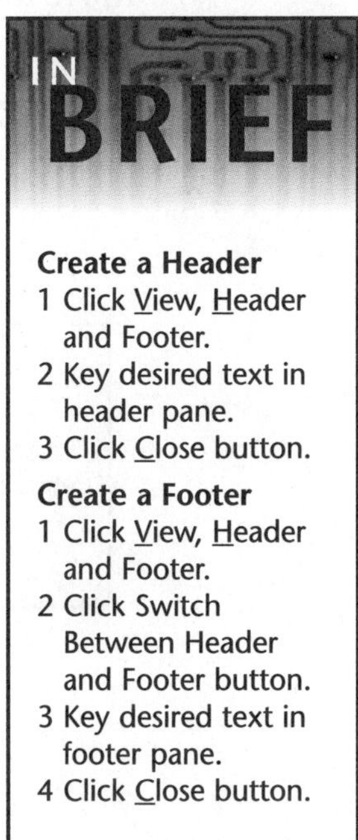

# In Brief

**Create a Header**

1 Click View, Header and Footer.
2 Key desired text in header pane.
3 Click Close button.

**Create a Footer**

1 Click View, Header and Footer.
2 Click Switch Between Header and Footer button.
3 Key desired text in footer pane.
4 Click Close button.

## 4.9 Modifying a Header or Footer

Header or footer text does not take on the character formatting of the document. For example, if you change the font for the document text, header or footer text remains at the default. If you want header or footer text character formatting to be the same as the document, format the header or footer in the header or footer pane. To edit a header or footer, click View and then Header and Footer. This displays the header pane. If you want to edit the footer, click the Switch Between Header and Footer button. Delete a header or footer from a document by displaying the header or footer pane and then selecting and deleting the text.

**PROJECT:** After looking at the printing of the Petersburg fact sheet newsletter, you determine that the header should be removed from the document and the footer should align at the left and include the page number at the right.

## STEPS

1. With Word S4-02 open, select the entire document, change the font to 11-point Bookman Old Style (or a similar typeface), and then deselect the text.
2. Make sure the insertion point is positioned at the beginning of the document, click View, and then click Header and Footer.

   This displays the header text in the header pane.
3. At the Header pane, select the text *Page 1* and then press the Delete key on the keyboard.

   This deletes the header text from the document.
4. Click the Switch Between Header and Footer button on the Header and Footer toolbar.

   Clicking this button displays the footer text in the footer pane.
5. Move the footer text back to the left margin by pressing the Delete key.
6. Move the insertion point to the right side of the footer text and then press the Tab key twice.
7. Key **Page**, press the spacebar, and then click the Insert Page Number button on the Header and Footer toolbar.

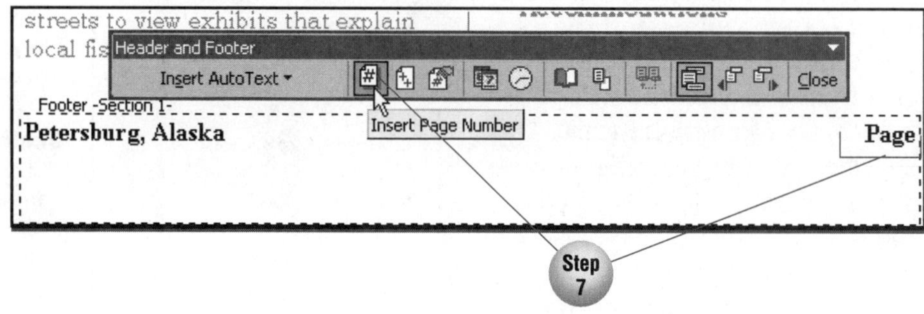

8. Select all of the footer text, change the font to 11-point Bookman Old Style bold (or the typeface you chose in step 1), and then deselect the footer text.
9. Click the Close button on the Header and Footer toolbar.
10. Scroll through the document and view the footer text.

    In Print Layout, the footer text displays dimmed.
11. Save, print, and then close Word S4-02.

# In Addition

## Creating Different Headers and Footers in a Document

By default, Word will insert a header or footer on every page in a document. You can create different headers or footers within one document. For example, you can create a unique header or footer on the first page, create different headers or footers for odd and even pages, or create different headers or footers for sections in a document. Create a unique header or footer with the two options in the Headers and footers section of the Page Setup dialog box with the Layout tab selected as shown at the right. Create a different first page header with the Different first page option or create a different header on odd and even pages by choosing the Different odd and even option.

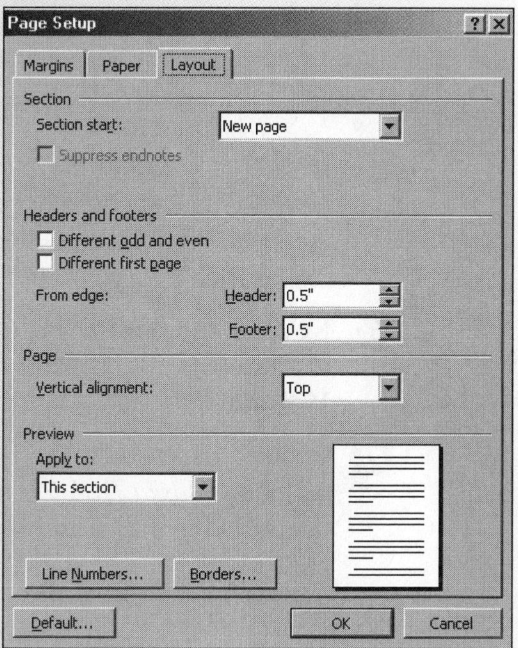

# 4.10 Saving a Document as a Web Page; Creating a Hyperlink; Using Web Page Preview

A Word document can be saved as a Web page and formatting can be applied to the Web page. When you save a document as a Web page, Word automatically changes to the Web Layout view. In this view, the page displays as it will appear when published to the Web or an intranet. Along with Web Layout view, you can also change to the Web Page Preview to view the page in the default Web browser and to view formatting supported by the browser. You can create a hyperlink in a document or Web page that connects to a site on the Internet or to another document.

**PROJECT:** Since many of First Choice Travel's clients have Internet access, you will insert a hyperlink from the Petersburg newsletter to the Alaska Division of Tourism's Web site. First, you need to save the newsletter as a Web page and then format it attractively.

## STEPS

1. Open Word S4-02 and save the document as a Web page by clicking File and then Save as Web Page.
2. Key **Petersburg Page** in the File name text box and then press Enter.

3. Apply a theme background to the Web page by clicking Format and then Theme.
4. At the Theme dialog box, scroll to the end of the Choose a Theme list box and then double-click *Sumi Painting* in the list box.

   Depending on your system setup, this theme may need to be installed.

PROBLEM? You may need to install additional themes.

5. Press Ctrl + End to move the insertion point to the end of the document. Position the insertion point a double space below the last line of text.
6. Key **For more information on Alaska, visit the Alaska Division of Tourism Web site.**
7. Create a hyperlink to the tourism site by selecting *Alaska Division of Tourism* and then clicking the Insert Hyperlink button on the Standard toolbar.

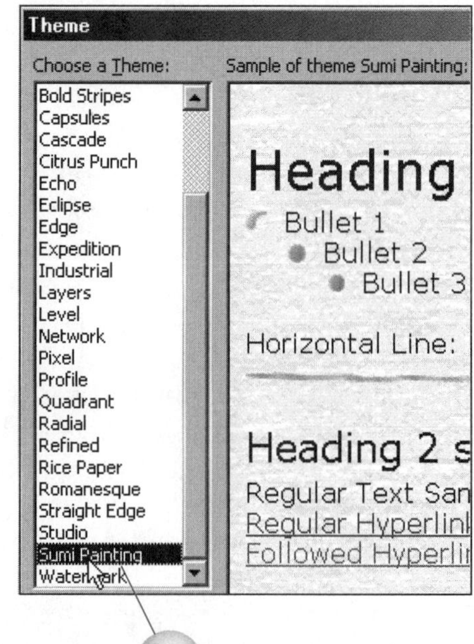

8 At the Insert Hyperlink dialog box, key **www.dced.state.ak.us/tourism** in the Address text box and then click OK.

Word automatically adds *http://* to the beginning of the Web address. When you click OK, the dialog box closes and the selected text changes color and an underline is inserted.

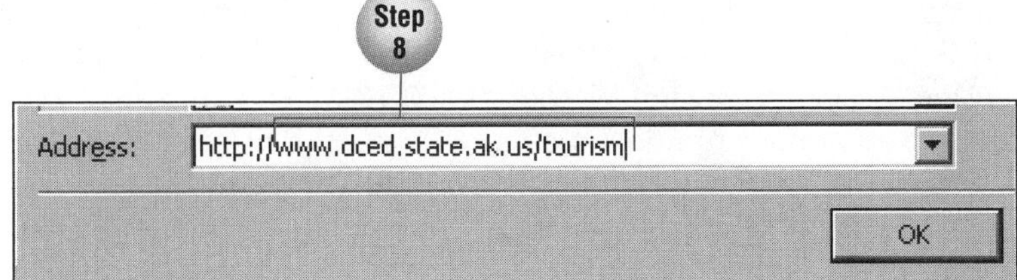


9 Make sure you are connected to the Internet. Position the mouse pointer over the Alaska Division of Tourism hyperlink until the pointer turns into a hand, hold down the Ctrl key, and then click the left mouse button.

10 At the Alaska Division of Tourism page, click on any hyperlinks that interest you. When you are finished, click File and then Close.

11 Click File and then Web Page Preview. (You may need to click the Maximize button located in the upper right corner of the browser to increase the size of the Web page.)

12 After viewing the document in the Web browser, click File and then Close to close the browser.

13 Save, print, and then close Petersburg Page.

The document prints with the original formatting applied.

## In Addition

### Downloading and Saving Web Pages and Images

The image(s) and/or text that displays when you open a Web page as well as the Web page itself can be saved as a separate file. Copyright laws protect much of the information on the Internet. Before using information downloaded from the Internet, check the site for restrictions. If you do use information, make sure you properly cite the source. To save a Web page as a file, display the desired page, click File on the Internet Explorer Menu bar, and then click Save As at the drop-down menu. At the Save Web Page dialog box, specify the folder where you want to save the Web page. Select the text in the File name text box, key a name for the page, and then click the Save button. A Web page is saved as an HTML file. A folder is automatically created when the Web page is saved. All images in the Web page are saved as separate files and inserted in the folder. Save a specific Web image by right-clicking the image and then clicking Save Picture As at the pop-up menu. At the Save Picture dialog box, key a name for the image in the File name text box and then press Enter.

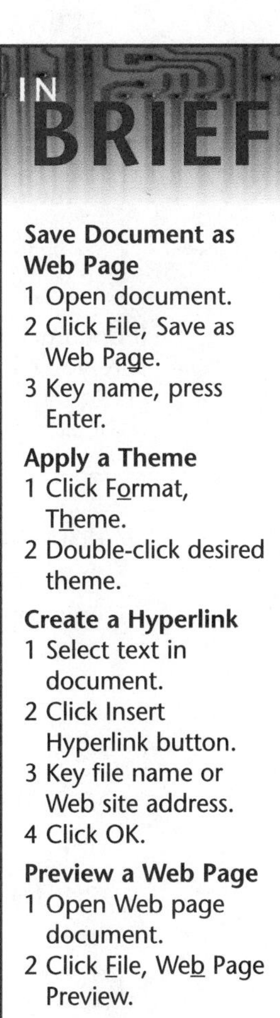

### IN BRIEF

**Save Document as Web Page**
1 Open document.
2 Click File, Save as Web Page.
3 Key name, press Enter.

**Apply a Theme**
1 Click Format, Theme.
2 Double-click desired theme.

**Create a Hyperlink**
1 Select text in document.
2 Click Insert Hyperlink button.
3 Key file name or Web site address.
4 Click OK.

**Preview a Web Page**
1 Open Web page document.
2 Click File, Web Page Preview.

## 4.11 Comparing and Merging Documents

Use Word's Compare and Merge feature to compare two documents and display the differences between the documents. This might be useful in a setting where multiple individuals in a workgroup make changes to separate copies of the original document. Merge all of the changes made by each individual using the Compare and Merge feature. When you compare and merge documents, you can choose to display the results in the original document, in the currently open document, or in a new document. In Print Layout view, the results display in the document as well as in balloons in the right margin. If you want to make comments in a document, or if a reviewer wants to make comments in a document prepared by someone else, insert a comment. A comment is useful for providing specific instructions, identifying critical information, or for multiple individuals reviewing the same worksheet to insert comments.

**PROJECT:** You want to keep track of the changes you made to the Petersburg fact sheet document so you decide to use the Compare and Merge feature to compare the edited document with the original document. You then will read over the newsletter and make a few comments about additions that should be made to the newsletter.

### STEPS

1. Open Word S4-02 and then make sure the view is Print Layout. (If not, click View and then Print Layout.)
2. Compare Word S4-02 with the original document. To do this, click Tools and then Compare and Merge Documents.
3. At the Compare and Merge Documents dialog box, make sure *Word S4* on your disk is the active folder and then click *FCT Petersburg* to select it.
4. Click the down-pointing triangle at the right side of the Merge button (located in the lower right corner of the dialog box) and then click *Merge into new document* at the drop-down list.

   Notice the marked changes that appear in the document.

PROBLEM? If document text displays in red, make sure you click *FCT Petersburg* before clicking the down-pointing triangle at the right side of the Merge button.

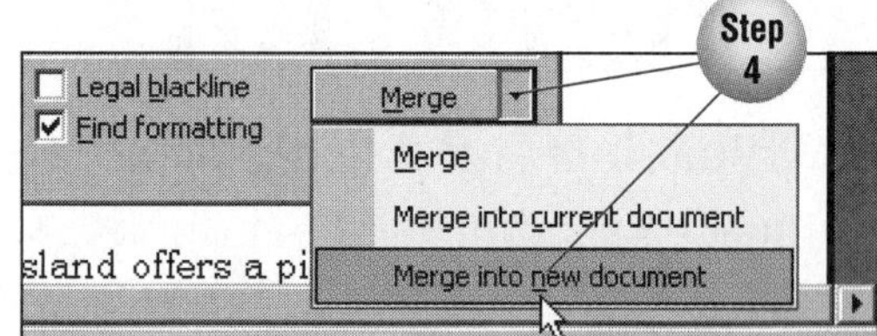


5. Print the document with the marked changes by clicking File and then Print. At the Print dialog box, make sure *Document showing markup* displays in the Print what option, and then click OK.

   The *Document showing markup* is automatically selected at the Print dialog box when a document contains marked changes.
6. Save the document, name it Word S4-03, and then close Word S4-03.
7. With Word S4-02 open, move the insertion point to the end of the first paragraph of text, click Insert, and then click Comment.

   This inserts a Comment balloon at the right side of the margin.

8. Key **Please include additional historical information.** in the Comment balloon.

9. Move the insertion point to the end of the first paragraph in the *Visitor Attractions* section, click Insert, and then click Comment.

10. Key **Include the admissions fee, if any, for the museum.** in the Comment balloon.

Step 8

11. Insert the comment **Please include average prices for hotels.** at the end of the first paragraph in the *Accommodations* section (located on the second page).

12. Print only the comments. To do this, click File and then Print.

13. At the Print dialog box, click the down-pointing triangle at the right side of the Print what option, click *List of markup* at the drop-down list, and then click OK.

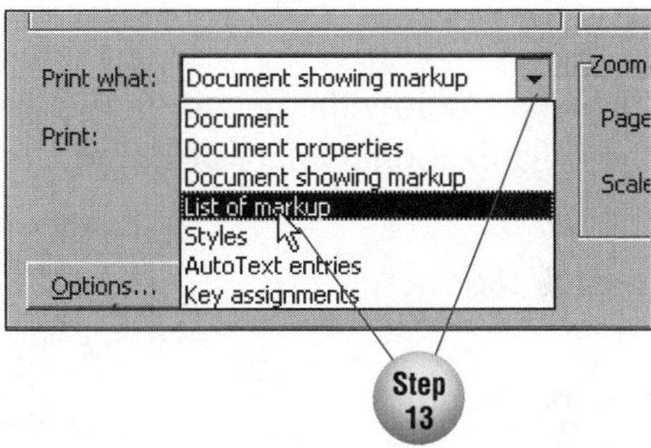


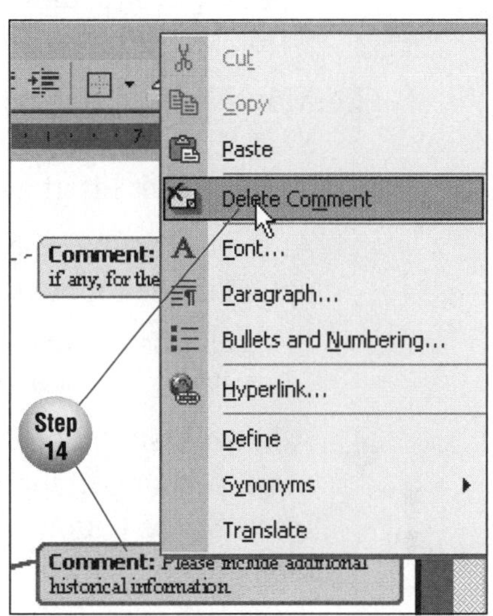


14. Delete the comment located after the first paragraph. To do this, right-click the Comment balloon that contains the text *Please include additional historical information*, and then click Delete Comment at the shortcut menu.

15. Click in the Comment balloon on the second page and then edit the comment so it reads *Please include average prices for hotels, motels, and bed-and-breakfast facilities*.

16. Print only the comments. (Refer to steps 12 and 13.)

17. Save and then close Word S4-02.

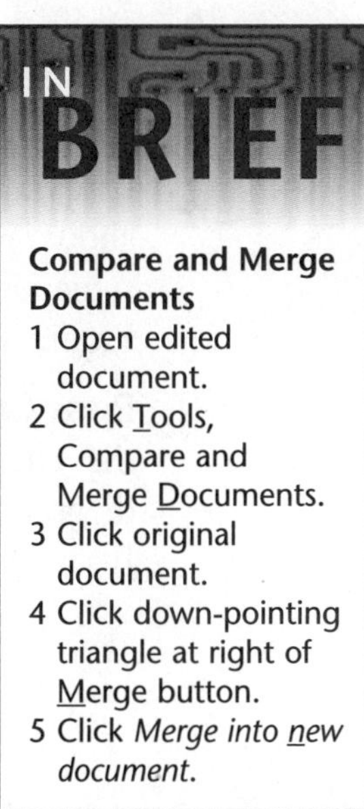

## 4.12 Creating Diagrams and Organizational Charts

If you need to visually illustrate hierarchical data, consider creating an organizational chart with options at the Diagram Gallery. At this gallery you can also create a diagram to illustrate a concept and enhance the visual appeal of a document. If you choose an organizational chart at the Diagram Gallery, chart boxes appear in the drawing canvas and the Organization Chart toolbar displays with buttons for customizing the chart. If you click a diagram option, the diagram is inserted in the drawing canvas and the Diagram toolbar displays with buttons for customizing the diagram.

**PROJECT:** Terry Blessing, president of First Choice Travel, has asked you to prepare a document containing information on the organizational structure of and services provided by First Choice Travel.

### STEPS

1. Open FCT Structure and then save the document with Save As and name it Word S4-04.
2. Move the insertion point a double space below the heading *ORGANIZATIONAL STRUCTURE* and then create the organizational chart shown in Figure W4.5. To do this, click Insert and then Diagram.
3. At the Diagram Gallery, double-click the first option in the top row.

   This inserts a drawing canvas in the document with an organizational chart inside.

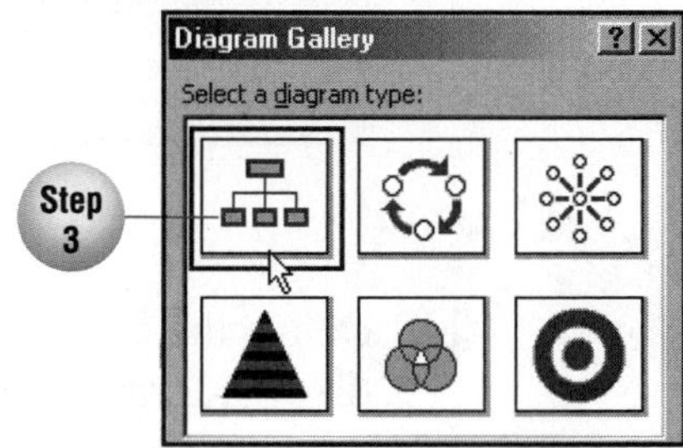


4. Add the assistant box to the chart by clicking the down-pointing triangle at the right side of the Insert Shape button on the Organization Chart toolbar and then clicking *Assistant* at the drop-down list.
5. Apply an autoformat to the chart by clicking the Autoformat button on the Organization Chart toolbar.

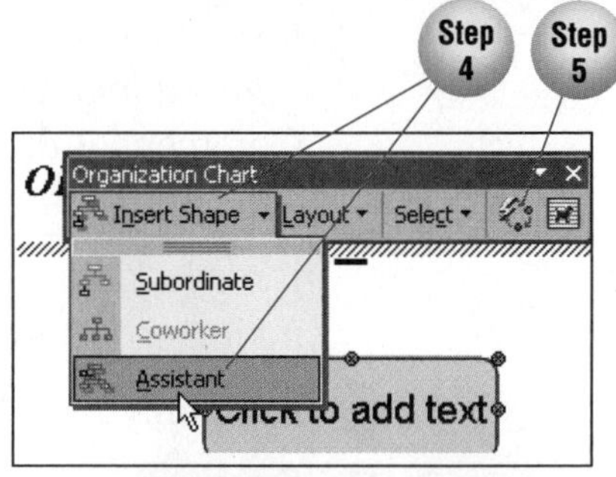


6. At the Organization Chart Style Gallery dialog box, double-click *Square Shadows* in the Select a Diagram Style list box.
7. Click inside the top box and then key the text shown in Figure W4.5. Click in each of the remaining boxes and key the text as shown in Figure W4.5.
8. Press Ctrl + End to move the insertion point to the end of the document and then insert the diagram shown in Figure W4.6. To do this, click Insert and then Diagram.

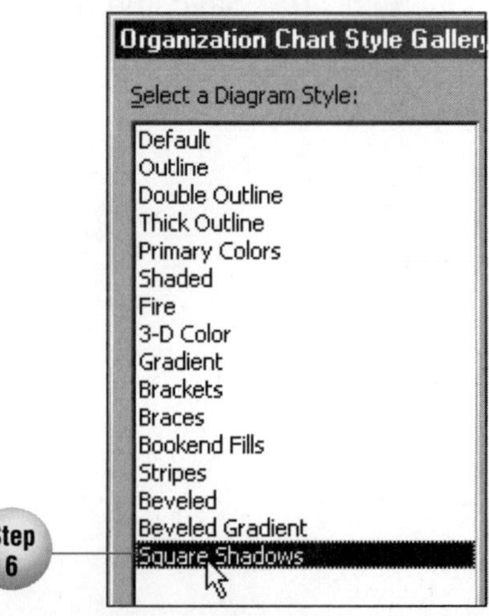

**FIGURE W4.5** Organizational Chart

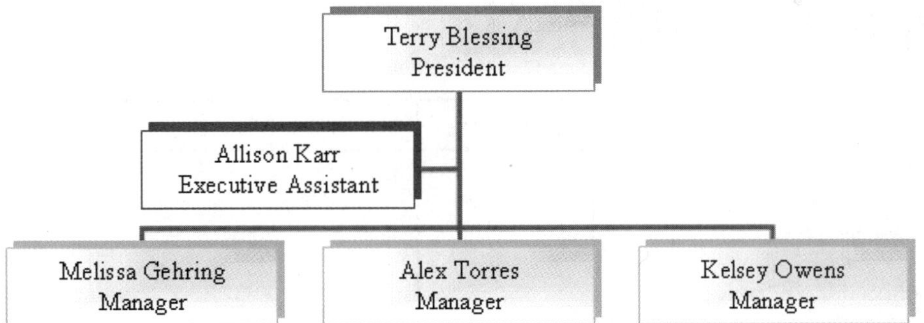


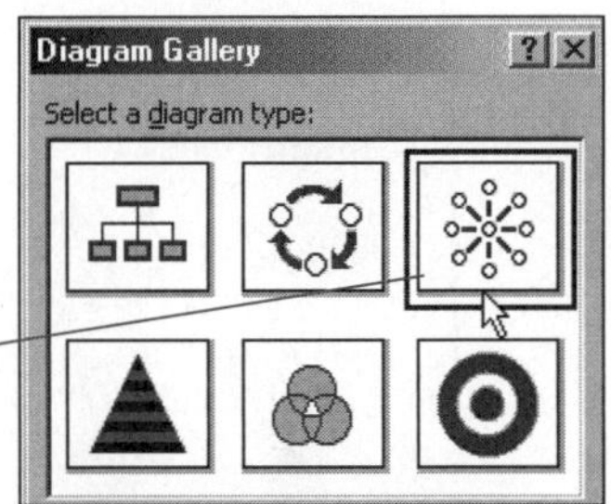


9 At the Diagram Gallery, double-click the last option in the top row.

This inserts a radial diagram in the drawing canvas in the document.

10 Click the Insert Shape button on the Diagram toolbar.

This inserts an additional circle in the radial diagram.

11 Click the AutoFormat button on the Diagram toolbar and then double-click *Thick Outline* in the Select a Diagram Style list box.

12 Click in the top circle in the drawing canvas, press Enter once, and then key **Cruise Packages** as shown in Figure W4.6. Click in each of the remaining circles and key the text as shown in Figure W4.6. (Press Enter before keying the text in each circle.)

13 Click outside the drawing canvas.

14 Save, print, and then close Word S4-04.

**FIGURE W4.6** Diagram

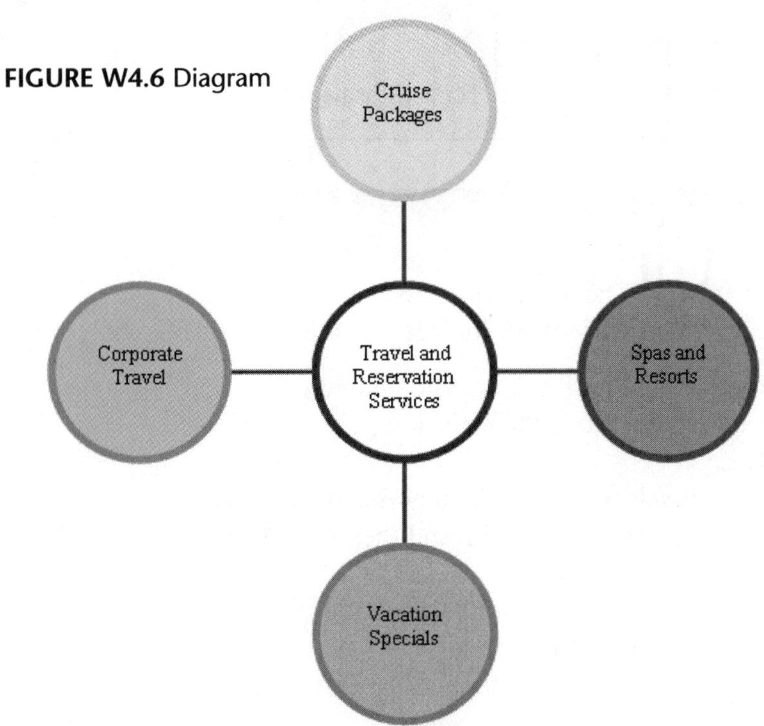


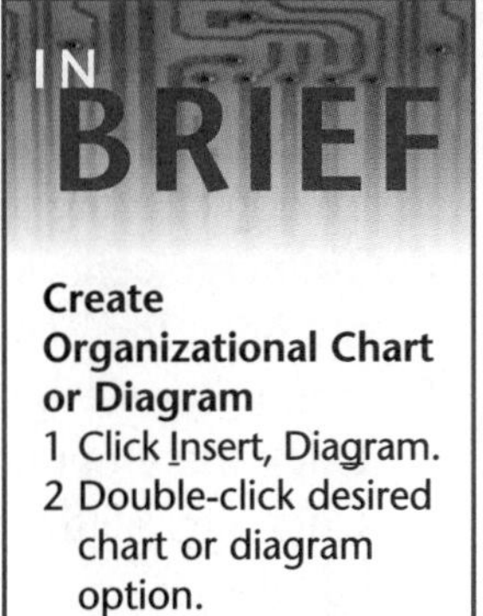


**Create Organizational Chart or Diagram**
1 Click Insert, Diagram.
2 Double-click desired chart or diagram option.

# FEATURES SUMMARY

| Feature | Button | Menu | Keyboard |
|---|---|---|---|
| Break dialog box | | Insert, Break | |
| Columns dialog box | | Format, Columns | |
| Compare and Merge dialog box | | Tools, Compare and Merge Documents | |
| Create columns | | | |
| Diagram Gallery | | Insert, Diagram | |
| Header pane | | View, Header and Footer | |
| Insert a column | | Table, Insert, Columns to Left or Right | |
| Insert comment | | Insert, Comment | |
| Insert Hyperlink dialog box | | Insert, Hyperlink | Ctrl + K |
| Insert a row | | Table, Insert, Rows Above or Below | |
| Insert Table dialog box | | Table, Insert, Table | |
| Save document as Web page | | File, Save as Web Page | |
| Select a column | | Table, Select, Column | |
| Select the entire table | | Table, Select, Table | |
| Select a row | | Table, Select, Row | |
| Table grid | | | |
| Theme dialog box | | Format, Theme | |

# PROCEDURES CHECK

**Completion:** In the space provided at the right, indicate the correct term, symbol, or command.

1. Use this button on the Standard toolbar to create a table. ____________
2. Use this keyboard command to move the insertion point to the previous cell in a table. ____________
3. To add shading to a cell or selected cells, display this dialog box. ____________
4. To merge cells A1 and B1, select A1 and B1 and then click this option at the Table drop-down menu. ____________
5. Choose predesigned table formats at this dialog box. ____________
6. Click these options to display the Break dialog box. ____________
7. Click this button on the Standard toolbar to create columns of equal width. ____________

8. Insert a line between columns with the Line between option at this dialog box. ________________
9. Display the header pane by clicking this option on the Menu bar and then clicking Header and Footer. ________________
10. Switch to the footer pane by clicking this button on the Header and Footer toolbar. ________________
11. Save a document as a Web page by clicking File and then this option. ________________
12. Apply a predesigned background to a Web page with options at this dialog box. ________________
13. Preview the Web page in the default browser at this view. ________________
14. Click these options to display the Diagram Gallery. ________________

# SKILLS REVIEW

### Activity 1: CREATING A TABLE

1 At a clear document screen, create a table with six rows and four columns.
2 Key the text in the cells as shown in Figure W4.7.
3 Save the table and name it Word S4-R1.

**FIGURE W4.7** Activity 1

| Course | Name | Days | Time |
|---|---|---|---|
| TR 101 | Intro to Theatre | MTWRF | 8:00 – 8:50 a.m. |
| TR 101 | Intro to Theatre | MW | 1:00 – 2:40 p.m. |
| TR 125 | Beginning Acting | MTWR | 9:00 – 9:50 a.m. |
| TR 211 | Set Design | MTW | 10:00 – 10:50 a.m. |
| TR 251 | Costume Design | MW | 3:00 – 4:20 p.m. |

### Activity 2: MODIFYING AND FORMATTING A TABLE

1 With Word S4-R1 open, insert a new column at the right side of the table.
2 Key the following text in the new cells:
    **Instructor**
    **Crowe**
    **Crowe**
    **Rubine**
    **McAllister**
    **Auve**
3 Insert a row above the first row.
4 Select the new row and then merge the selected cells.
5 In the top row, key **THEATRE ARTS DIVISION – FALL SCHEDULE**.
6 Bold and center *THEATRE ARTS DIVISION – FALL SCHEDULE* in the cell.
7 Select the second row (contains the text *Course*, *Name*, *Days*, etc.) and then bold and center the text in the cells.
8 Decrease the width of the cells so the table appears as shown in Figure W4.8.

9 Move the table so it is positioned between the left and right margins.
10 Save Word S4-R1.

**FIGURE W4.8** Activity 2

| THEATRE ARTS DIVISION - FALL SCHEDULE | | | | |
|---|---|---|---|---|
| **Course** | **Name** | **Days** | **Time** | **Instructor** |
| TR 101 | Intro to Theatre | MTWRF | 8:00 – 8:50 a.m. | Crowe |
| TR 101 | Intro to Theatre | MW | 1:00 – 2:40 p.m. | Crowe |
| TR 125 | Beginning Acting | MTWR | 9:00 – 9:50 a.m. | Rubine |
| TR 211 | Set Design | MTW | 10:00 – 10:50 a.m. | McAllister |
| TR 251 | Costume Design | MW | 3:00 – 4:20 p.m. | Auve |

### Activity 3: APPLYING BORDERS AND SHADING TO A TABLE; APPLYING AN AUTOFORMAT

1 With Word S4-R1 open, apply a thick/thin border to the table and add light green shading to all cells in the table.
2 Select the second row in the table (contains *Course*, *Name*, *Days*, etc.) and then add light gray shading to the row.
3 Save and then print Word S4-R1.
4 Apply the Table Colorful 1 autoformat to the table.
5 Save, print, and then close Word S4-R1.

### Activity 4: INSERTING A SECTION BREAK; CREATING AND MODIFYING NEWSPAPER COLUMNS

1 Open FCT Hawaiian Specials.
2 Save the document with Save As and name it Word S4-R2.
3 Complete a spelling and grammar check on the document. (*Molokini* is spelled correctly.)
4 Position the insertion point at the beginning of the heading *White Sands Charters* and then insert a continuous section break.
5 With the insertion point positioned below the section break, format the text below the section break into two columns of equal width with 0.6 inch of space between the columns and a line between the columns.
6 Balance the two columns on the second (last) page in the document.
7 Save Word S4-R2.

### Activity 5: INSERTING AND MODIFYING A FOOTER

1 With Word S4-R2 open, select the entire document, and then change the font to a typeface (other than Times New Roman) of your choosing.
2 Bold the title *HAWAIIAN SPECIALS* and the headings (*White Sands Charters*, *Air Adventures*, *Deep Sea Submarines*, *Snorkeling Fantasies*, and *Bicycle Safari*).
3 Move the insertion point to the beginning of the document and then insert a footer that prints centered and bolded at the bottom of each page and reads *Hawaiian Specials - #* (where the page number is inserted in place of the # symbol).

4 Select the footer and change the font to the same typeface as chosen in step 1. (Make sure the footer is bolded.)
5 Save Word S4-R2.

### Activity 6: SAVING A DOCUMENT AS A WEB PAGE; CREATING A HYPERLINK; USING WEB PAGE PREVIEW

1 With Word S4-R2 open, save the document as a Web page and name it Hawaiian Newsletter.
2 Apply a theme background of your choosing to the Web page.
3 Move the insertion point toward the end of the document approximately a double space below the text.
4 Key **For more information on Hawaii, visit the Hawaii Tourism Authority Web site**.
5 Select the text *Hawaii Tourism Authority* and then insert a hyperlink to the Hawaii Tourism Authority at *www.hawaii.gov/tourism*.
6 Make sure you are connected to the Internet, hold down the Ctrl key, and then click the *Hawaii Tourism Authority* hyperlink.
7 At the Hawaii Tourism Authority site, click on any hyperlinks that interest you. When you are finished, click File and then Close.
8 Preview the Web page in Web Page Preview.
9 After viewing the page, click File and then Close to close the browser.
10 Save, print, and then close Hawaiian Newsletter.

### Activity 7: COMPARING AND MERGING DOCUMENTS

1 Open Word S4-R2.
2 Compare Word S4-R2 with FCT Hawaiian Specials and merge the results to a new document.
3 Save the merged document and name it Word S4-R3.
4 Print and then close Word S4-R3. (Make sure the results print.)
5 With Word S4-R2 open, move the insertion point to the end of the only paragraph in the *White Sands Charters* section and then insert the comment *These times have changed. Please call the charter company for the current times.*
6 Move the insertion point to the end of the heading *Air Adventures* and then insert the comment *Please include prices.*
7 Print only the comments.
8 Save and then close Word S4-R2.

### Activity 8: CREATING AN ORGANIZATIONAL CHART

1 Open MP Prod Dept.
2 Save the document with Save As and name it Word S4-R4.
3 Press Ctrl + End to move the insertion point to the end of the document and then insert the organizational chart shown in Figure W4.9. Apply the Bookend Fills autoformat to the chart.
4 Save, print, and then close Word S4-R4.

**FIGURE W4.9** Activity 8

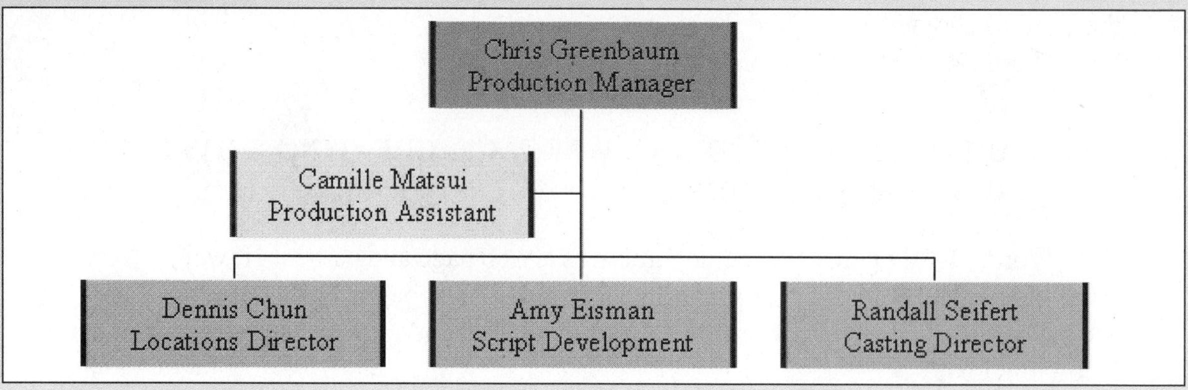


# PERFORMANCE PLUS

## Activity 1: CREATING A TABLE FOR THE WATERFRONT BISTRO

1 At a clear document screen, create the table shown in Figure W4.10 for The Waterfront Bistro. Be sure to include the modifications and formatting as shown in the table. Set the title *CATERED LUNCH OPTIONS* in 16-point size.
2 Save the completed table and name it Word S4-P1.
3 Print and then close Word S4-P1.

**FIGURE W4.10** Activity 1

| CATERED LUNCH OPTIONS | | | |
|---|---|---|---|
| **Option** | **Contents** | **Cost Per Person** | **Discount Price** |
| Option A: Hot | Vegetarian quiche, Caesar salad, vegetables, dressing, dessert, and beverages | $8.75 | $7.95 |
| Option B: Deli | Turkey or ham sandwiches, chips, vegetables, dressing, brownies, and beverages | $7.50 | $6.55 |
| Option C: Continental | Bagels, rolls, cream cheese, vegetables, dressing, cookies, and beverages | $6.75 | $6.00 |

## Activity 2: FORMATTING A THEATRE ARTS DIVISION NEWSLETTER

1 Open NPC Theatre Newsletter.
2 Save the document with Save As and name it Word S4-P2.
3 Select the entire document and then change the font to a font of your choosing.
4 Bold the title *THEATRE ARTS DIVISION* and the headings (*Division Description*, *Division Faculty*, and *Division Productions*).
5 Insert a continuous section break at the beginning of the heading *Division Description* and then format the document into newspaper columns (you determine the number of columns and the formatting of the columns).
6 Balance the columns on the last page in the document.
7 Insert a footer of your choosing in the newsletter. Format the footer in the same font as the document text.
8 Save, print, and then close Word S4-P2.

### Activity 3: COMPARING AND MERGING DOCUMENTS

1 Open Word S4-P2.
2 Compare Word S4-P2 with NPC Theatre Newsletter and merge the results to a new document.
3 Save the new document and name it Word S4-P3.
4 Print and then close Word S4-P3.
5 Close Word S4-P2.

### Activity 4: CREATING AN ORGANIZATIONAL CHART

1 Open PT Design Dept.
2 Save the document with Save As and name it Word S4-P4.
3 Move the insertion point to the end of the document and then create an organizational chart (you determine the autoformat) with the following information:

| | Camilla Yong<br>Design Manager | |
|---|---|---|
| Scott Bercini<br>Designer | Terri Cantrell<br>Designer/Sewer | Paul Gottlieb<br>Designer/Sewer |

4 Save, print, and then close Word S4-P4.

### Activity 5: INSERTING FORMULAS IN A TABLE

1 Use Word's Help feature to learn how to perform calculations in a table and specifically how to total numbers in a row or column.
2 Open WE Sales, save the document with Save As, and then name it Word S4-P5.
3 Using the information you learned about totaling numbers in a row or column, insert a formula in the cell immediately below *Total* that sums the amount in the cell immediately below *First Half* and the amount in the cell immediately below *Second Half*.

4 Insert a formula in each of the remaining cells in the *Total* column that sums the amount in the *First Half* column with the amount in the *Second Half* column.
5 Save, print, and then close Word S4-P5.

### Activity 6: CONVERTING A TABLE TO TEXT

1 Use Word's Help feature to learn how to convert a table to text.
2 Open Word S4-R1.
3 Save the document with Save As and name it Word S4-P6.
4 Convert the table to text separating text with tabs.
5 Save, print, and then close Word S4-P6.

### Activity 7: LOCATING INFORMATION AND WRITING A MEMO

1 You are Camille Matsui, production assistant for Marquee Productions. You have been asked by Chris Greenbaum, the production manager, to find information on renting a car in Toronto. Connect to the Internet and search for a car rental company in the Toronto area. Locate pricing information on economy and midsize cars and also minivans. Find out both the daily and weekly rental fees for each vehicle.
2 Using the information you find on the Internet, write a memo to Chris Greenbaum that includes a table containing the information you found on car rentals. Modify and format the table so the information in the table is attractive and easy to read.
3 Save the completed memo and name it Word S4-P7.
4 Print and then close Word S4-P7.

# INDEX